Creation, Rationality and Autonomy

INGERID S. STRAUME
GIORGIO BARUCHELLO
(EDS.)

Creation, Rationality and Autonomy

ESSAYS ON CORNELIUS CASTORIADIS

NSU Press

Contents

Preface

Several symposia and workshops have been arranged around the thought of Cornelius Castoriadis, in and beyond his lifetime, but rather few publications have emerged from them. The editors are pleased to see this publication become a reality.

In the years 2007–2009, the Nordic Summer University (NSU) hosted a series of workshops entitled "Creation, Rationality and Autonomy". These sessions took place in the winter and in the summer in various locations: Stockholm, Wik (near Uppsala, Sweden), Akureyri (Iceland), Brandbjerg (Denmark), the Norwegian and Swedish institutes in Athens, and finally at Tyrifjord (Norway). Prior to the sessions, a symposium was held at the Maison des Sciences de l'Homme in Paris, for which we wish to thank the Fondation Maison des Sciences de l'Homme for practical and financial support. Most of all, we are grateful to the NSU for making all these arrangements possible, and to all those who have assisted and supported the network over the years. Thanks to you, fruitful and creative discussions have emerged in what we see as a unique type of network.

The sessions had a notable amount of attendants from diverse backgrounds, geographically and academically. Some were new to Castoriadis, others were from his closest circle; and many came from what could be called the periphery. The present collection is but an example of all the creativity and exchange that took place during these sessions. It should also be mentioned that most of the authors have written their contributions in what is their second or third language.

The collection reflects the currently growing interest in various aspects

7

of Castoriadis's thought, and the ways in which his ideas are able to stimulate new research into established domains: the will to think with and beyond Castoriadis in what could perhaps be called the spirit of creation, rationality and autonomy.

A special thanks goes to Anders Ramsay, who was a co-editor in the initial phases of the project and one of the coordinators of the NSU network. Also, thanks to all of those who have contributed in various ways, bringing their papers to workshops, participating in discussions and not least, assisting in the practical arrangements over the years. This book is a collective project!

March 12th 2013
The editors

Abbreviations

ASA *A Society Adrift, Interviews and Debates, 1974–1997* (2010), eds. Enrique Escobar, Myrto Gondicas and Pascal Vernay, trans. Helen Arnold. New York: Fordham University Press.

CR *The Castoriadis Reader* (1997), trans. and ed. David Ames Curtis. Malden, MA and Oxford: Blackwell.

FT *Figures of the Thinkable* (2007), trans. Helen Arnold. Stanford, CA: Stanford University Press.

IIS *The Imaginary Institution of Society* (1987), trans. Kathleen Blamey. Cambridge, Mass: MIT Press (note, first paperback version of the *IIS* with alternative pagination Cambridge, England: Polity, 1998).

PPA *Philosophy, Politics, Autonomy. Essays in Political Philosophy* (1991), trans. and ed. David Ames Curtis. New York: Oxford University Press.

WIF *World in Fragments. Writings on Politics, Society, Psychoanalysis, and the Imagination* (1997), trans. and ed. David Ames Curtis. Stanford, CA: Stanford University Press.

Creation, Rationality and Autonomy – a Brief Introduction

Ingerid Straume and Giorgio Baruchello

Cornelius Castoriadis (1922–1997), one of the most original thinkers of the 20th century, is currently gaining increasing attention from a wide range of academic disciplines. As a radical leftist, thinking beyond both Marxism and anarchism, and as a philosopher who was able to draw together classical thought with psychoanalysis and modern social theory – a thinker in the tradition of the Enlightenment, yet with Romanticist leanings (Adams 2005, Arnason 1989) – Castoriadis created his own new, original categories of thought and interpretation.

One of his central concerns was to flesh out the full implications of the fact that social-historical reality is a *created* reality, a meaningful 'world', which implies thinking the social-historical *as itself* and not in terms of something else, be it 'human nature', the 'laws of the market', social 'functions' or similar constructs. The insight that the social-historical world is a created world does not mean that the world has no independent existence outside of a given social subject, but that the world, such as it exists, is *organisable* and that it is always represented as a specific world. This ontological conception transgresses the crude subjective-objective divide that informs the most part of the Western philosophical tradition. As a result, Castoriadis was able to elaborate his philosophy into one of the most original, stimulating and open-ended *oeuvres* in the history of philosophy.

Castoriadis's philosophy does not belong to the contemporary 'social constructionism', whose field of investigation is limited to human beings' meaning-making processes. As one of the first social theorists to take a serious interest in biology and systems theory, Castoriadis also elaborated on the living being and its world (Castoriadis 2011: 58–73; see also Adams 2011). His concern for biology was not merely academic, since Castoriadis also drew attention to the ongoing threatening ecological breakdown from a very early stage, and treated it in essays and talks (see, e.g., Castoriadis 1981). Throughout his life, Castoriadis participated in numerous public debates, and in his later years he was deeply concerned for the future of what he called *the project of autonomy*, which he regarded as a unique creation of the Graeco-Western world. Though ancient in its origins, this project is not given once and for all, for it must be lived and enacted continuously as a vital, public, collective questioning of the instituted order. In this connection, Castoriadis clearly foresaw the totalizing effects of neoliberalism as a general disinvestment of meaning, conformism, lack of distinctions, cynicism and a "rising tide of insignificance" (Castoriadis 2011).

As these few remarks should illustrate, it is not possible to adequately understand, re-present or discuss Castoriadis's work without actually having studied its defining categories of thought and interpretation. This is probably one of the reasons why a relatively small number of established scholars have made use of this thought in their own projects. Notable exceptions are the distinguished social theorists Johann P. Arnason and Peter Wagner, who have both been invaluable contributors – through their advice and encouragement as well as inspiration – to much of the research presented in this volume.

This book is not the place, however, to find an introductory pre-sentation of Castoriadis's work. Since the discussions developed in its chapters are all of a fairly advanced level, readers unfamiliar with Castoriadis should refer to introductions in English such as Castoriadis (1997a), Curtis (1997), Rockhill (2011), Tovar-Restrepo (2012) and the forthcoming Adams (ed).[1]

Castoriadis in the Nordic world

For the reasons outlined in the paragraphs above, the whole scope of Castoriadis's thought will probably remain a special interest for the few. Still, various aspects of his thought have already found fertile ground, also in the Nordic region. Parts of his work were translated into the Scandinavian languages relatively early, sometimes before translation into English, e.g. the first part of his main work, *L'institution imaginaire de la société*, which was translated into Danish in 1981, six years after its publication in French and another six years before it emerged in English in 1987.[2] Some of his political pamphlets – published under the pseudonym Paul Cardan – were translated from English into Swedish and Norwegian in the early 1970s and circulated among left-wing activists. The aforementioned public talk on ecology and autonomy (Castoriadis 1981) was published in Swedish already in 1982[3], and a Swedish translation of some of his most important essays emerged in 1995 in a collection edited by Mats Olin.[4] Eight years later, the Swedish journal *Res Publica* launched a special issue on Castoriadis,[5] and in 2008 a special issue of the Icelandic scholarly journal *Nordicum-Mediterraneum* devoted to Castoriadis originated from a winter symposium in the NSU network, in what might be dubbed a northern

1 See also two special journal issues on Castoriadis: Baruchello (ed. 2008) and Adams and Straume (eds. 2012). A major English language source is the journal *Thesis Eleven*, which has published several special issues and commentaries on the work of Castoriadis.
2 *Marxisme og revolutionær teori* (Copenhagen, Bibliotek Rhodos: 1981), translated by Poul Eriksson og Frans Storr-Hansen, with a postscript by Dominique Bouchet.
3 *Från ekologi till självstyre*. Stockholm: Federativs.
4 Castoriadis, Cornelius (1995) *Filosofi, politik, autonomi*. Stockholm/Stehag: Brutus Östling.
5 *Res Publica* nr. 58/2003.

outpost even in a Nordic setting: Akureyri.

We can only speculate why Castoriadis's work is currently finding resonance in the Nordic world. One key could be the concept of equality, which for Castoriadis – *pace* much liberal thought – is another side of freedom (Straume 2008). For a long time, the Nordic nations have been known for their egalitarian ideals. Inclusion is valued, if not always practiced. Capitalism, it is often argued, has been civilized in the Nordic countries and turned into an instrument of human progress, rather than mere cutthroat competition, as recently noted and unexpectedly appreciated even by free-market flagship journal *The Economist*.[6]

Castoriadis's thought offers a set of ideals that come rather close to traditional Nordic ideals, such as egalitarianism, but also the questioning of established authorities and dogma. Farmers and fishermen in the Nordic nations – especially the smaller ones, who have endured colonial domination – have a long history of opposition as well as self-organization and self-education. In a time of increasing differences between the super-rich and the poorest groups in society, the Nordic nations are still on top of the world scale – along with Japan – of the countries with the narrowest income differentials. As the studies of epidemiologists Wilkinson and Pickett (2010) have demonstrated, drawing on a large amount of independent statistical sources, countries with high income equality experience far fewer problems on a wide set of social and medical variables, ranging from physical and mental health to, e.g., teenage births, drug use, crime and imprisonment rates. Not least, these nations experience a high level of trust: trust between fellow citizens and trust in public institutions. The countries with the widest income gap – the United States, the United Kingdom and Portugal – do worst on the same variables.

Of late, this 'Nordic model' is being set under pressure as adaptation to globalized capitalism has been enforced in the Nordic nations too –

---

6 "The Next Supermodel", February 2nd 2013.

at the moment of writing with Sweden as a neoliberal spearhead. This phenomenon has triggered critical reflection among those who would like to preserve (or revive) the traditional Nordic ideals and the solidarity of the political left. The current interest in Castoriadis's thought has co-emerged with major political developments that can lead either to a general depoliticization, or worse, to antipolitical currents. An obvious place to look for alternative thought, we think, is the work of Castoriadis and the group Socialisme ou Barbarie, who were able to theorise autonomy without and beyond liberal dilemmas and dichotomies.

In short, for the authors of this collection, the way Castoriadis's thought is able to integrate politics with complex scientific and philosophical matters is precisely the kind of thought that is needed today: A thought that is bold, creative, cutting-edge, comprehensive, and yet, always open for new developments.

On the papers

The collection is organized around the three themes of creation, rationality and autonomy, which were key themes for Castoriadis. Some of the papers comment upon Castoriadis's thought and its reception, while others are more creative, setting forth new ideas inspired by Castoriadis's project of unbound questioning and thorough elucidation in various regions of thought and *praxis*.

Creation

The concept of creation is a core concept in the work of Castoriadis, a fountainhead for reflections upon the whole philosophical tradition, elaborated especially in his principal work, *The Imaginary Institution of Society* (*IIS*). All the themes explored in the *IIS* – Marxism, theory, praxis, history, society, imagination, psyche, time, language, epistemology, ontology, social imaginary significations and the social-historical –

are explored through the prism of *creation* and its *modus operandi*, the *imagination*, which Castoriadis believed to have been occulted in traditional philosophy since Plato, with very few exceptions (*IIS*, see also *WIF*: 213–45 and 246–72).

In the opening chapter, "Chaos and Creation in Castoriadis's Interpretation of Greek Thought", Angelos Mouzakitis introduces Castoriadis's concept of creation as it was developed in his engagement with the Greek experience of the world in his seminars held at the EHESS.[7] Mouzakitis relates how Castoriadis, in his engagement with pre-Socratic thinkers, sought to overcome the phenomenological-hermeneutical perspective of Heidegger and Gadamer, whose purpose was to unearth the meaning of texts. In its place, Castoriadis set forth to identify the core significations that shaped the very meaning of the Greek civilisation. In a careful reading of the early seminars, Mouzakitis traces the relationship between chaos and creation in the Greeks' notion of the world, where chaos is always a present dimension, and leads the reader through the core concepts in Castoriadis's ontology, such as creation *ex nihilo*, mortality and *apeiron* (the infinite/inderterminate). He ends the chapter by showing how Castoriadis's interpretation of Sophocles' tragedy *Antigone* differs significantly from that of Heidegger; not surprisingly, in its political import. In *Antigone*, Castoriadis recognises the ambiguous conditions of human beings' self-creation, where the joy of creation is always threatened by its shadow: *hybris*. In the domain of human creation, hybris entails the denial of mortality and of the chaos that, in the end, is the foundation-less source of all creation.

In the second chapter, "Origins as a Sign of Pathology in Architectural Thinking", Catharina Gabrielsson discusses a problem that is haunting architectural thinking, namely the invocation of architectural *origins*,

---

7 École des hautes études en sciences sociales, Paris. The seminars are published in French as *Ce qui fait la Grèce I–IV* (Paris: Seuil).

or more specifically, the idea that there is a pure, primitive, original origin – a principle underlying later historical developments that can, at least in theory, be sought out. In effect, Gabrielsson argues, such ideas often play a heteronomous role in the history of architecture, serving the purpose of disciplinary self-preservation. Drawing on Castoriadis's idea that each society is a unique form, closed onto itself, Gabrielsson asks how is it possible to turn to societies other than one's own as a source for knowledge. By overriding simple dichotomies and pointing out alternative narratives for the history of architecture, for instance the construction of the Greek temple, she points toward a narrative of beginnings and uncertain foundations. Gabrielsson further questions the utility of a sharp heteronomy/autonomy divide in the domain of creation, arguing that the paradoxes evoked by the discursive creations of architectural origins expose a tension in the heteronomy/autonomy divide that point toward deeper questions concerning the construction of a discipline, such as architecture, and the need to discuss the applicability of Castoriadis's concepts in interdisciplinary research.

The chapter by Suzi Adams, entitled "Castoriadis, Arnason and the Phenomenological Question of the World", is the result of an enduring scholarly debate about the thought of Cornelius Castoriadis and one of its main interpreters, Johann P. Arnason. In particular, Adams's chapter addresses the conceptions of 'the world' in their intellectual production. For both authors, 'the world' constitutes the fundamental creative ground for the emergence of any rationality whatsoever, which is social as much as it is individual, for only individuals can think, yet solely within the milieu of a society that allows for and at times cultivates human thought. Both Castoriadis and Arnason echo Merleau-Ponty and the notion of 'world horizon', but while Castoriadis's conception of the world focuses upon ontological issues, Arnason's concerns are primarily *culturological*. This difference in approach generates tensions that Adams investigates and discusses in fine detail. Arnason's elaboration of 'the world' is said to offer a *shared and interpretative horizon*, whilst Castoriadis's depicts it as an *ontological creation ex nihilo*. Adams's chapter assesses the strengths and weaknesses of both accounts and argues that there is a dimension in Castoriadis's notion of the world that scholars have regularly overlooked, especially as it reappears in his later poly-regional ontology of the *for-itself*.

Rationality

Rationality is a challenging notion, and a challenged one in Castoriadis's *oeuvre*. In this context, only some general remarks are possible. First of all, there can be no question that Castoriadis valued the rationality of what he called 'the quest for truth' that characterises the Graeco-Western tradition (see, e.g., "Done and To Be Done", *CR*: 361–417). However, in the same tradition, rationality is an ambiguous figure. In his political texts he would often refer to the phrase 'pseudo-rational pseudo-mastery', a perverted form of the 'rational mastery' he saw to be one of modernity's two core significations (along with autonomy).[8] These two significations are in a state of perpetual tension, which is at the same time ambiguous and productive (a point elaborated by Peter Wagner in numerous publications, e.g. Wagner 2012; see also Theodoridis 2008). From another perspective, there is *rationalism qua* philosophical perspective – as exemplified by Plato and Hegel – which is a kind of reductionism that constitutes the main obstacle for Castoriadis's alternative philosophical approach, *elucidation*. In another context, Castoriadis mocks the tendency to postulate the existing state of affairs as the rational (or 'axiomatic') one, as he accuses his co-philosophers Nozick and Rawls of doing (*FT*: 135). But none of these aspects of rationality is exhaustive: There is also rationality as a quality of *thought*. When we study the philosophical style of Castoriadis, it is clear

8 Cf. "The 'Rationality' of Capitalism", *FT*: 47–70 and "What Democracy?" in *FT*: 118–50.

that he values rationality in his own (and others') thought, and he was certainly no epistemological relativist or postmodernist. Like his great inspirer, Max Weber, he considers rationality to be a constitutive aspect of modernity, and his thinking is rational in this specifically modern sense, always asking for reasons/grounds and justification, placing high value on the quest for truth, and more specifically, by distinguishing between different forms of validity (see especially "Done and To Be Done", CR: 361–417). Rationality, or more broadly, reason, is a social imaginary signification of modernity, which holds a special status in what we, with Habermas, could call rational discourse. Consider the following statement:

> We pose the question: What is valid *de jure* (as thought, as law etc.)? We are told: You also have to demonstrate that the question of *de jure* validity is itself valid *de jure*. We are told, you have to prove rationally that reason is valid [*vaut*], you have to furnish a 'rational foundation'. But how can I even raise the question of the *de jure* validity [...] without having already raised it and having thus posited both that it makes sense and that it is valid *de jure*? How can I rationally found reason without presupposing it? If a foundation of reason is rational, it presupposes and utilizes what it wants to prove; if it is not [...], it contradicts the result it is aiming at. Not only social-historically, but logically ('transcendentally'), the positing of reason is inaugural, it is *self-positing* (*CR*: 391).

Once rationality has been instituted, it becomes a measuring stick for various other significations and meanings, rendering them rational, irrational or a-rational. However, in contemporary times, which Castoriadis sees as an age of insignificance, 'pseudo-rationality' has become a dominant feature: especially the pseudo-rationality of so-called progress and market capitalism (cf. "The 'Rationality' of Capitalism", *FT*:

47–70). This signification is a perversion of rationality that overstretches the domain of the rational to the detriment of autonomy. In other words, pseudo-rationality puts a stop to thinking and creation.

In the chapter entitled "Odd Bedfellows: Cornelius Castoriadis on Capitalism and Freedom", Giorgio Baruchello discusses how 'capitalism and freedom' is not only the title of a 1962 book by Milton Friedman playing a pivotal role in asserting worldwide the neoliberal paradigm of alleged rationality, but also a slogan that leading statesmen, politicians and opinion-makers have been heralding in recent decades in order to provide a rationale for, amongst other things, the slashing of welfare states and the invasion of foreign countries. In particular, 'capitalism' has been coupled regularly with 'democracy', the latter being seen as the political system that better entrenches and promotes 'freedom' or 'autonomy'. Thus, 'capitalism' and 'democracy' have been described as the two sides of one and the same project for human emancipation, which is said to characterise modernity and crystallise the modern standard of rationality. However, Castoriadis's *oeuvre* reminds us inexorably of their different historical origin and of their different defining axiology, which is highlighted in further depth by references to the works of Adam Smith and Karl Marx. In particular, Castoriadis's work highlights how little emancipation is actually present in the alleged liberal democracies of the world, whose adoption of capitalism promotes money-making conformist inanity and market-serving irrationalities, rather than autonomous self-creation *via* robust rational self-analysis and radical self-interrogation.

Sophie Klimis's chapter is entitled "From Modernity to Neoliberalism: What Human Subject?" and as such it furthers the exploration of Castoriadis's reasoning-prone democratic project of autonomy and the actual heteronomous subjects of modern alleged democracies. Contrary to the official neoliberal mantra that would want us to believe that we live in the most free and efficient, hence rational, societies ever created by humankind, Klimis argues that modern societies operate upon a higher-level irrational principle of endless expansion on a finite planet and a lower-level plethora of irrationalities aimed at securing equally endless consumption and the related generation of profit for private money investors. Successively, Klimis offers a positive definition of the autonomy-seeking Castoriadean subject and discusses its similarities and differences with respect to the classical Cartesian *ego* and the capitalist individual. Additionally, Klimis outlines and assesses the conditions that could revive the capitalist individual's desire for self-transformation into a genuine autonomous subject. Also, she examines the question of whether modernity, capitalism and its contemporary hegemonic manifestation as neoliberalism have to be considered as three altogether different types of society, or rather as one and the same society that has been altering itself through time. In connection with this examination, Klimis recalls Aristotle's analysis of money in order to reveal the profound antinomy that exists between today's economy-defining desire for money and the desire for autonomy praised by Castoriadis, as well as their very different anthropological and socio-political implications.

Andrea Gabler's chapter, called "Artistic Critique? Socialisme ou Barbarie's and Castoriadis's Concept of Revolutionary Work Research", draws attention to the fascinating and original research of the group Socialisme ou Barbarie, where Castoriadis was a key figure. Even though the group itself is well-enough known, its rich research on work life, undertaken by French industry workers and published in the journal *Socialisme ou Barbarie* has not received the attention it deserves. In their analysis of capitalism, May 68 and various forms of protest (*Le nouvel esprit du capitalisme,* 1999), French sociologists Luc Boltanski and Eve Chiapello draw attention to the group, and discuss their role in the restructuring of power and protest in post-Fordist capitalism. However, Gabler argues, their categorisation of Socialisme ou Barbarie, as 'artistic critique' – as distinct from 'social critique' – misses the point. The context of their work research is clearly 'non-artistic', she argues; thus, the group presented a critique whose target was the social organisation as a whole, consisting, as they saw it, of order-givers and order-takers or executors. The 'testimonies' of the worker-researchers clearly showed the irrationality of industrial rationalisation processes, elucidating a point, later elaborated by Castoriadis, that, in order to work, capitalist production relies heavily on the creativity of workers to avoid and, indeed, compensate for the attempts at rationalisation by capitalist-bureaucratic management. Moreover, *pace* Boltanski and Chiapello, Socialisme ou Barbarie and Castoriadis were able to point out the irreducible complexities of modern work life, where inclusion and exclusion processes exist at the same time (rather than as poles in a pendulum movement). Thus the new spirit of capitalism is able to veil, but not override, the tensions and conflicts that still exist in the social organisation – a point overlooked by Boltanski and Chiapello. Gabler concludes that the ('social') critique of the group is able to steer future analyses and critiques of capitalism onto their proper target.

Autonomy

Castoriadis's concept of autonomy must be distinguished from its traditional (liberal) understanding, where the concept of autonomy is *per* definition restricted to individuals, and attached to the ideal of independence of others. For Castoriadis, autonomy is always at the same time collective and individual, and – building on the assumption that the 'fabric' of individuals is social-historical – a full realisation of autonomy *qua* independence would for him signify a state of autism or psychosis. Autonomy holds a special position in Castoriadis's thought, as a signification that – once it has been created – puts all other significations into relief as the very condition for choosing (be it autonomy or heteronomy), questioning and asking for justifications (*CR*: 394). The status, significance and multiple aspects of autonomy are elaborated by Castoriadis in numerous contexts: as a social-historical signification; as effectively embodied in a democracy; as a philosophical and political *project*; and on the level of the individual *qua* reflective subjectivity. The four chapters in this section deal with all these aspects.

In "The Power of the Imaginary", Harald Wolf draws attention to the concept of power in Castoriadis's work and relates it to the prospects of autonomous – conscious and explicit – transformation of society. By comparing Castoriadis's conception of power to other well-known conceptions, notably those of Weber, Foucault, Nietzsche, Heidegger and Bourdieu, Wolf demonstrates how Castoriadis's notion holds more political potential, in the deepest sense of the term. The 'power of the imaginary' – which is 'radical infra-power' or 'ground-power' – makes things and phenomena emerge as parts of a specific social-historical imaginary, that is, the instituted society. By conceptualising this infra-power Castoriadis highlights the potential in a society for breaking its state of (or drift towards) heteronomy. While most theorists theorise power as something 'pseudo-natural', i.e. heteronomous, Castoriadis's focus on autonomy and the notion of the 'instituted' *vis-à-vis* the 'instituting' society open for a more politicized perspective, Wolf argues. However, this capacity is always ambiguous, and in contemporary Western society it is severely weakened. The ongoing erosion of signification and meaning haunts not only organised politics, but also undermines the project of autonomy as a whole, leaving the ground-power unthematised, and thus, in a sense, total. Still, as Wolf concludes, despite his reasons for pessimism, every dead end may also be a prospect for new openings.

In the ensuing chapter, "Castoriadis, Education and Democracy", Ingerid Straume focuses on autonomy in its institutional embodiment: democracy. Straume brings Castoriadis's ideas on democracy and *paideia* into a broader debate concerning theories of democracy in the philosophy of education. Although democracy and education (or *paideia*) were connected in Castoriadis's thought, he did not undertake a systematic discussion of their relationship. Drawing mainly on three of Castoriadis's texts on democracy, Straume argues that the notion of *paideia* holds a double meaning for Castoriadis which has not been adequately distinguished: the former being *paideia* as socialization and the latter what Castoriadis refers to as *paideia* in the 'full' or 'true' sense. Only the latter meaning brings out the essence of a democracy (a 'true' democracy as understood by Castoriadis), that is, a society that consciously creates and re-creates itself. As argued by Straume, this emphatic notion of democracy adds significance to educational practices, and strengthens the connection between education and democracy beyond the understanding that dominates the field of education, inspired by, on the one hand, John Dewey's notion of democracy as a 'way of life' and, on the other, the politically defensive liberalism of John Rawls. In short, Straume argues that, even though his concept of *paideia* needs some further distinctions and elaborations, the relationship between democracy and education gains nevertheless more importance – meaning and significance – in the perspective offered by Castoriadis than the conceptions that dominate the educational field.

In her essay "The Wreath of Subjectivity and Time", Kristina Egumenovska challenges the reader to engage in the intriguing question of *time*, which for Castoriadis is essentially the question of creation, or in another term, the emergence of 'otherness'. As demonstrated by Egumenovska, notions of subjectivity have often been entangled with the question of time, and many classical discussions about how to understand and conceptualise time also tell us something about subjectivity. Egumenovska engages with several well-known accounts of time, such as time *vis-à-vis* space, showing that time and space, but also subjectivity, have traditionally been thought reductively by conceptualising one category through another. She further brings into play Heidegger's discussion of private and public time in *Being and Time* as well as contemporary personality psychology to demonstrate the aporias that emerge when time and subjectivity are abstracted from their proper contexts, that is, without any reference to Castoriadis's notion of *the social-historical,* which provides the 'content' of the thinking subject. In this context, Aristotle's definition of time "as a number of change" is invoked to elucidate Castoriadis's conception of time as the emergence of otherness. In short, as Egumenovska argues, subjectivity cannot be explained in terms of an algorithm, however sophisticated, or as in any way given, but, rather, that the birth of the social imaginary and human psychism are consubstantial. Her essay thus exemplifies the centrality of creation in all of Castoriadis's work, and reminds us that all of his key topics and ideas were really interrelated.

The final chapter, "Autonomy and Self-Alteration" by Stathis Gourgouris, furthers and deepens the idea of the subject as emergence of otherness, or *alterity.* Through a careful discussion of the conditions of sublimation – elucidated by the idea of creation *ex nihilo* – Gourgouris puts the (psychoanalytical) question of sublimation into the largest possible perspective: the *poietic* side of ontology and politics. How is it possible, Gourgouris asks, that an autonomous subject emerges from a heteronomous order? In his reading of Judith Butler and Castoriadis, Gourgouris is able to broaden the perspective of sublimation – which, following Castoriadis is always social-historical – into a question of *power*. Power first emerges as the power of the other, but power is also a force in the subject's act of self-alteration, which thereby exceeds the power that brought the subject into existence in the first place. We see here a parallel to the chaos/cosmos characteristic of the formation of a social-historical world in the formation of the subject, where the unconscious is a chaos that can only by partially ordered. Thus, the creative power of the subject is brought to light. In conclusion, Gourgouris argues that the notion of autonomy brings forth dimensions of performativity, self-othering, perpetual questioning and *poietic* experience, all with implications that far exceed the traditional notions of *autopoeisis*.

References

Adams, Suzi (2005) "Interpreting Creation: Castoriadis and the Birth of Autonomy". *Thesis Eleven*, Vol 83 no. 1, 25–41.

Adams, Suzi (2011) *Castoriadis's Ontology: Being and Creation.* New York: Fordham.

Adams, Suzi (forthcoming) (ed.) *Cornelius Castoriadis: Key Concepts.* London: Bloomsbury.

Adams, Suzi and Straume, Ingerid S (2012) (eds.) Cornelius Castoriadis: Critical Encounters. Special issue of *European Journal of Social Theory.* Vol. 15, no. 3, August 2012.

Arnason, Johann P (1989) "The Imaginary Constitution of Modernity", in Busino, Giovanni (ed) *Autonomie et autotransformation de la société. La philosophie militante de Cornelius Castoriadis.* Genève, Libraire Droz.

Baruchello, Giorgio (2008) (ed.) *Nordicum-Mediterraneum* volume 3 no. 2 December 2008 (available at http://nome.unak.is/previous-issues/issues/vol3_2/)

Castoriadis, Cornelius (1981) (avec Daniel Cohn-Bendit et le Public de Louvain-la-Neuve), *De l'écologie à l'autonomie.* Paris: Seuil, ix-xxxix.

Castoriadis, Cornelius (1987) *The Imaginary Institution of Society,* trans. Kathleen Blamey. Cambridge: MIT Press.

Castoriadis, Cornelius (1997a) "Democracy as Procedure and Democracy as Regime", trans. David Ames Curtis. *Constellations* vol. 4, no. 1, 1–18.

Castoriadis, Cornelius (1997b) An introductory interview, in *The Castoriadis Reader,* trans. and ed. David Ames Curtis. London: Blackwell, 1–34.

Castoriadis, Cornelius (2011) *Postscript on Insignificance. Dialogues with Cornelius Castoriadis.* Edited with an introduction by Gabriel Rockhill, trans. Gabriel Rockhill and John V. Garner. London: Continuum.

Curtis, David Ames (1997) "Translator's foreword", in Castoriadis, Cornelius *World in Fragments,* trans. and ed. David Ames Curtis. Stanford Ca: Stanford University Press, xi-xxxix.

Rockhill, Gabriel (2011): "Editor's introduction. Eros of Inquiry: An aperçu de Castoriadis' life and work", in Castoriadis, Cornelius *Postscript on Insignificance. Dialogues with Cornelius Castoriadis.* London: Continuum.

Straume, Ingerid (2008) "Freedom and the Collective", *Nordicum-Mediterraneum,* volume 3 no. 2 December 2008 (available at http://nome.unak.is/previous-issues/issues/vol3_2/).

Theodoridis, Fotis (2008) "Beyond the Reductionist Thinking-Doing", *Nordicum-Mediterraneum,* volume 3 no. 2 (available at http://nome.unak.is/previous-issues/issues/vol3_2/).

Tovar-Restrepo, Marcela (2012) *Castoriadis, Foucault and Autonomy.* London: Continuum.

Wagner, Peter (2012) *Modernity: Understanding the present.* Cambridge: Polity.

Wilkinson, Richard and Pickett, Kate (2010) *The Spirit Level: Why equality is better for everyone.* London: Penguin

Part I

Creation

Chaos and Creation in Castoriadis's Interpretation of Greek Thought

Angelos Mouzakitis

Introductory Remarks

In one of the talks he delivered in Greece under the title "Ancient Greek democracy and its importance for us today", Castoriadis explicitly links the rekindling of his interest in Greek antiquity with the period of his intellectual development, when he subjected Marxism's conception of revolution to thorough critique. In the same text Castoriadis (1999: 10–11) maintains that this critique was essential for the development of his position that in Greece one finds for the first time in history the emergence of the political domain proper. This assertion might seem intriguing to the uninitiated reader, since it implies that all forms of government preceding the democratic *polis* – and all non-democratic forms of government that historically followed the decline of Greek democracy – are not essentially – or truly – political. However, this seemingly audacious claim is clearly premised on Castoriadis's under-standing of social creation as consisting of two moments or instances. Indeed, Castoriadis claims that human creation takes the form of freely 'instituting' the conditions of social life, but it is also always confronted by the already 'instituted', i.e. by already established norms and forms of life that are often presented as allegedly objective conditions of social life. In this manner, Castoriadis depicts the social-historical as "the union *and* the tension of instituting society and of instituted society, of history made and history in the making" (*IIS*: 108).

Now, given that creation proper is for Castoriadis always *creation ex nihilo*, i.e. largely unconditioned by the established 'reality', it is easy to surmise that in his thought creation is identified with the act of instituting, namely with the creation of new forms of collective and individual life (*WIF*: 84). Moreover, in his seminars originally published under the title *Ce qui fait la Grèce*[1] Castoriadis explicitly describes politics as identical with the very act of instituting; in other words he defines politics as the domain of human creation, the domain where human freedom takes concrete forms (*Gr.*: 95). More specifically, in the Greek *polis* Castoriadis traces the birth of the first political community that actively engages not in the deliberation of action within the horizon of an always already established, fetish-like legal order, but in the radical incessant *creation*, destruction and recreation of its laws and institutions (*Gr.*: 410–11). Importantly, the *polis* is explicitly acknowledged as both the foundation and the guarantor of this legal order. Consequently, without being a *model* for contemporary thought and political action, the *polis* contains the seed of autonomy; it is for Castoriadis the historical theatre where autonomy emerged *qua* primary *signification* and therefore also as *praxis*, since for Castoriadis significations always include the "identitary/ensidic dimension" (*Gr.*: 82). Thus, Castoriadis's interpretation of Greek civilisation in all its guises aims at the uncovering of the elements that made such an understanding of the world, of nature, of the sacred and the profane, of society and of the human being *possible* in the first place. Castoriadis maintains that the primary imaginary significations characterising the Greek conception of the world from Homer to classical antiquity, rest on the fundamental disclosure of the

---

1 Hereafter referred to as *Gr.* Here I use the first volume of the Greek edition entitled *Η Ελληνική Ιδιαιτερότητα: Από τον Όμηρο στον Ηράκλειτο,* 2007, Athens: Κριτική (Kritiki).

world as *chaos*. Or rather, the Greeks seem to conceive of a unity of chaos and 'world', which entails that the 'world', i.e. the sum total of ordered elements, is possible only as a partial order, emerging out of – and ultimately depending on – chaos (*Gr.*: 92).

The first inference Castoriadis draws from this insight is that the Greek experience of the world entails the acknowledgement that the 'world' is at the same time thinkable and un–thinkable, i.e. that there is always a substratum sustaining the world, which is not amenable to representation. A further consequence of this point is that *Logos* touches only the *surface* of this abysmal, chaotic condition of the world. The second important inference concerns the identification of this abyss (of the non-representable *nihil*) as the common ground for the development of both myth and philosophy in ancient Greece. Both points are of great importance, since they place the foundations of reason *beyond* the realm of logic, while also putting the relationship between myth and reason under a new, philosophically fruitful perspective. In other words, by relating myth and reason to their common abysmal origin, Castoriadis resists the temptation of modern philosophy to explain reason as a gradual development of myth. Therefore he is able to avoid both positions that follow from this premise, namely that myth is but an early, incomplete mode of reasoning (Hegel) and its critical modification that sees in reason what I could take the liberty to call the 'eternal return of myth', or a 'vicious dialectic' between myth and enlightened reason. For how else could one interpret the thesis expressed in the *Dialectic of Enlightenment* according to which the "unending process of enlightenment" is deeply rooted in mythology, while the enlightenment's propensity to subject every new attainment of 'truth' to criticism results in a state-of-affairs where "the very notions of spirit, of truth, and, indeed, enlightenment itself, have become animistic magic" (Adorno and Horkheimer 1986: 11)?

In addition to this, Castoriadis maintains that the conception of the unity of chaos and cosmos entails the acknowledgment of radical finitude. This notion, which will be explored in detail below, is central to his philosophy where it is always thought as a prerequisite of autonomous socio-historical creation and therefore also of democracy (*Gr.*: 297). Moreover, this essential belonging together of chaos and world signifies for Castoriadis that in Greek culture there is no radical breach between the human and the divine, since despite the postulated *difference* between the two realms the divine is not thought as *transcendent* (*Gr.*: 192). This fundamental concurrent disclosure of the world and of the human being entails the abolition of *hope* for a redemptive state-of-affairs established *beyond* the realm of life, without succumbing to nihilism or hedonism. In other words, *hope* is not altogether extinguished from this culture, but it rather takes the form of an exaltation of κλέος/*kleos* (meaning good report, fame, glory) and Κύδος/*kudos* (meaning glory, especially in war) (Liddell and Scott: 435 and 455). In Castoriadis's view these two principles are formative of Greek civilisation and creation, while they give an agonistic character to the Greek world, which is epitomised in the motto αιέν αριστεύειν/*aien aristeuein* (i.e. always excel).

The difference between the Greek conception of excellence and the modern one is perhaps marked by the fact that the former is part and parcel of the pre-established *solidarity* within the *polis* (*Gr.*: 238–39). It follows that Castoriadis's interpretation of Greek thought develops from the perspective generated by this fundamental insight. In particular Castoriadis sets as his explicit aim to overcome the hermeneutic–phenomenological perspective introduced by the early Heidegger and taken up by Gadamer, in order to capture the fundamental imaginary significations characterising the sum of artistic, political, scientific and philosophical creations of ancient Greece. Thus, his meditations on Greek civilisation are characterised by a shift of emphasis from the hermeneutic unearthing of the meaning of 'texts' to the identification of core imaginary significations that support and shape this 'meaning'. In other words, texts, works of art and institutions are but pointers of fundamental, often non-thematised – but ultimately thematisable, elements or imaginary significations, which *condition* a given social-historical formation.

Chaos and Creation: Conceptions and Representations

Castoriadis thus traces in Hesiod's *Theogony* a two-fold conception of chaos corresponding to the two fundamental conceptions of creation informing philosophical, religious and even scientific accounts from antiquity to modernity. The first meaning of chaos is derived etymologically from the verb χαίνω/*chainō* and points to a conception of chaos as void and abyss. The second meaning entails a conception of chaos as κυκεών/kykeon (mixture, medley) stemming from the verb κυκάω/ *kykaō* (to stir up, mix, bit up) (see Liddell and Scott: 454–55) and signifying "an amorphous, terrible mixture" of elements that "embraces and nurtures" everything that is (*Gr.*: 266). Importantly, Castoriadis maintains that the former meaning implicitly entails the idea of radical creation, i.e. the emergence of radically new forms and *eidē ex nihilo* that he champions in his works, while the latter was destined to play a pivotal role in the development of Greek philosophy (*Gr.*: 265–66). In particular, Castoriadis detects in the concept of ἄπειρον/*apeiron* (infinite) ever since Anaximander the philosophical modification of this originary conception of chaos as embracing-nurturing abyss.

Although Castoriadis acknowledges that with the passage of time – and after Aristotle's era – the ἄπειρον comes to signify the end-less, that which has no end (πέρας/*peras*), he is still able to trace behind this modification a primary – and more important for his philosophical and political agenda – conception of ἄπειρον signifying the '*indeterminate*', a sense Castoriadis derives also with recourse to the word πεῖρα/*peira* (knowledge, experience). Now, Castoriadis believes that the sense of ἄπειρον mentioned above, viz. as something that resists our knowledge and comprehension because of its intrinsically indeterminate character has been systematically covered up by identitary logic and philosophy.

However, this suppression has not been entirely effective, as remnants of this fundamental interpretation are not confounded in mythical accounts but are present under different guises in the thought of the pre-Socratic philosophers. In effect Castoriadis argues that this interpretation always resurges even in Greek philosophy of the classical times, haunting the works of Plato and Aristotle (*Gr.*: 267).

The conception of an indeterminate substratum conditioning and supporting every determinate being is preserved – and transformed – in Thales' conception of a primal water (ὕδωρ/*hydōr*) as the ultimate cause of being. Castoriadis even takes the liberty to call this primal water, *Urwasser*, presumably pointing to the idea of *Urgrund* which is pivotal in Schelling's writings and which is important also for Heidegger's interpretation of *Being*. Castoriadis finds another important transformation of this primal, quasi–conscious understanding in Anaximander's conception of ἄπειρον as the source of the cosmos, which according to Castoriadis signifies again the non-representable and the indeterminate (*Gr.*: 284). The acknowledgment of this fundamental indeterminacy is equally forceful in Castoriadis's interpretation of the fragments of Heraclitus. It is equally present in the renowned interpretation of becoming in terms of πόλεμος/*polemos* (war), in the postulation of universal unity (εν το παν/*en to pan*) and in the identification of this unity with primal fire (*Gr.*: 357ff.). As for philosophy in classical antiquity, Plato's conception in the *Timaeus* of a divine demiurge[2] that puts a pre–existent chaotic mixture of elements into order and Aristotle's insight that matter

---

2 The English translation of the relevant passage that reads "he [i.e. the god/demiurge] does his utmost to bring to completion the character of what is most excellent" (*Timaeus* 46d: 1249) is slightly misleading as it fails to capture the sense of incompleteness implied by the Greek κατά το δυνατόν (*kata to dynaton*) in the original text and on which Castoriadis rightly insists claiming that in Plato's conception the chaotic elements are not entirely tamed by the logical order established by the divine demiurge. Perhaps we could translate more efficiently "κατά το δυνατόν" as "as far as it is possible". This squares with Plato's claim in the same dialogue (48a) that creation is the outcome of necessity's succumbing to νους/*nous*, a word that is normally translated as mind or sense (Liddell and Scott: 535) but which is difficult to accurately capture in terms of its philosophical significance because of the different connotations the word 'mind' bears in modernity.

includes the infinite (ἄπειρον/*apeiron*), both point in Castoriadis's view to the acknowledgment of an indeterminate substratum supporting the ensidic dimension of all–that–is and defying the attempts of logic to comprehend and sublate it.

Even more characteristic is in this respect the Platonic conception of the *Chora* (Χώρα), of a third kind (εἶδος/*eidos*) mediating between the indestructible and non-generated being on the one hand and the destructible, generated kind on the other (*Timaeus* 52a and 52d). The *Chora* is the abysmal womb supporting everything that is, undifferentiated space, the indeterminate and indestructible receptacle through which birth is given to all beings that are accessible to the senses (*Timaeus* 52b), and which in Plato's own definition can be thought only through a form of illegitimate and barely convincing reasoning (*Timaeus* 52a). Castoriadis draws the conclusion that despite Plato's claim (*Timaeus* 52c) that reason can help us understand indestructible being, the insight of the essentially indeterminate character of being is preserved even in the idealism of Platonic philosophy (*Gr.*: 269–73).

Castoriadis's interpretation attempts from the outset to show that in the context of Greek civilization cosmic creation is not severed from human creation. In other words, he maintains that the principles of Greek ontology are applicable to what we call 'natural' and 'human' worlds, although the latter dimension often remains unacknowledged. We encounter here in yet another fashion Castoriadis's fascination with the *mysterium magnum* posed by a concurrent compatibility and infinite distance between being and being-human, chaos and logic, nullity and existence. Thus, in Greek thought Castoriadis traces an early – although not explicitly and not thoroughly worked out – intimation of his own position, according to which human creation, the creation of laws and institutions happens also *ex nihilo*. And although Castoriadis pays heed to – and leaves open – the question concerning the cosmological dimension, his writings suggest that irrespective of their truth or falsity the cosmological principles of the Greek – I believe that we could also say of cosmologies in general without violating his position – could be understood as projections in the psychoanalytic sense of the term. In other words they are more helpful in elucidating the – often concealed – self-image of whole civilizations as it emerges from the core significations of the anonymous unconscious and as preserved in their collective representations. Importantly, his analysis implies that certain aspects of Greek culture are responsible not only for the depiction of this fundamental human trait – i.e. of creation – but also for the *development* of this trait. To put it in even bolder terms, the various forms of Greek culture pay witness to the gradual emergence of the human being *qua* human, an emergence best depicted in tragedy. Although it would be impossible to trace the various moments of this transformation, Castoriadis maintains that at least two such pivotal moments are still identifiable in tragedy, while coinciding with great shifts in Greek culture.

The first concerns the acknowledgment of radical finitude that Castoriadis finds expressed with force in Aeschylus' *Prometheus Bound*. We are familiar with the theme of this play. Zeus condemns Prometheus, a Titan, for having helped humans survive by giving them the gift of the fire, which he had stolen from the Gods. *Prometheus Bound* can be seen as a play depicting the conflict between the cult of the Olympian Gods, the cult of Dionysus and that of Orpheus. In any case, in a passage of this play Prometheus clearly foresees the end of the Olympian divine order. In reply to Hermes' demand that he should reveal the secret that threatens Zeus' dominion, Prometheus says that he has already seen two tyrants falling from their thrones and he is about to see the third tyrant (Zeus) falling with shame and force (verses 969–72). However, Castoriadis's interpretation shifts the emphasis from the divine order and Prometheus' ultimately unjustified torture to the conception of death and mortality that the play depicts. As Castoriadis emphatically writes, the "text says: I put an end to the condition whereby mortals did not foresee their death", which means that Prometheus taught human beings "that they are mortal" (Castoriadis 2001: 146). In other words, Castoriadis argues that the acknowledgment of human mortality is the most significant element this tragic play brings to the fore.

The *Antigone*: Being-human *qua* being-political

The second pivotal 'moment' mentioned above, is arguably more radical and Castoriadis unearths it via an interpretation of Sophocles' *Antigone*, the tragedy that has often fascinated philosophers. It is worth looking more closely at Castoriadis's reading, which is from the outset directed against two major interpretations of Sophocles' text, those of Hegel and Heidegger.

In brief, Hegel's position in the *Phenomenology of Spirit* is that the *Antigone* exemplifies the battle between two opposing forms of the ethical order[3], of which Antigone as woman represents the 'natural' realm, i.e. the ethical law that derives from familial relations (paragraphs 470 and 476). This position is repeated in Hegel's *Elements of the Philosophy of Right*, where it is stated that Antigone represents "the law of emotive subjective substantiality ... the law of the ancient gods and of the chthonic realm", which stands "in opposition to the public law, the law of the state" (paragraph 166). Indeed, Hegel seems to think that this play exemplifies a moment of crisis in the *Sittlichkeit* of the

---

3 The term *Sittlichkeit* is often translated in English as 'ethical order'. Solomon describes *Sittlichkeit* quite successfully and clearly as "morality as established custom, not a set of principles ... shared activity, shared interests, shared pleasures; it is not first of all, and perhaps not at all, rational reflection on the [ethical] rules" (Solomon 1983: 534). Hegel introduced this term in his critique of Kantian ethics, in order to account for a state-of-affairs that supports and makes morality possible. Hegel's argument is twofold. On the one hand he stresses the fact that the Kantian 'good will' is inadequate as an ethical ground insofar as it is not yet expressed or 'objectified' in concrete institutions. Furthermore, Hegel maintained that it makes no sense to understand individuals as isolated rational agents in the Kantian sense, since one becomes a self only via interaction, or as he states in the *Phenomenology of Spirit* just in the beginning of his famous Master and Slave dialectic: "A self-consciousness exists for *a self-consciousness*" (paragraph 177) and "Self-consciousness exists in and for itself when, and by the fact that, it so exists for another; that is it exists only in being acknowledged" (paragraph 178).

ancient Greek world, the waning of the old ethical order expressed by the law of the family and the emergence of a new order expressed by the state's exclusive claim to power. Since for Hegel freedom and self–fulfillment are only possible when there is a harmonious coexistence between the particular and the universal, it would not be inaccurate if following Solomon (1983: 549) we described this state-of-affairs as one of *alienation* (*Entfremdung*). Moreover, Hegel interprets Antigone's sense of duty towards the 'divine' laws and her consequent defiance of Creon's orders as indicative of the alleged 'fact' that the ethical order of the family preceded that of the state (see Solomon 1983: 547). Indeed, this is a point Hegel repeats in the *Elements of the Philosophy of Right*, where he defines family as the "immediate substantiality of spirit" that is based on love (paragraph 158). Now, although Antigone's slain brothers already express the political realm, they represent equally partial powers and they both commit the crime of failing to acknowledge the "highest form of consciousness, the Spirit[4] of the Community" (paragraph 473). In all these cases Hegel detects the danger of *contingency* and this is why he treats them as necessarily *sublated* forms of the human spirit. This holds truth despite the fact that in the *Phenomenology* Hegel has not yet formulated an explicit understanding of the state as "the actuality of the ethical idea" and "the rational in and for itself", as he did later in his *Elements of the Philosophy of Right* (paragraphs 257 and 258).

Now, Castoriadis downplays Hegel's interpretation *via* a simple statement that the *Antigone* is not really about the conflict between the law of the family and the law of the *polis*. Regrettably, apart from this nothing else is said of Hegel and Castoriadis's strategy is to oppose the main points of Heidegger's interpretation of this tragic play. In effect, Heidegger's interpretation aims at the uncovering of a primordial mode

---

4 Hegel uses the term 'Spirit' (*Geist*) in the *Phenomenology* in order to denote an objective, collective, unifying principle. Spirit therefore is "this absolute substance which is the unity of the different independent self–consciousnesses which, in their opposition, enjoy perfect freedom and independence" (paragraph 177).

of truth *qua* un-concealment (α-λήθεια/*a-letheia*), which he believes is preserved in poetic modes of discourse and transmitted by tradition. He even attempts to locate the "poetic project of being human" in a stasimon of the chorus (verses 332–75) from the *Antigone* (Heidegger 1959: 146). The first significant 'step' of Heidegger's interpretation revolves around the verses that characterise the human being as δεινόν/*deinon*. It has to be noted that δεινόν is a polyvalent word stemming from δέος/*deos* (fear, alarm, affright, etc.) and primarily signifying the fearful, terrible, dread, dire, mighty, able, clever, etc. (Liddell and Scott: 179 and 176–77). Heidegger translates δεινόν as "*Unheimlich*", which in the English edition of the *Einführung in die Metaphysik* (*Introduction to Metaphysics*) is translated as 'strange', or 'uncanny'. Castoriadis attacks this interpretation arguing that even the German word *Unheimlich* is "terribly insufficient", while the word *deinon* itself presents immense difficulties for "those not fortunate enough to understand a bit of Greek" (Castoriadis 2001: 150). Indeed Castoriadis indicates a first meaning of the word δεινότης/*deinotes* as "creative vehemence", which points also to a "division" within human nature and to the fact that the human being's skillfulness leads it "sometimes to good and sometimes to evil", good and evil understood in a political, non-moralistic sense (Castoriadis, 2001: 150). At any rate, Heidegger claims that the word δεινόν/*deinon* exemplifies in the best possible manner the Greek experience of *anthropos* (i.e. of the human being) and consequently also of the cosmos. In a sense in the context of Heidegger's philosophy, as an important event of disclosure it also points to a specific conception of 'Being'.

Although it is undeniable that Sophocles here gives a powerful interpretation of *anthropos*, Castoriadis rightly observes that Heidegger's interpretation suffers from the systematic "disregard" of the significance of the democratic institutions of the *polis* (Castoriadis 2001: 140). This disregard becomes rather disquieting given the inextricable historical bonds between the cultivation of philosophy and the development of democracy, which far from being a mere co–incidence binds together these supreme manifestations of human activity also on the level of meaning (Klimis 2006: 10).

In any case, Heidegger argues that the image of the human being that emerges from his interpretation of the Antigone is far deeper than modern philosophical interpretations of human existence. He furthermore believes that having pointed to the abysmal character of 'Being' and having severed his ties with a long metaphysical tradition that understands human otherness in terms of personhood, he has unearthed a more primordial interpretation of human life. Understood from this perspective, his statement that "among the Greeks there were no personalities (and for this reason no supra-personality)" (Heidegger 1959: 148), clearly signifies the belief in a pre-metaphysical, primordial conception of humanity.

Central to Heidegger's interpretation of the human being is the notion of δεινόν as the powerful "in the sense of one who uses power, who not only disposes of power [*Gewalt*] but is violent [*gewalt-tätig*] insofar as the use of power is the basic trait not only of his action but also of his being-there" (Heidegger 1959: 149–50). Heidegger explains that his aspiration in this context is to introduce a notion of violence that goes beyond the "common usage of the word, as mere arbitrary brutality". He thereby seems to imply that this common interpretation of violence is the product of a moralizing discourse, which he ultimately finds detrimental for our attempt to grasp the "mysteriousness of the essence of being human" (Heidegger 1959: 164). This interpretation of δεινόν served Heidegger to claim that the human being – the Dasein to be more faithful to the philosophical idiom introduced in *Being and Time* – is fundamentally *homeless*. In fact, in Heidegger's view the concept of homelessness describes in the best possible way both Dasein's being in the "midst of the overpowering" and its ability to "surpass the limit of the familiar [*das Heimische*]" (Heidegger 1959: 151). In a further appropriation of the chorus from the *Antigone*, Heidegger treats two words used by the chorus to characterise the human being, i.e. the words '*pantoporos aporos*' as a couplet, despite their being separated by a semi-colon in the play's text (lines 357–62) as Castoriadis (2001: 140) rightly points out. The importance of this interpretative move becomes apparent once we consider the transformation that this passage of Sophocles' text underwent in Heidegger's hands. Indeed, Heidegger's translation reads: "Everywhere journeying, inexperienced and without issue, he [i.e. the human being] comes to nothingness" (Heidegger 1959: 151). Having hermeneutically appropriated the text, Heidegger argues that the passage describes the human being's violent making a path out of the familiar, only to be befallen by ruin and catastrophe (Heidegger 1959: 151–52).

Now, a careful look at the play shows that the chorus is clear that despite their dexterity and inventiveness humans cannot escape death (see verses 357–62). This point is maintained in Heidegger's translation, which reads: "Through no fight can he [i.e. the human being] resist the one assault of death" (Heidegger 1959: 147). Here we encounter an acknowledgment of finitude, which however as mentioned above is for Castoriadis already present in Greek culture before the writing of Sophocles' play.

Heidegger employs the same interpretative strategy with regard to the verses that explicitly point to the *polis* as the historical place where the unconcealment of being–human is inaugurated. Here he stresses the antithesis between υψίπολις/*hypsipolis* and άπολις/*apolis*, the former term indicating the praised citizen, the latter the disgraced one, someone who because of one's own actions does not deserve to bear the name of the citizen any longer. In this context it is important to note that Heidegger wishes to establish a close linkage between the historical and the political, always from the perspective of the disclosure of human essence as this latter emerges from Dasein's partaking in 'Being'. The powerful is rendered again the overarching principle of this disclosure and

Heidegger turns his gaze to the tragic dimension of historical-political creation. However, as shown above, his interpretation of historical-political creation revolves around the idea of *power* – in the guise of *violence* – as the principle underlying the allotment of fortunes between humans. In other words violence is seen as the principle that allows certain human beings to become historically pre–eminent (υψίπολις/ *hypsipolis*) while marginalising others (άπολις/*apolis*) (Heidegger 1959: 152). It is easy here to recognise a transformation of the Heraclitean theme of *polemos* which renders some people free and others slaves and Nietzsche's *will to power*, i.e. of a principle that permeates all forms of life, natural and human.

In place of a conclusion: Being-human as creation and *hybris*

It is true that in deliberately breaking with ethics Heidegger's interpretation uncovers violence as an essential characteristic of human life. At the same time it arguably disregards other, equally fundamental characteristics of human existence – like *eros*, love and solidarity – assuming that these have been addressed – and shaped – by metaphysics. Especially through his interpretation of the *Antigone*, Heidegger furnishes us with a 'heroic' account of human existence, which despite its unquestionable merits is rather unsatisfying and often even ideological. Levinas (1969) explicitly directed his critique against Heidegger's 'heroic' conception of humanity and attempted to show its limits. His thesis against Heidegger could be briefly summarised in his belief that Heidegger glorifies death but remains blind to the fact that death is primarily *murder*. A consequence of this blindness, which is nothing less than indifference towards the Other – is that the 'heroic' subject remains ultimately enclosed to itself, that it fails to open up to other persons. It is not accidental that Levinas's *Totality and Infinity* culminates with the identification of "the heroic existence" with "the isolated soul" and postulates that the finitude of this existence relies exactly on its inability to break free from the continuous time of subjective identity and to open up to the discontinuous time of *humanity* (Levinas 1969: 307).

However, Castoriadis's critique of Heidegger focuses not so much on its alleged cruelty but mainly on Heidegger's fundamental misunderstanding of the Greek experience of the world in all its manifestations (divine, human and natural). This misunderstanding entails the inability – or unwillingness – on Heidegger's part to grasp the true essence of the *polis*, the emergence of democracy. Time and again Castoriadis has stressed in his writings that tragedy itself was consubstantial with democracy as it uncovered three fundamental dimensions of human existence, namely mortality, *hybris* and the acknowledgment of the need to collectively decide about our common affairs (see *WIF*: 93–94). This fundamental insight concerning the inextricable link between tragedy and democracy clearly informs the interpretative twist Castoriadis gives to the notions of υψίπολις (*hypsipolis*) and άπολις (*apolis*). Indeed, Castoriadis points to the non–translatability of the word υψίπολις, which he explains literally as "standing high within one's city" and furthermore as indicating the "sublime" human being as member of a political community. Άπολις, is then the citizen who "for the sake of daring" or because of "imprudence" transgresses the established limits of action. This interpretation allows Castoriadis to claim that the conceptual couplet 'υψίπολις–άπολις' points the reader to the real theme of this tragic play, viz. *hybris*. For Castoriadis, although Kreon and Antigone represent "adversary principles", they still both commit *hybris* against the polis; they both violate the principle that gave birth to the *polis*, namely thinking collectively and thinking on equal terms – *ison phronein* (Castoriadis 2001: 148–49).

For Castoriadis the *Antigone* shows exactly the human being's "terrific power (*deinotes*)", which results mostly in the self-destruction of *hybris* but has also the potential to reach "the sublime domain of *hypsipolis*" provided that the "equitability of collective thought" is not violated (Castoriadis 2001: 150). Addressed from this perspective, Sophocles' exaltation of the human being as δεινόν (*deinon*) irrevocably shows for Castoriadis that in creating its 'worlds' the human being creates itself, that the "essence of anthropos is self–creation" (Castoriadis 2001: 151). However, there is no unequivocally triumphant tone behind this insight, as the joy of creation is always threatened by the shadow of *hybris*. Castoriadis seems to suggest that the essence of *hybris* is the isolation of individual existence, a claim that squares with his interpretation of *hybris* in relation to Anaximander, where Castoriadis understands the very existence of beings, their differentiation from chaos to which they ultimately have to return, as *hybris* and injustice (*Gr.* 299). Similarly, there is no refutation of destruction in Castoriadis's account of human creation but there is *defiance* in the face of it. This defiance is then rather based on the concurrent acknowledgment of finitude and of a mode of 'infinity' emerging out of *agon* and *solidarity* as prerequisites of significant and lasting human doings.

References

Adorno, Theodor and Horkheimer, Max (1986) (2nd ed.), *Dialectic of Enlightenment*, trans. John Cumming. London and New York: Verso.

Castoriadis, Cornelius (2001) "Aeschylean Anthropology and Sophoclean Self-Creation of Anthropos", in Johann P. Arnason and Peter Murphy (eds.), *Agon, Logos, Polis: The Greek Achievement and its Aftermath*. Stuttgart: Franz Steiner Verlag.

Castoriadis, Cornelius (1987) *The Imaginary Institution of Society*, trans. Kathleen Blamey. Cambridge: MIT Press (*IIS*).

Castoriadis, Cornelius (1997) "The Greek and the Modern Political Imaginary", in *World in Fragments*, ed. and trans. David Ames Curtis. Stanford CA.: Stanford University Press.

Hegel, G.W.F (1991) *Elements of the Philosophy of Right*, ed. Allen W. Wood and trans. H. B. Nisbet. Cambridge: Cambridge University Press.

Hegel, G.W.F (1977) *Phenomenology of Spirit*, trans. A.V. Miller with analysis of the text and forward by J.N. Findlay. Oxford: Oxford University Press.

Heidegger, Martin (1959) *An Introduction to Metaphysics*, trans. Karl Manheim. New Haven and London: Yale University Press.

Levinas, Emmanuel (1969) *Totality and Infinity: An Essay on Exteriority*, trans. Alphonso Lingis. Pittsburgh, Pennsylvania: Duquesne University Press.

Plato, "Timaeus" in John M. Cooper (ed.) and D. S. Hutchinson (Associate ed.) (1997), *Plato: Complete Works*. Indianapolis and Cambridge: Hackett Publishing Company.

Klimis, Sophie (2006) "Explorer le labyrinthe imaginaire de la création grecque : un projet en travail", in S. Klimis and L. Van Eynde (eds), *L'imaginaire selon Castoriadis. Thèmes et enjeux, Cahiers Castoriadis*, n.1, Bruxelles: Publications des Facultés Universitaires Saint-Louis, 9–58.

Solomon, Robert C. (1983) *In the Spirit of Hegel*. Oxford and New York: Oxford University Press.

In Greek

Αισχύλος (Aeschylus) (1992), Προμηθέας Δεσμώτης (Prometheus Bound). Athens: Κάκτος (Cactus).

Καστοριάδης (Castoriadis), Κορνήλιος (Cornelius) (2007), Η Ελληνική Ιδιαιτερότητα: Από τον Όμηρο στον Ηράκλειτο. Αθήνα: Κριτική.

Καστοριάδης (Castoriadis), Κορνήλιος (Cornelius) (1999), Η αρχαία ελληνική δημοκρατία και η σημασία της για μας σήμερα. Athens: Ύψιλον (Ypsilon).

Πλάτων (Plato) (1996), Τίμαιος (Timaeus), translated and with an introduction by Βασίλης Κάλφας (Vassilis Kalfas). Athens: Πόλις (Polis).

Σοφοκλής (Sophocles) (1994), Αντιγόνη (Antigone). Athens: Κάκτος (Cactus).

Dictionaries

Liddell and Scott (1889), *Greek–English Lexicon*, 7th abridged edition, impression of 1997. Oxford: Oxford: Oxford University Press.

Origins as a Sign of Pathology in Architectural Thinking

Catharina Gabrielsson

In "The Imaginary: Creation in the Social-Historical Domain" (*WIF*: 3–18), Castoriadis gives a condensed account of the basis for his thinking. "Each society, like each living being or species, *establishes, creates its own world*" he writes, relating to his thesis that there is no meaning or truth beyond the realm of social imaginary significations (WIF: 9). But if every society is different and institutes its own reality, how is it possible to turn to societies other than one's own as a source for knowledge? Castoriadis himself returns to antiquity, like countless others have done before him, in search of principles that are essential to philosophy, democracy and the arts. It would be a contradiction to Castoriadis's terms if such a return did not amount to an act of creation in itself. It is not a return in an archaeological sense, set on un-digging evidence from the past, but a radical re-reading of ancient sources that contextualises them as well as their present setting. This kind of return means to create a new space for thought and action.[1]

In this essay, I will draw the outlines for the sort of 'return' that

---

1 See Hal Foster's opening discussion in "Who is Afraid of the Neo-Avant-Garde?" concerning the creative reuse of the past and "the radical" as the literal re-reading of roots *(radix)*, drawing on Michel Foucault's seminal article *What is an Author?* (Foster 1996: 2).

predominates in architectural thinking. The role and importance of history in and for architecture is, of course, impossible to summarize; yet there are certain traits that seem to recur, a way of thinking that is strangely consistent and which is what interests me here. Exposing it means to generalize, thus missing out on nuances and details, but it has the asset of focusing on the problem directly – which is how the architectural discipline, throughout the ages, maintains the illusion of its independency from the outside world.

We might begin by recalling one such instance, the famous *querelle* of the Ancients and the Moderns in the late 17th century – a heated debate in the French Academy involving a critical questioning of progress (cf. Barasch 2000: 360–65). While neither side disputes the authority of antiquity, the quarrel concerns the degree to which the achievements of the past should determine activities in the present. For the Ancients, classical architecture was posited as a collection of formal ideals that reduces the status of any later achievements to that of the faithful copy. But for the Moderns, followers of the Cartesian *cogito*, historical forms merely establish principles that may be interpreted, and indeed surpassed, by later creations (Rykwert 1989: 57–61). The essence of architecture, according to the radical architect Claude Perrault, is not to slavishly imitate the ancient but to produce a beauty that is "positive and convincing", even allowing for the arbitrary products of taste. In questioning the existence of universal aesthetic principles, he suggests that proportions in architecture are agreeable "for no other reason than that we are used to them" (quoted in Wittkower 1973: 144). In their inherent relativism, these ideas challenge the very stability of architecture's foundations: they cannot be allowed to ferment. Thus Perrault arrives at the conclusion that even if architecture ultimately aims to please, it is not enough to merely repeat the words used by the ancients. They must be used with eloquence, and it is only the Architect who has the education and skill to do so. What we see here is how the potentially destabilizing notion of a practise that merely aims to please is brought to a close by the insertion of authority; the architect as the professional maker of pleasing and meaningful things; the Architect as Author.

This scurry to close the rupture that opens whenever architecture is confronted with an expanded social sphere – the emotions, imaginations and activities of others – is typical for the mindset I will explore here. Escaping precise diagnosis but made manifest in a wide array of behaviours and ideas, the pathology I am alluding to may be identified with what Cornelius Castoriadis refers to as *heteronomy*, which he in fact compares to "a psychotic person suffering from paranoia", one who has "created once and for all his own all-encompassing and totally rigid interpretative system, and nothing can ever enter his world without being transformed according to the rules of this system" (*WIF*: 17). Castoriadis sees heteronomy as marked by cognitive closure, an inability to recognize the self-inflicted character of mental limits. He opposes this to *autonomy*, the capacity to question one's thinking as well as the forms and ideas produced by the society at hand.

It is important, I think, to recognize heteronomy and autonomy as perhaps primarily psychic states and notice how our minds tend to fluctuate from one state to another. But in Castoriadis's writings, frequently crossing between political and psychoanalytic theory, there are larger issues at stake. Stressing their literal Greek meanings, heteronomy is seen to signify the laws (*nomos*) deriving from another (*heteros*), suggesting the existence of some exterior, absolute principle or force as ultimately defining society. Conversely, autonomy in Castoriadis's thinking is attaining the full recognition that the laws derive from oneself (*auto*), that is, from inside the social sphere having no other source than the human imagination and ability to create (*WIF*: 86–88). The paradoxes and complexities inherent to the discursive creations of architectural origins, however – which is what I will focus on here –

exposc a tension in the autonomy/heteronomy divide, one that opens up for discussions at a more in-depth level: on the one hand concerning the construction of the architectural discipline, on the other concerning the applicability of Castoriadis's concepts in interdisciplinary research.

The mythological origins of architecture

According to a persuasive Western mythology, recounted by a wide range of thinkers, society emerges along with language around the primordial fireplace. In *Civilization and its Discontents*, Sigmund Freud posits that "the first acts of civilization were the use of tools, the gaining of control over fire and the construction of dwellings" (Freud 1961: 90). Although tools, fire and dwellings seem to be allocated equal importance here (while remarkably omitting language), the acquisition and control of fire is regarded by Freud as sexually charged and therefore of primary significance.[2] For the antique architect and scholar Vitruvius, however, what primarily arises from the discovery of fire is social cohesion and language – and through that, shortly thereafter, architecture. Partly through competition, partly through acts of collaboration, primitive man is drawn into a flurry of activities set on improving his living conditions: "some of that company began to make roofs of leaves, others to dig hollows under the hills, yet others made places for shelter in imitation of the nests and buildings of swallows out of mud and wattle" (quoted in Rykwert 1989: 105). The simplicity of this Ur-scene is what allows its content and focus to shift with each separate interpretation. Architects and historians have returned to it repeatedly throughout history, at

2 In a theatrical aside, Freud makes a curious suggestion as to how the acquisition and control of fire may be seen as constitutive for the differences and hierarchies between the sexes. Since "primal man had an infantile desire to put out fire with a stream of urine … an enjoyment of sexual potency in homosexual competition", he finds it reasonable that woman was appointed guardian of the fire and permanently positioned by the hearth since "her anatomy made it impossible for her to yield to the temptation of this desire" (Freud 1961: 90, note 1).

each moment denoting a particular stance in terms of the identity and legitimacy of architecture.

Thus the origin of architecture has never been quite as innocent as these myths may lead us to believe. In providing a persistent point of reference in architectural thinking, origins have served as a source for determining that which is considered essential to architecture. Whether appropriated, fabricated or based on scanty archaeological evidence, origins have always been charged with ideology and intent. As I hope to make clear in what follows, conjuring up an origin for architecture is an operative act, one embedded in the social, political and discursive context of its time but with the precise intent to act upon, and ultimately transform, that context. One of the most famous historical examples is the view put forward by Abbé Marc-Antoine Laugier in his influential *Essai sur l'Architecture* (1753). His allegorical story of 'architecture returning to its natural model' entails the famous depiction of the rustic hut:

> The little hut which I have just described is the type on which all the magnificences of architecture are elaborated. It is by approximation to its simplicity of execution that fundamental defects are avoided and true perfection attained. The upright pieces of wood suggest the idea of columns, the horizontal pieces resting on them, entablatures. Finally, the inclined members which constitute the roof provide the idea of a pediment (quoted in Rykwert 1989: 44).

With this minimal definition of an ideal architecture, Laugier is said to "break with the renaissance tradition of *mimesis* and redefine architecture not as a civic art, whose meaning lies in the decorous representation of social, religious, or philosophical values, but as the material art of construction" (van Eck, quoted in Hvattum 2006: 34). In other words, Laugier is said to do away with decoration by grounding architecture in the rational laws of construction. But although it may be regarded as a proto-functionalistic approach, stressing form as evolving through the proper use of materials, Laugier does not break with *mimesis* as such – he merely shifts the focus as to *what* architecture should represent. According to the German scholar Karsten Harries,

> Laugier pleads for an architecture that is *doubly representational*: architecture should represent Greek architecture, and by doing so it will most adequately represent the primitive hut that is supported by the authority of human nature. Representing the primitive hut, architecture recalls us to the essence of building, to its *arche*, its timeless origin (Harries 1997: 113).

This comment suggests that the very root of the problem I am addressing here derives from the etymology of architecture, its *arche* [Greek: *archē*, to begin, the original or first]; implicating architecture as ultimately determined by its origins, even as constituting an origin in itself – the unyielding, permanent and stable ground of civilisation that, in Harries wording, is supported by "the authority of human nature".

Laugier's view is a severe, almost religiously ascetic position articulated as a defence against the caprice of decoration and the vagaries of individual taste. But the set of distinctions thus implied – between structure and ornament, substance and appearance, building and architecture – are continuously at stake whenever origins are brought into question. The chapter headings in the architectural historian Joseph Rykwert's seminal account, *On Adam's House in Paradise: The Idea of The primitive Hut in Architectural History* (1989) serve to illustrate the crucial issues at hand: Thinking and Doing, Necessity and Convention, Positive and Arbitrary, Nature and Reason, Reason and Grace (followed by a chapter on anthropological rites, and one speculating on psychology). So although origins may be rethought and reinvented to serve the problem at hand, the issues they raise seem to remain the same throughout early Modernity.

Paradoxically, however, the massive intellectual shift in the 19th century – the 'discovery' of history, the fascination for the multiplicity of nature and the search for its underlying principles – merely serves to reinforce the significance of origins, albeit now in another sense. In architecture, it means that the primitive hut (in various forms and materials) ceases to be regarded as a conceptual or once existent ideal and rather becomes like a seed; a prototype that serves to explain variety and differences in building, particularly in terms of style (Hvattum 2006).

In his *Dictionary of Architecture* (1832), Antoine Quatremère-de-Quincy hence stresses the contextual, multiple and diverse nature of architectural origins. From the basis of three primordial kinds of human life – hunters, shepherds and farmers – he identifies the cave, the tent and the wooden hut as the three archetypical building structures from which the architecture of the Egyptians, the Chinese and the Greeks have evolved. The evolutionary theme does not eradicate a normative or ideological content, however. Because of its eternal and absolute beauty, Quatremère finds only the architecture of the Greek to be worthy of imitation (a view he later legitimizes by reference to geographic, moral, climatic and racial conditions). Resounding with Hegelian aesthetics, the Greek (*la belle architecture)* is seen as the model for "a thinking man's architecture", an eternal ideal that is unsurpassed by later achievements (Lavin 1992: 30). With the advent of eclecticism, however – constitutive for the weaning of *one* classical tradition – the contextualised, historicised and multiplied conception of origins generate a new set of applications. Faced with a sudden abundance of styles, origins are used to justify choice from a bewildering array of possibilities. It is now original function, rather than form, that becomes decisive: thus Chinese for a pavilion, Gothic for a church, Neo-classical for a court building etc. (Hvattum 2004). Despite this shift as to how origins are conceived and made operative, their basic purpose remains the same: to stabilise the architectural practice by eradicating the arbitrariness of evaluation and choice. The evolutionary theme introduced by Quatremère will be pushed further by others – most notably by Viollet-le-Duc, whose rationalistic approach is in better alignment with the ambitions of the times. The turbulent 19th century brings about an increase in mobility, an increased access to distant sources in space and time (i.e. through archaeological and geographical discoveries) and provides new technological means for the production and dissemination of knowledge. The development of society creates new architectural conditions and new assignments, but is also a challenge to any tradition or inherited form. The crisis of Modernity therefore promotes a repetition of origins; a continuous production of *assertive statements* meticulously forged by a merging of facts and fictions.

Viollet-le-Duc's version of the primordial Ur-scene, for instance, is deliberately fictitious in order to bring the point across. In his *Histoire de l'habitation humaine* (1875), with "unshakable faith in the power of reason", Viollet-le-Duc builds his doctrine on the activities of two fictitious characters, Doxi and Epergos, in order to argue for an architecture based on constructive rationality (Rykwert 1989: 38). In distinction to Doxi, his weak and hesitant partner, Epergos resolutely steps into the course of events and *teaches* primordial man how to build. The conceptual clarity of Viollet-le-Duc's myth is suggestive of the historian as *fictor*, "the modeller, the artisan, the author, the inventor of whatever past he offers us" (Didi-Huberman 2005: 2). But it is precisely the fictitious nature of Viollet-le-Duc's account that serves to underline his strategy: to establish an absolute, timeless basis for architecture. It serves to enforce the 'tone of certainty' that a historiographical critic like Didi-Huberman sets out to undo.

Eradicating uncertainty

Residing on the problematical and widespread conception that the first is somehow *right*, origins are (as Edward Said has noted) teleological in nature and therefore divine (Said 1997: xxiii). Carrying the content and structuring the logic of all that is expected to follow, origins form part of the causal and linear epistemology that has allowed architects and historians, well into the present day, to use history as "at once source, verification, and authorization" (Vidler 2008: 12). Following onto this, origins have less to do with the past than with the future, in setting out the path for architecture ahead; thus "speculations intensify when the need is felt for a renewal of architecture" (Rykwert 1989: 183). But if the origin has a privileged position in Western thinking – if not as a source for truth and authenticity, then at least as morally or aesthetically superior (Gombrich 2002) – its use in writings on architecture reveal an almost obsessive need, not merely to argue for a particular architectural conception or style, but to justify the discipline as such (Forty 2006: 4). Le Corbusier famously linked nomad temples to fishermen's shacks to argue for what he called 'the principle of the straight line' – thereby promoting an architecture which, in its basic adherence to reason, would be of eternal value. And this kind of thinking re-emerges whenever architecture is grounded in so-called essential principles. It finds its most explicit form in uncritical phenomenological writings, but is equally embedded in the humanist tradition whereby form is supposed to harmonize with the idealized human body (Hight 2008: 17–31). The underlying consistency of these moves is unmistakable. While the return to origins, as pointed out by Foucault, always carries the potential of transforming discourse (Foucault 1969), it seems that its primary aim in architectural thinking has been to put an *end* to discourse.

According to Castoriadis, social forms cannot be derived from "physical conditions, from 'antecedents' or from permanent characteristics of 'man'", and the tendency to do so perpetuates an inability to grasp society as humanly created and self-instituted (*WIF*: 13). But while architectural origins may be seen to epitomise heteronomous thinking, they also have the effect of bringing two distinctively different conceptions of

57

autonomy into view. One as defined by Castoriadis, which might in fact be understood as the outcome of psychoanalysis (acknowledging one's defence mechanisms, knowing the limits of one's capacity, accepting responsibility for one's relationships), which at a social level finds its equivalence in democracy and philosophy (e.g. *FT*: 227); the other denoting an independent and self-sufficient object, organism or form, more in alignment with a biological model. The work that origins perform in architectural thinking is basically to prove and support this latter form of autonomy, for understanding architecture as a self-referential, aesthetic structure that takes its cues – not from the individual maker (the author), neither from the reality of the present society (e.g. use or programme) – but from an extra-social source, whether configured in terms of climate, material, necessity, reason or the human body.

Architectural autonomy finds its most explicit articulation in Leon Battista Alberti's *De re aedificatoria*, written about 1450. In his plan for an ideal church, autonomy is primarily attained through the adherence to a divine proportional system that, as derived from a neo-Platonic ontology, is believed to permeate the universe. But it resounds throughout, in every requirement, ranging from the physical isolation of the building, its being elevated from the ground, its windows only allowing for a view of the sky to its absence of decoration (Wittkower 1973: 9) – all used as means to make a decisive break with the everyday. Arguably, it is at this point that the architectural discipline finds its 'true' origin in being hinged onto an authored, professional practice. With Alberti, architecture enters into its tormented double bind to universalism and authorship, and is distanced from the craft of building through its elevation into art endowed by theory. And it is the impossible closure of this disciplinary structure that appears to be in need of constant re-enforcement by later writers, based on a conception of autonomy that Castoriadis defines as "false", as heteronomy, an "organisational, informational, cognitive closure" that ultimately signifies an inability to encompass the contradictions inherent to social existence (*WIF*: 16).

In commenting on the idea of the primitive, Adrian Forty remarks that the constant need for justifying and grounding the discipline sets architecture apart from other aesthetic practices. He claims that the interest in cave paintings, African and Indian art, the content and structure of dreams etc. within the cultural avant-garde and the subsequent import of these influences into practice were driven by the desire to topple the dominant (bourgeois) conception of art – not to affirm it (Forty 2006: 4). Thus notions of the primitive in architecture – including rustic huts and other mythological origins – have primarily served as means for sustaining and enforcing essential values in architecture, rather than questioning them or posing alternatives. What Forty fails to recognize, however, is that the production of origins in architecture is also a critical practice – perhaps not intended to shock, but certainly fused by a desire to transform the dominant culture. The main difference *vis-à-vis* art, in how I see it, lies in what origins in architecture reveal: an unreasonable fear of uncertainty that works compulsively to put an end to experimentation whenever the stability of the discipline is at risk. A towering monument in these processes of self-analysis, the Greek temple holds a special position in the history of architectural origins; we may turn to it here to see how the fear is made manifest.

The origins of the Greek temple

According to Vitruvius, whose authority relies precisely on being the 'First' (reducing all others, according to Rykwert, to mere commentaries) and whose legacy has been handed down through the ages, the essential architectural principle is symmetry.[3] It is established by the general proportional relationship of the Greek temple, based on a module that

---

3 Recent re-readings of Vitruvius bring out the reductive and distorted character of this legacy. Bernard Cache has pointed out that large sections of Vitruvius' *Ten Books of Architecture* are characterised by a managerial approach and is devoted to war machines and movable parts, not building *per se* (Cache 2010).

is half the diameter of a column, a mathematical unit derived from the idealized human body. Vitruvius describes how two of the Greek *genus* (orders) – the Doric and the Ionic – originate from the male and the female body (while the third order, the Corinthian, emanates from a narrative, mythological source). Vitruvius is clear on the point that this proportional system was already practiced on earlier, wooden temples that constitute the origin for the temple. The ornamentation of the orders is seen to derive from carpentry, whose constructive logic and material details were transferred to and imitated in later stone structures.

This idea of the temple's wooden origins has been enormously influential – we have already encountered it in Laugier's ideal hut. For Vitruvius, "the notion of origins had cardinal speculative importance ... his whole theory of architecture flowed from it" (Rykwert 1989: 112) – so clearly the issue of wooden origins is important, but less in an archaeological sense and more for what it reveals concerning the construction of the architectural discipline. Appropriated as a source to explain the Greek orders, the issue of wooden origins encapsulates the question of representation in architecture; *mimesis*, structure, ornament and a building's capacity to 'speak'; that is, all that is slippery in architecture in that it exceeds the necessities of construction. If Vitruvius' writings are based on practice, basically describing what he knows and has heard, his recommendations are re-worked during the renaissance and transformed into a rigid law (Barletta 2001: 2). In *De re aedificatoria*, Alberti thus makes a distinction between Beauty and Ornament as one of substance verses surface. Beauty is "the harmony and concord of all the parts achieved in such a manner that nothing could be added or taken away or altered except for the worse", whereas ornament is "a kind of additional brightness and improvement to Beauty ... something added and fastened on" (Wittkower 1973: 33). The distinction between beauty and ornament, between eternal values and temporary taste, between substance and surface, between that which is 'proper and innate' to architecture and arbitrary additions, is a prevailing theme in architectural thinking that indeed resounds unto the present.[4] What needs to be noted, however, is the resemblance to another dichotomy, that between *episteme* and *doxa*, between certified knowledge (absolute truth) and mere opinion, expressed for instance in the opposition between Plato/Socrates and the sophists' teachings in rhetoric (Rosengren 2002). There are therefore ontological and epistemological issues involved when Ornament (arbitrary *doxa*) is rejected in favour of Beauty (structural *episteme*). It also means to reject the immanent, social and practised reality as a source of knowledge, similar to prioritizing language to speech, rationality to desire, objective laws to subjective perception. Curiously, however, the Greek temple refuses such distinctions between the essential and the non-essential – it may even be seen as a display of an ultimate *sophistic* position. As described by Percy Gardner:

> The whole building is constructed, so to speak, on a subjective rather than an objective basis; it is intended not to be mathematically accurate, but to be adapted to the eye of the spectator. To the eye a curve is a more pleasing form that a straight line, and the deviations from rigid correctness serve to give a character of purpose, almost of life, to the solid marble construction (quoted in Dinsmoor 1973: 39).

Such observations open up to the particularities of the Greek perception of the world, its reality of social imaginary values, based on what we might call an *embodied* knowledge that goes beyond entrenched dichotomies. We see here how the definition of ornament as an imitation of a former constructive detail serves as a means of rationalisation; it transforms

4 An evident example is how the modernist adherence to rational construction, honesty of materials and universal style is replaced by the post-modern re-appropriation of classicism, which according to Charles Jencks is precisely to restore architecture as "an enjoyable art" based on its communicative capacity (Jencks 1973: 389). It should also be noted that the distinction between substance/structure and surface/decoration is profoundly gender-loaded: concrete versus curtains, so to speak.

ornament into a necessity, *not* because of its communicative or sensual powers, but as a manifestation of reason. Thus for Quatremère-de-Quincy, the inherent rationality of the temple is "the principal reason for the very pleasure which Greek architecture gives us, and this pleasure is the very same which we find so desirable in other arts of imitation" (quoted in Rykwert 1987: 63).

According to Sylvia Lavin, Quatremère's thinking revolves around an understanding of architecture structured like language; an alignment of systems seen "as equally fundamental to society ... the distinguishing characteristics of civilisation", thus abiding to the idea of a shared genesis around the primordial fire (Lavin 1992: xi). In pointing to his conceptualisation of architecture as a social art, as artifice and thus *removed* from nature, Lavin shows how matters of representation, decoration and meaning are central to Quatremère's inquiries. There is evidently a difference at stake in Quatremère's position, that between a classical conception that sees architecture as an imitation of nature, and a more modern view where architecture is put in correspondence with social, historical or scientific structural laws. Despite the fact that origins are played out as cards in different contextual settings, I nevertheless venture to suggest that it is language, rather than speech that has remained a priority in architectural thinking, indicating that architectural anxieties primarily flow from the fundamental ambiguity of meaning.

Thus the pathology of architectural thinking is a difficult complex, psychologically speaking, for it is precisely the *expressivity* of architecture that distinguishes it from (mere) building. Whether defined as an art of imitation, a materialization of spirituality, a capacity to evoke emotions or something else, architecture cannot be unhinged from aesthetics. Meanwhile, ornamentation must be justified, rationalised or standardised (within the Academy) or banned (in Modernity), all in order to prevent arbitrary utterances, or even worse: noise. The vagaries inherent to speech, the uncertainties of communication, and the groundlessness implied by what Rosengren denotes 'doxology' (Rosengren 2002) provide a fundamentally *uncertain* foundation for architecture that has never been fully considered in theory. For these uncertainties are not without significance – it is rather a case of the reverse, for the unknowable enters into architecture silently and indirectly, its very omission highlighting the compulsion to certify architecture beyond the realm of the social. "Determinations are there with an effort" Renata Tyszecuk notes, regarding even the language of architecture as "indicative of an obsession with determination: we have projects, models, specifications, details, efficiency: all is determined" (Tyszcuk 2007: 154). And so the effort to close the gap, the abyssal indeterminacy that threatens to undo architecture as structure, discipline and ground, is also made manifest in how speech (the Greek orders) is rationalised into language (universal structure) – if not indicative for a rejection of the Real, as Tyszecuk suggests, then certainly for a fear of uncertainty and an almost autistic inability to grasp what is actually worth saying.

Alternative beginnings

The question of wooden origins may have been a contested issue in the 18th and 19th century academies, but contested within a discourse that was firmly structured by rationality and logic (Barletta 2001: 17). In so far as it remained within a framework of constructive reason, the interpretation of architectural expressivity was sustained by an epistemology of linear progress and hierarchy and may therefore be seen as yet another symptom of heteronomy.[5] There is, however, a remarkable exception to this

---

5 Recent archaeological research casts interesting new light on this old debate. Barletta claims that rather than a step-by-step progression from primitive to advanced, the two primary materials – mud-brick and stone – seem to have coexisted for the entire period defined by what was available locally (Barletta 2001: 25). There is thus little support for wooden origins – in fact, the discovery of 7th century temples in Corinth and Isthamia has recently yielded fresh evidence for a primary stone tradition. While there is, indeed, some evidence that supports the idea of early wooden structures, what is *not* clear is the relationship between wooden and

trail which deserves special attention – precisely because it highlights what an alternative way of thinking architecture might be. For it is with the second major source of disagreement – that of the colouring of the Greek temple – a significant shift occurs. If Winckelmann had celebrated the Greek for the pristine grandeur and simplicity of their art, the discovery of traces of paint on the remaining stone structures in Greek and Italy shook this aesthetic doctrine at its foundations. For Gottfried Semper it brings about another idea of origins altogether; not as form or physical structure, but one based on the experience and use of space. To paraphrase Edward Said, it constitutes thinking *beginnings* in architecture; beginnings as a socio-historical, dynamic and constantly evolving process of starting and starting again (Said 1997: xxiii).

Initiated by his study on the polychromy of Greek architecture in the 1830s (a doxological aspect *par excellence*), Semper sets out to write a theory on architecture as based on a gradual, socio-historical evolvement of material skills. In his unfinished life work from 1860, *Style in the Technical and Tectonic Arts or Practical Aesthetics,* Semper defines the primordial 'elements' or motives in architecture as the terrace, the hearth, the wall and the roof – each one evolving out of a certain practice or technique (pottery, weaving etc.). For him, the primary architectural element is the wall, seen as originating from tapestry and the practice of subdividing space by mounting textiles, thereby reducing the supporting structure (whether in wood, stone or bricks) into mere scaffolding. Semper's *Bekleidung* theory implies that ornamentation is not an addition, a superstructure to architecture: it is the primary architectural element. Furthermore, in suggesting the making of space as the central architectural motivation – the wall being "the earliest vertical spatial

---

stone forms in the architectural orders. Barletta stresses the high degree of experimentation expressed in the great variety of temple forms: the "extant remains contradict the idea of a rigid canon ... Instead, the architect seems able to choose from various models and even to invent his own" (Barletta 2001: 82). Again: the weakest link lies in the question of ornament, in the architectural rhetoric, in that which – maybe – merely aims to please.

enclosure that man invented", "the inner life separated from the outer life" (Semper 1989: 254) – the formal rigidity of structural origins are replaced by shifting, relational and social forms of spatial emergence.

Although Semper's work is clearly aligned with the morphological interests of his time, and 'materialistic' in that architecture is seen to originate from practical skills, much of Semper's thinking goes beyond these constraints (Hvattum 2004). Under the enigmatic heading of paragraph 60, "The Most Primitive Formal Principle in Architecture Based on the Concept of Space and Independent of Construction. The Masking of Realities in the Arts", he offers a radically different approach to the interpretation of the Greek temple. Arguing for the importance of the temporary event, he sees it as a symbolic materialization of social or religious celebration made evident by its original polychrome appearance. The ornamentation and colouring of the Greek temple are thus representations of a former "festival apparatus", what was once an "improvised scaffolding ... covered with decorations, draped with carpets, dressed with boughs and flowers, adorned with festoons and garlands, fluttering banners and trophies" (Semper 1989: 256). In an extensive footnote, he goes on to say:

> I think that the dressing and the mask are as old as human civilisation, and the joy in both is identical with the joy in those things that drove men to be sculptors, painters, architects, poets, musicians, dramatists, in short, artists. Every artistic creation, every artistic pleasure presupposes a certain carnival spirit, or to express myself in a more modern way – the haze of carnival candles is the true atmosphere of art. The denial of reality, of the material, is necessary if form is to emerge as a meaningful symbol, as an autonomous creation of man. ... [but] only these men in times of high artistic development also masked the material of the mask (Semper 1989: 256).

This quote points to more than a reversal of the standard architectural logic – it signals a radical shift of framework. Although Semper retains the idea that the ornament is a symbolic representation of an earlier form, he does it in a completely different way. Semper's main interpreter H. F. Mallgrave suggests that "the painted marble does not imitate the logic of its timber prototype, but denies its material basis altogether. In effect, the material disappears behind the radiant polychrome dressing and becomes pure form" (Mallgrave 1989: 40). But what Mallgrave identifies as pure form – announcing a modern aesthetics – is also form as rhetoric, a generator of actions, ideas and emotions. Semper's origin of architecture is essentially not of a formal kind, but concerns the human capacity to endow materials with affective qualities. It is an evaporation of the origins of architecture, taking as its source a ritual and collective spatial practice. Elsewhere, Semper suggests that civilization begins with rhythm, "the regularities of the oarstroke and the handbeat ... the wreath and the bead necklace" (Rykwert 1982: 127); the creation of order through gesture and speech, rather than form and language. There is an affinity here to a way of thinking recently framed as "non-representational theory" (Thrift 2008), drawing largely on the philosophy of Gilles Deleuze and Félix Guattari; enough ambiguity for us to see it as an *opening*, rather than a closure, of what architecture is and could be. But Semper is the major exception to how origins in architecture have been perceived. Hvattum characterises his thinking as a "resistance" to the architectural culture of his time, and the misunderstandings and simplifications of his theories continue to this day (Hvattum 2006: 36–42; Rykwert 1989: 26, 29–33, 191; Mallgrave 1989). Semper's thinking is a challenge to the kind of pathological thinking I try to unravel here.

The dualism of autonomy and heteronomy reconsidered

While heteronomous thinking predominates in architecture, there is also something else going on that is difficult to resolve. For what is rarely brought to the fore is the wilful creativity of these acts, how origins are *invented* and made operative in discourse, imbued with a critical intent. There is a tactical and rhetorical side to architecture's engagement with origins – indeed to the effect of transforming the discursive practice itself (Foucault 1969) – but one that is haltered by, and enters into almost complete contradiction with, the formal and cognitive closure that origins are taken to represent. On the one side there is the desire to re-invent practice in accordance with new ideals, on the other the urge to do so by calling on the timeless and the absolute.

Castoriadis's understanding of autonomy is radically different from the liberal conception, which he sees as a cognitive closure – stemming from a conception of reality as given once and for all. It means that the content of the social imaginary is seen to correspond to an exterior principle – whether Reason, Rationality, God, Nature or Capitalism – summed up as "the myth of being as determined" (Rosengren 2006: 58). Aligning with autonomy in the architectural sense, this kind of reasoning characterises the belief system of most societies: the full implications of the fact that society, power and knowledge are socially produced have great difficulties in sinking through. Meaning is continuously pushed outside discourse, attributed to principles in science, religion or economy, instead of being seen as socially produced and hence subjected to desire, will and judgement. In contrast to this, true autonomy, 'in the proper sense' (according to Castoriadis) is not closure but *openness*. Autonomous societies (and, remember, this is also at an individual level) are those that:

> ... call into question their own institution, their representation of the world, their social imaginary significations. ... [something which] open[s] up a space where the activities of thinking and politics lead

to putting again and again into question not only the given forms of the social institution and of the social representation of the world but also the possible ground for any such forms. Autonomy here takes the meaning of a self-institution of society that is ... more or less *explicit*: we make the laws, we know it, and thus we are responsible for our laws and have to ask ourselves every time, 'Why this law rather than the other one?'(*WIF*: 17–18).

For Castoriadis, the potentiality of political emancipation, freedom, critique and creation all stem from this recognition, which is ultimately of an ethical kind. The construction and use of architectural origins, however, seem to balance between heteronomy and autonomy. What is initially recognizable as an explicit case of heteronomy – origins epitomizing 'the myth of being as determined' – runs in parallel to the *invention* of origins as a critical and creative act. Indeed, their purpose as means for questioning the existent state of affairs carries an autonomous impulse. So how may this matter be resolved? On the subject of learning from history, Castoriadis writes:

> There is ... an immense, indeed interminable, useful and meaningful research around the question: What was there in the 'old' that was somehow or other 'preparing the new' or related to it? But here again, the principle of closure heavily intervenes. Briefly speaking, *the old enters into the new with the signification given to it by the new and could not enter it otherwise* (*WIF*: 14, orig. emphasis).

Clearly, architectural origins are such a case of reworking 'the old' – whatever goes as a historical fact is always secondary to the intentions, the project as such. The psychology of these moves may be elucidated by the psychoanalytical concept *Nachträglichkeit*. Attributed to Jacques Lacan in his re-reading of Freud, it is taken to signify how "experiences, impressions and memory-traces may be revised at a later date to fit with fresh experience" at which time they may "be endowed not only with a new meaning but also with physical effectiveness" (Laplanche and Pontalis 1973: 111). Capturing the complexity of influence and how the past is re-worked, re-arranged and brought into effect, *Nachträglichkeit* is a fruitful reminder of the selective or even fictitious character of past events (Foster 1996; Didi-Huberman 2005). Therefore, the 'physical effectiveness' (identified by Freud as neurosis) may also be identified with the creative aspect of inventing origins and their critical use in discourse. What ultimately becomes important, then, is the operative aspect of origins: to what end are they being used, to *claim what* precisely? What kind of space do they produce, is it open or closed, and what is their potential for practice?

The rigidity of a discipline characterised by determination, claims of autonomy and an obsession with authorship – embedded into its culture with the inherent contradictions unresolved – suggests that it is the refusal, or inability, to take responsibility for its creations at a *social* level the brings the architectural mindset to a close. But the social is in itself ambiguous. Rather than constituting an alternative reality excluded by the architectural discipline, it gives rise to a series of questions that refuse final answers. For although the notion of autonomy in architecture is anti-social in character, who can say whether the *fabrication* of this protective shield – the establishment of ideals within the domain that is *controllable* to architects – is a social or anti-social act? Is it not the withdrawal from others in order to eradicate uncertainty a sign of disempowerment, indicative of an inability to cope with a multifarious, complex, relational and thus ultimately *social* context?

Therefore, as we gain recognition of the complexities of these stubborn returns – simultaneously dealing with psychological, social and aesthetical issues – it seems that Castoriadis's autonomy/heteronomy divide also comes to a close. The terms become too rigid, too dichotomised, too determined in themselves and unyielding to interdependent in-betweens and fluctuations. In "The Social-Historical: Mode of Being, Problems of Knowledge" (*FT*: 223–35), Castoriadis explicitly discusses the problem of learning from the past. Here, he elaborates on the essential closure of socio-historically produced meanings, stressing the difficulty to obtain deeper knowledge of alien (past or distant) societies beyond the realm of some basic, biological or structural universals. He concludes by pronouncing the project if not "vain", then at least marked by "essential lacunarity" (*FT*: 235). Although he recognises the desire to know as a breach out of our own confinements, constitutive for a project of autonomy – that of "go[ing] over and beyond the *closure of meaning* of our own institution" (*FT*: 227) – the creative potential of these returns is left unconsidered. Here, we come to a crucial limit regarding the conditions of interdisciplinary research. For while concepts developed in one field of thinking might aid advancements in another, they must be recognized as essentially nothing but vehicles or tools that must be discarded and/or replaced by others whence new problems arise. In other words: old meanings taken into the new are always secondary to the project, subjected to the intensions and meanings of the work at hand.

Conclusion

Given the role of architecture as a social construct; structuring needs, economies, significations and movements; reflecting subjectivities while simultaneously producing them; involving vast sums of money and tied up with temporalities often exceeding those associated with other works of art – clearly, what I have referred to as a pathology may be a natural response, a socially induced defence mechanism that protects the architect from being overwhelmed by the responsibilities involved. While we may only speak of a pathology when the defence mechanisms attain such strength that the subject is incapacitated from partaking in everyday life, one may indeed question my use of the term here. What I have attempted to show is how a certain rationality is embedded in the architectural disciplinary structure in such a way that even those who argue for a more 'open' conception find themselves up against an ontology that will not be changed.[6] And in so far as this ontology prevents architects from responding to social needs in a sensible and sensitive way – it is, in fact, hindering architects to engage with the uncertainties of time, gender, atmospheres, meanings and affects – we may indeed consider it a pathology, one furthermore maintained by a predominantly patriarchal discipline.

For if architecture is to be understood as something *other* than building, it cannot escape the ambiguity of interpretation, the uncertainty of meaning and the fluctuations of use. If we truly are to understand architecture as a social art, the only foundation for its production lies in what Castoriadis conceptualises as the social imaginary – by which we would be free to imagine architecture differently, as a creator of a different world, perhaps not even as structure primarily. But in so far as architecture forms a significant part of the material world created by each society, the pathology I have set out here is ultimately a case in point for the power of social institutions; for the slow-moving forces of magma and the ossification processes that turn acts of self-institution into solidified Law. In that sense, it stands token for what Castoriadis denotes as tragedy (*WIF*: 93): a perpetual reminder of mortality, the most radical and ultimate limitation of humankind.

---

6 A problem succinctly articulated by Belkis Uluoglu: "Every time there is a pressure for a change in the definition of architecture – usually a matter of 'limits' provoked by societal and economic changes – a drive for change in theory occurs; yet the ontological premises stay the same, limiting replies either to isolated practices with no long-term repercussions, or to dispersed theoretical attempts" (Uluoglu, 2005: 29).

References

Barasch, Moshe (2000) *Theories of Art: From Plato to Winckelmann*. New York and London: Routledge.

Barletta, Barbara A. (2001) *The Origins of the Greek Architectural Orders*. Cambridge: Cambridge University Press.

Cache, Bernard (2010) *Projectiles*. London: Architectural Association Publications.

Castoriadis, Cornelius (1997) *World in Fragments. Writings on Politics, Society, Psychoanalysis and the Imagination*, trans. and ed. David Ames Curtis. Stanford Ca.: Stanford University Press (*WIF*).

Castoriadis, Cornelius (2007) *Figures of the Thinkable*, trans. Helen Arnold. Stanford Ca.: Stanford University Press (*FT*).

Didi-Huberman, Georges (2005) *Confronting Images: Questioning the Ends of a Certain History of Art*, trans. J. Goodman. University Park, Penn: Pennsylvania State University Press.

Dinsmoor, William Bell (1973) *The Architecture of Ancient Greece: an Account of its Historic Development*. New York: Biblo & Tannen.

Freud, Sigmund (1961) *The Future of an Illusion, Civilization and its Discontents and other works*, trans. James Strachey. London: Hogarth Press.

Forty, Adrian (2006) "Primitive: the word and concept", Jo Odgers et al (eds.) *Primitive: Original Matters in Architecture*. London: Routledge .

Foster, Hal (1996) *The Return of the Real: The Avant-Garde at the End of the Century*. Cambridge, Mass./London: MIT Press.

Foucault, Michel (1969) "What is an Author?", modified version translated by Josué V. Harari available at: http://www.generation-online.org/p/fp_foucault12.htm (accessed 2013.01.19)

Gombrich, Ernst H. (2002) *The Preference for the Primitive*. London: Phaidon.

Harries, Karsten (1997) *The Ethical Function of Architecture*. Cambridge Mass./London: MIT Press.

Hight, Christopher (2008) *Architectural principles in the Age of Cybernetics*. London: Routledge.

Hvattum, Mari (2004) *Gottfried Semper and the Problem of Historicism*. Cambridge: Cambridge University Press.

Hvattum, Mari (2006) "Origins redefined: a tale of pigs and primitive huts", in Jo Odgers et al (eds.) *Primitive: Original Matters in Architecture*. London: Routledge.

Jencks, Charles (1973) *Modern Movements in Architecture*. London: Penguin.

Laplanche, Jean and Pontalis, Jean-Bertrand (1973) *The Language of Psycho-Analysis*, trans. D. Nicholson-Smith. London: Hogarth Press.

Lavin, Sylvia (1992) *Quatremère de Quincy and the Invention of a Modern Language of Architecture*. Cambridge Mass./London: MIT Press.

Panofsky, Erwin (1991) *Perspective as Symbolic Form*. New York: Zone books.

Mallgrave, Harry Frances (1989), introduction to Semper, Gottfried, *The Four Elements of Architecture and Other Writings*. Cambridge Mass: Cambridge University Press.

Rosengren, Mats (2002), *Doxologi: en essä om kunskap*. Åstorp: Rhetor.

Rosengren, Mats (2006) *För en dödlig som ni vet är största faran säkerhet*. Åstorp: Rhetor.

Rykwert, Jospeh (1989) *On Adam's House in Paradise*. Cambridge MA/London: MIT Press.

Rykwert, Joseph (1982) *The Necessity of Artifice*. London: Academy Editions.

Said, Edward (1997) *Beginnings: Intention and Method*. London: Granta.

Semper, Gottfried (1989 [1869]) *The Four Elements of Architecture and Other Writings*, trans. Harry Frances Mallgrave and Wolfgang Herrmann, introduction by Harry Frances Mallgrave. Cambridge: Cambridge University Press.

Thrift, Nigel (2008) *Non-Representational Theory: Space, Politics, Affect*. Oxon and New York: Routledge.

Tyszczuk, Renata (2007) "Games of Skill and Chance", *field:* 1:1, 151–67.

Uluoglu, Belkis (2005) "The Speciality of the Singular Building and the Everydayness of the City", *City, Architecture in Between Past and Future*. Istanbul: Istanbul Technical University.

Vidler, Anthony (2008) *Histories of the Immediate Present: Inventing Architectural Modernism*, Cambridge, MA/London: MIT Press.

Viollet-le-Duc, Eugène-Emmanuel (1990) *The Architectural Theory of Viollet-le-Duc*, trans. Millard Fillmore Hearn. Cambridge MA/London: MIT Press.

Wittkower, Rudolf (1973) *Architectural Principles in the Age of Humanism*. London: Academy Editions.

Castoriadis, Arnason and the Phenomenological Question of the World

Suzi Adams

The present essay emerges from an ongoing discussion at the intersection of the thought of Cornelius Castoriadis and Johann P. Arnason. It forms part of a larger work-in-progress.[1] Part of its overall problematic is to elucidate the notion of 'the *world*' as it appears in their respective intellectual trajectories. Each might be said to take a post-Merleau-Pontian approach to the 'world horizon', but while Castoriadis's post-phenomenological account of the world takes an ontological turn, Arnason's phenomenological-hermeneutical path elaborates a distinctive *culturological* perspective. Their differing elucidations of the quasi-concept of the *world* have provided a point of enduring contention between them. Arnason elaborates it as a *shared and interpretative horizon*, whilst Castoriadis views it as an *ontological creation ex nihilo*.[2] The problematic of the world undergoes several mutations in Arnason's thought, but, whereas Castoriadis retreats from (but never fully exorcizes) the phenomenological problematic of the world, for Arnason

---

1 An earlier, shorter version of this essay appeared as "The Retrieval of the World Problematic in Castoriadis's Thought" (Adams 2011b).
2 See the Busino collection of papers devoted to Castoriadis's thought (1989). In this vein, see especially Arnason's essay "The Imaginary Constitution of Modernity" (1989a) and Castoriadis's response to his critics, 'Done and to be Done' (1997, *CR*). I return to their respective differences concerning 'creation' and 'interpretation' later.

'the world as a shared horizon' becomes an increasingly important and explicit dimension of his project. The present essay argues that there is an overlooked dimension in Castoriadis's notion of the world, however, especially as it reappears in his later poly-regional ontology of the *for-itself*. Castoriadis did not systematically pursue this line of reflection and, as such, it requires hermeneutical reconstruction. The essay further argues that the implications that appear from the appearance of 'the world' at the level of 'the living being' point to lacunae in Arnason's thought, and puts into question his understanding of the phenomenal field as the sole province of *anthropos*.

I

The question of the world in Castoriadis's thought is underdeveloped, but not insignificant; overall it remains an indefinite half-presence. His changing elaborations of the world horizon give a specific twist to the general inquiry into human relations to the world in modernity; these can range from an image of 'world alienation' (Arendt) to opportunities for new forms of 'worldhood' (Blumenberg).[3] Castoriadis's engagement with 'the world' undergoes several transformations throughout his intellectual trajectory. Three main phases can be distinguished.

First, Castoriadis's early thought can be situated within pheno-menological Marxism. Here the world appears as a phenomenological problematic that is, if not *the* focus of his philosophical work, then at least a distinct theme. For example, at the beginning of a significant passage in "Marxism and Revolutionary Theory" (*IIS: 9–164*), Castoriadis writes:

> Theory in itself is a doing, the always uncertain attempt to realize the project of clarifying the world. And this is also true for that supreme or extreme form of theory – philosophy – the attempt to conceive of the world without knowing, either before or after the fact, whether the

---

3 I discuss this at greater length elsewhere (Adams 2007a).

world is actually conceivable, or even just what conceiving of something exactly means (*IIS*: 74).[4]

In the same vein, in the penultimate paragraph of the 1964–65 section of the *IIS*, Castoriadis reframes the 'eleventh thesis' as part of his 'roads beyond Marx':[5]

> And yet, what appears to speculative reason as an insurmountable antinomy undergoes a change of sense when we bring the consideration of history back into our project of the theoretical elucidation of the world, and in particular of the human world, when we see in it a part of our effort to interpret the world in order to change it [...] (*IIS*: 164; emphasis in original).

Second, with his ontological turn in the second part of the *IIS*, the problematic of the world becomes transformed in Castoriadis's thought.[6] At this point, the 'world' as an overarching meta-context and horizon recedes from focus, especially in its phenomenological aspects, whilst its mode of being – as the creative 'magma' – becomes a cornerstone of his maturing ontology of time and creation. In this vein, following Arnason's argument (1989b), Castoriadis can be said to have ontologized the world (as magma). The ontologization of the world occurred in tandem with an increasing emphasis on modes of social-historical *signification* and a concomitant marginalization of the mode of being of social-historical *doing* in the 1975 section of the *IIS*. The increasing focus on the 'imaginary significations' culminates in a long discussion in the final chapter ("Social Imaginary Significations"), with

4 See, too, his early homage to Merleau-Ponty first published in 1971(1984a). See also Joas (2002) and Adams (2009a).
5 See Arnason's "Roads Beyond Marx" (2006).
6 The first part of the IIS was written in 1964–65 and published in *Socialisme ou Barbarie*, whilst the second part was composed over the period 1970–74. The two sections were first published together in 1975.

no mention of the being of 'doing' at all. In that final chapter of the *IIS* Castoriadis tells us that '[t]he institution of society is in each case the institution of a magma of social imaginary significations, which we can and must call a *world* of significations for it is one and the same thing to say that society institutes the world in each case as its world or its world as the world (*IIS*: 359; emphasis in original).

As I have discussed elsewhere, however, it is *not* 'the same thing'; in agreement with Arnason, I argue that Castoriadis at this point reduces 'the world' as an overarching and shared horizon common to the human condition as cultural humanity to a particular creation of each social-historical formation, and thus seems to overly emphasise the constructivist 'world-making' capacity of the social-historical (Adams 2007a). In this vein, the social-historical creation of its world through the purely generative core significations seems to occur in a worldless vacuum.

Third, even though 'the world' *qua* phenomenological problematic that, as an overarching horizon of experience and cultural interpretation, is clearly marginalized after Castoriadis's ontological turn (with the *IIS* 1987[1975]), it is never fully jettisoned. Indeed, 'the world' returns as part of his rethinking of 'the living being' during the 1980s. This rethinking had profound effects on his overall ontology and was central in facilitating his expanding 'magmatic modes of self-creating being' from '*anthropos*' to 'nature', as well as through a rethinking of *à-être* as creative *physis*. Also, Castoriadis's rethinking of the living being saw the problematic of the world introduced within a new context, thereby altering the parameters of discussion (I return to this later).[7]

In addition to these different phases of 'world articulation' in Castoriadis's philosophical trajectory, there are (at least) three incipient trends in his work, all of them post *IIS*, that open onto renewed consideration of 'the world' (although these would need to be

---

7 For a more systematic discussion, see Adams (2011a).

reconstructed, as Castoriadis did not systematically pursue them). The first concerns a shift in his articulation of 'the sacred' at the time of the *IIS* to a different elaboration in the slightly later and important essay "The Institution of Society and Religion" (1993). The second involves Castoriadis's later concern with art and aesthetic forms of autonomy and his reference to art as opening a 'window' onto the abyss (Arnason 1989c, Arnason 2011, Rockhill 2011). Finally, Castoriadis's later insights into Plato's *chora* (2007), especially with respect to its chaotic residue, differ markedly from his earlier account in the *IIS*. The opening onto a rethinking of the *chora* offers opportunities to reflect on a dynamic notion of place/space as a cultural clearing of the anthropic world, and to radicalize this further as a broader phenomenal field (I return to this later).[8] Although these instances show the ambiguous but enduringly present concern for 'the world', they also open onto a broader question concerning the relation between ontology and phenomenology, 'being' and 'appearance', 'being' and 'the world'.

The problematic of 'the world' is central to understanding Arnason's phenomenological hermeneutics, which is an interdisciplinary endeavour situated between philosophy and historical sociology. If Arnason (1989b) showed some earlier hesitations in embracing 'the world' as a trans-historical horizon, his more recent work has elevated 'the world' to central stage as part of his project on world histories and inter-civilizational encounters (e.g. Arnason 2003). Arnason elaborates 'the world' as part of a decentred anthropology where *anthropos* is not only a 'self-interpreting' animal, as *per* Charles Taylor, but also 'world interpreting'.[9] The world as

---

8 Karl Smith (2010) has likened Castoriadis's notion of 'magma' to Merleau-Ponty's elucidation of 'flesh', but without taking it any further. In this context, it seems pertinent to note that Richir (1993) has compared Merleau-Ponty's notion of 'flesh' to Plato's *chora*.

9 Although the phenomenological problematic of the world horizon is not absent from Taylor's considerations, neither is it brought systematically into the horizon of his philosophical anthropology. In the same vein, the tension between *anthropos* as 'self-interpreting' and as 'expressive' has not been fully recognized either by Taylor or by his interlocutors. For a discussion of Taylor's philosophical anthropology in relation to Castoriadis, see Smith (2010).

an enigmatic horizon is known to us through our encounter with it and its consequent 'cultural articulation'.

Here Arnason gives Merleau-Ponty's *'mise en forme du monde'* a distinctive culturological twist. Specifically, Arnason's articulation of the cultural element of the social world decentres socio-centric definitions of society. Socio-centric approaches to social creativity were central to Durkheim's cultural turn in *The Elementary Forms of the Religious Life* (1995[1912]). In this book Durkheim saw the sacred as 'society divinized' but, more broadly than sociological currents alone, this approach to 'social creativity' belongs to the humanist imaginary and imaginary of sovereign subjects as inaugurated by Descartes, and, by extension as sovereign world makers.[10] The *re-centring* of 'the world' at the level of culture, that is to say, the trans-subjective field–i.e. the social level of reality beyond the inter-subjective domain–brings in the world as *transcensus,* to draw on Jan Patočka, that goes beyond the radical immanence of Castoriadis. It is also important for Arnason's enduring criticism of functionalist images of society, on the one hand, and of images of the human condition as over-socialized and overly normative, on the other (e.g. Arnason 1988, 2003). Instead, his philosophical anthropology emphasizes social creativity, where 'meaning' is a central dimension of the human condition of 'being-in-the-world'. In modernity, this cultural surplus of meanings engenders a conflict of interpretations that partially structure modernity as a 'field of tensions'.

The enigma of 'the world' has been of enduring interest to pheno-menological thinkers, whose reflections form various conjunctions of heterogeneous currents of thought rather than a continuous tradition.[11] Arnason's phenomenology of the world is situated within the nascent field of post-transcendental thought. For Arnason, articulation of a

---

10 See Alexander and Smith (2005). See also Arnason (1976), especially the section on the three kinds of humanism.
11 In this vein, see Bermes' (2004) study on the problematic of the world as a philosophical theme.

non-subjectivist theory of meaning in relation to the world horizon and to culture has become a central problematic. His contribution to this fields developed via engagement with Merleau-Ponty, Patočka and Castoriadis, but also Weber's early theory of culture as a 'patterning of the world' (Arnason, 1982, 1988, 1993, 2003). Arnason emphasizes 'cultural meaning' as 'figurative' (a dimension that was not prominent in Castoriadis's thought) and demonstrates that the indeterminate horizon of the world can only be made manifest through concrete cultural configurations (which his historical-sociological analyses have pursued within a civilizational context). Thus Arnason's turn to philosophical hermeneutics (in the 1980s) and historical sociology (in the late 1980s and early 1990s) addresses interweaving aspects of the same problematic.[12] In other words, to adequately address the phenomenological problematic of *the world as a shared horizon*, both philosophical hermeneutics and historical sociology are needed.

Arnason's hermeneutic phenomenology highlights 'interpretability' as the basic element of 'the world', and that our necessary encounter with it requires a cultural articulation. In contrast, Castoriadis emphasizes the creative aspect of 'world' to the detriment of the interpretative dimension. By focusing on trans-subjective contexts and problematics, Arnason wants to move not only beyond the idea of a *subjective* or 'egological' constitution of the world, but also beyond its *intersubjective* constitution. What he terms the "post-transcendental field" emphasizes the trans-subjective problematic of world interpretation, and the links between culture and meaning as *cultural articulations of the world*, thereby relativising the distinction between "imposed meaning and meaningless world" (Arnason 2003: 206).

Arnason has recently begun to speak of his hermeneutic phenome-

---

12 See Knöbl (2000) and more generally *Johann P. Arnason: Modern Constellations, Civilizational Horizons,* special issue of *Thesis Eleven* (2000: 61) and Adams, S., K.E. Smith, and G. Vlahov (eds.) *Johann P. Arnason: Encounters and Interpretations*, special issue of the *European Journal of Social Theory* (2011).

nology as a *culturological* approach. To my knowledge, Arnason first uses the concept in an essay on Castoriadis (Arnason 1989b), and most recently in a paper on Merleau-Ponty and civilizations (Arnason 2013). Therefore, Arnason's *culturological* approach can be situated as an alternative to the ontological turn in French phenomenology, on the one hand, and as a radicalization of the hermeneutical turn, on the other. In earlier works he has tended to use the term 'culturalist' (for example, 1982 and 1994); his recent articulation of a 'culturological' approach may be used to distinguish it from the Eisenstadtian 'culturalist' version of civilizational analysis, which Arnason argues not to take in adequate account the phenomenon of historical variation. The culturological context is seen as inseparable from the post-transcendental field, and highlights the importance of a philosophy of culture more generally. Although 'culture' and 'meaning' appear at various *niveaux* in Arnason's multi-layered social theory, the cultural articulation of the world is the precondition for the concretization not only of other domains of social life, but also of civilizational constellations.

The historical world as an anthropologically shared horizon is a key aspect to Arnason's (inter)cultural hermeneutics and phenomenology of the world.[13] It also provides a point of enduring difference between Castoriadis and himself, with Arnason's 'culturological' perspective contrasting Castoriadis's ontological approach of the *IIS* years.[14] In this

---

13 It should be noted that Arnason's work is not reducible to phenomenology; rather, he fuses together phenomenological insights and problematics within social theoretical and historical sociological contexts. His work is not, then, 'phenomenological' in the conventional sense, although it clearly falls within a broad understanding of the phenomenological movement, which has continued to transform itself since its inception with Hegel (as opposed to its self-labelling turn with Husserl).

14 For a discussion of Arnason's culturological approach to phenomenology, see Adams (2009b; 2011). To my knowledge, Arnason was the first to notice the implications of Castoriadis's fragmentary later work on art as a possible rapprochement with the phenomenology of the world (Arnason 1989c). Although Arnason critiques Castoriadis's emphasis on the ontological creation of the social world to the detriment of a more phenomenological-hermeneutical approach, he does not in this case look to Castoriadis's pre-ontological thought for contexts of meaning amenable to hermeneutical reconstruction.

vein, whereas Castoriadis insists on the social-historical creation of a world *ex nihilo*, Arnason upholds that the social-historical creation of a world is as much interpretative as it is creative (Castoriadis 1989, Arnason 1989a). In this he argues for an account of 'interpretation' as inherently creative, and of 'creation' as inherently interpretative. Or, to put it another way, Arnason argues for creation as *culturally contextual* rather than *ontologically absolute*.[15] At stake is a conception of 'the world' as a philosophical problematic. For Castoriadis, the ontological creation of a social-historical "world as the world" (*IIS*: 359) is achieved *ex nihilo* and *via* central social imaginary significations, such as 'God' or 'autonomy'. For Arnason, Castoriadis obfuscates the interpretative dimension of 'social-historical creation', at least in part, due to his prior fudging of the phenomenological problematic of the 'world horizon' or, more specifically, of the 'world as a *shared horizon*'. Specifically, if 'the world' is considered as an overarching and shared horizon, then it is not only of significance to a variety of autonomously culturally articulated worlds, but also to an overarching inter- and trans-cultural field of *interpretation*.

The idea of the world 'as a shared horizon' encapsulates another enduring theme in Arnason's thought, i.e. the problematic of the 'human condition' as a 'unity in diversity'. This presumes 'the world' to be an anthropological as well as historical horizon, and makes it both 'shared' and 'intercultural'.[16] In this way 'the world' as an overarching and shared horizon of anthropic encounters and cultural articulations opens up questions of anthropological horizons of being-in-the-world as a common cultural 'clearing' that draws on and reconfigures

---

15 I discuss this at greater length in Adams (2011a). Castoriadis's later qualification that creation might be *ex nihilo* but it was not *in nihilo* or *cum nihilo* seems to indicate that it can be 'conditioned', but this falls short of acknowledging the interpretative element and its attendant implications.

16 For a discussion of the intercultural implications of Arnason's thought see Adams (2009b) and Smith (2009).

Heidegger's notion of a clearing of being (*die Lichtung*).[17] Arnason's early roots in phenomenological Marxism would suggest Heidegger as a plausible source for his culturological-phenomenological configuration of a 'cultural clearing' (although he has not used this actual term), which becomes visible in his interpretation of Weber: "'The general definition of culture is evidently meant to capture a common ground which enables different cultures – in some degree – to understand each other, and which can therefore not be seen as a domain of sovereign and arbitrary world-making" (Arnason 2003: 206). 'The clearing' is a feature of 'the world' as a shared and cultural horizon of interpretation, whereas Castoriadis's account of 'the social-historical creation of a world' seems to fall within a current of thought that privileges 'sovereign and arbitrary world-making' and as such cannot accommodate the shared and therefore also interpretative aspect of 'the world' as an overarching horizon and meta-context.

Arnason's approach to ontology has changed over time. If initially he seemed to reject it entirely, he now appears rather to transform it through his culturological approach to 'the world horizon'. This change notwithstanding, it remains true that he has not embraced the ontological turn and the corresponding 'question of being' that was paramount not only for Heidegger, but also for Castoriadis. The issue remains whether, analogous to the ultimate intertwining of the orders of '*nomos*' and '*physis*' as apparent in Castoriadis's later philosophical thought, there might not be an intertwining between 'being' and 'appearance' in Arnason's thought. Although Arnason's focus grapples with the historical context as the pre-condition of appearance, it is open to question whether the *Seinsfrage* can be totally dismissed. This is not to say that ontology should be upheld as a-historical, but neither can it be reduced to 'cultural ontologies'. If there can be a variety of cultural ontologies, then an overarching ontological horizon (if I may use this term) with a particular if partial grasp on the

---

17 See for example, his "Letter on Humanism" (1998) and *Being and Time* (1996).

world must be a precondition. The phenomenal order intersects with an ontological order that is refracted through the world.[18] The aim then becomes to elaborate ontology in its trans-historical and trans-human interplay with the phenomenal field in its historical and contextual aspects, on the one hand, and its anthropological, trans-anthropological features and pre-conditions on the other.

From a different perspective, Arnason's phenomenology emphasizes 'the world' as an anthropological horizon, but an account of the anthropological and natural interplay is downplayed in his thought (at least post-dating his hermeneutical turn).[19] In that his anthropology focuses on humankind in general, and cultural humanity under the condition of civilizations in particular, this is not surprising. Nor is it surprising that his phenomenology may want to stress the notion of social creativity in history, which removes it from both functionalist and evolutionary accounts of society and civilizations. However, in these times of renewed urgency surrounding the issues of global warming, the environmental crisis and the emerging debates in the human sciences concerning humans and animals – and the divide between them (see for example, Nik Taylor 2007) – elaborations of 'nature' as the perennial,

---

18 Renaud Barbaras' important book on Merleau-Ponty *The Being of the Phenomenon* (2004) makes this trend most explicit.

19 Although not emphasized in his thought since his hermeneutical turn in the 1980s, the intersections of the subject between nature and society was the theme of Arnason's *Habilitationschrift*, published as *Zwischen Natur und Gesellschaft: Studien zu einer kritischen Theorie des Subjekts* (1976). After his shift to a cultural hermeneutics, Arnason sometimes writes of 'anthropological preconditions' (for example, Arnason 1994: 155) but without elaborating further on what they might be: His emphasis remains the elaboration of a cultural anthropology of civilizational anthropos as historical modes of being-in-the-world. Implied in the notion of 'anthropological preconditions' would seem to be the sense that they would be rooted in biology or zoology, that is as such not a task for the human sciences. This in turn presumes a more or less clear division between 'humankind' and 'nature'. More generally, 'nature' or 'the non-human' do not feature in Arnason's discussion, in general, or, specially, in his schema of a twofold tripartite division of social processes into economic, political and cultural spheres (although it must be noted that for Arnason 'culture' is not only a sphere of social processes but an element of the world and as such goes beyond the 'social') and the further three categories of wealth, power and meaning as the foci of institution building (Arnason 2003: 198-99).

unspoken 'other' of 'the social' need to be jettisoned, and, within that, the cultural images (or imaginary significations) of nature in modernity require urgent attention, and renewed theoretical endeavour, not to mention political action. At the level of overarching interpretative frameworks, theoretical work is needed including the reconsideration of the lines of continuity and discontinuity between 'anthropic' and 'natural' forms of being, whose ontological splitting in modernity provides a partial precondition for the contemporary world articulation that can envisage the natural world as an inert realm inviting (or requiring) human mastery, on the one hand, and infinite human intervention on the other, with far-reaching ecological consequences that we are seemingly only beginning to recognize.

II

In an important if too little discussed paper on Castoriadis's thought, Arnason has rightly emphasized that Castoriadis's theorization of a 'creation' of a world of significations can only have ontological import at the social-historical level and not at the psychical one (Arnason 1989c). In terms of Castoriadis's engagement with the problematic of *nomos* and *physis*, it can be said the psyche is more than *physis*, yet not quite *nomos*. Arnason's overall point is that although Castoriadis could not be accused of psychoanalytic reductionism in regards to his elucidation of the properly social level of reality, there was nonetheless a tendency to smuggle psychoanalytic terms into the social-historical arena. At that time in Arnason's thought, however, Castoriadis's later rethinking of 'the living being' during the 1980s was not taken into account. In other words, Castoriadis's elucidation of the ontological creativity of the living being, as well as the ontological significance of its *Eigenwelt*, was not given its proper due. Central to this rethinking on Castoriadis's part was the elucidation of a poly-regional ontology of the *for-itself* on the one hand – with 'the living being' as the 'archetypal' instance – and the return of the problematic of 'the world' on the other – albeit cast in ontological rather than purely phenomenological terms and with ensuing implications for philosophical anthropology, phenomenology and biology.[20]

Castoriadis's elaboration of a poly-regional ontology of modes of being 'for-itself' in the 1980s has remained little remarked in the secondary literature (but see Klooger 2009, Adams 2007b, 2011a). The poly-regional ontology advanced by Castoriadis hinges on his rethinking of 'the living being', on the one hand, and of the Aristotelian notion of *physis*, especially its creative aspects, on the other. The rethinking of the creative aspects of *physis* in turn relocates, even broadens the scope of the *nomos* and *physis* problematic into the natural realm, especially in considering Varela's notion of *biological autonomy*. The problematic of *physis* and *nomos* is central to understanding Castoriadis's philosophical trajectory (I elaborate this in more detail below).[21] Its significance is not apparent at first glance, however, and needs hermeneutical reconstruction. At the time of writing the *IIS* – or at least the second part, that is, chapters four to seven, where he elaborates his shift from phenomenological Marxism to ontology – Castoriadis was interested to provide an elucidation of the ontological preconditions of autonomy. At this juncture, the opposition of *physis* and *techne* was perhaps more visible in this work: *Techne* for Castoriadis signified human 'creative doing' and the 'making-be' of ontological forms; it was central at that stage to his understanding of the mode of being of autonomy. In the fifth chapter, dealing with the primordial institutions of *legein* and *teukhein*, where the former is understood as a precursor for theoretical reason and the latter as practical reason, *teukhein* is articulated as potentially the more

---

20 Castoriadis's notion of the 'for-itself' arguably continues the undue emphasis on sovereign creation as was the case in his elaboration of the social-historical creation of a world of imaginary significations *ex nihilo*. Surely the living being is as much 'for-the-world' as 'for-itself'. In that it is via the living being's rupture with physical strata of being that the world first appears as a horizon at all. In brief, further reflection and elaboration is needed on this point.
21 See Adams (2011a) for extended discussion of the shifting configurations of *nomos* and *physis* in Castoriadis's thought.

radical and 'transformative' of the two, and is closely aligned to modes of *social doing*.[22] Whilst writing *IIS*, however, Castoriadis sidelined the importance of elucidating the being of 'doing' and focussed upon the being of 'signification'. This change of focus culminates in the final chapter of *IIS* elucidating the being of social imaginary significations, which marks as well the reduced attention paid to *techne* as praxis and creative *making-be*.[23]

At the time of the *IIS*, the orders of *nomos* and *physis* were seen in mutual opposition. Castoriadis's consideration of *physis* was limited to its relevance to the human condition; therefore he understood *physis* in the sense of 'natural norm'. As such, the notion of '*physis*' was antithetical to an elucidation of the social-historical. Instead, the elaboration of the intermittent philosophical tradition of the order of *nomos*, for which 'no ontological place exists' (1984b: 326), stood behind Castoriadis's elucidation of anthropic being as the creative imagination in its modes *qua* radical imagination of the psyche and radical imaginary of the social-historical. The 'order of *nomos*' as human institution is, as he put it in "*Physis* and Autonomy", "our creative imaginary institution by means of which we make ourselves qua human beings. It is the term *nomos* that gives full meaning to the term and project of autonomy" (Castoriadis *WIF*: 332).

The reconfiguration of the *nomos* and *physis* problematic in the 1980s saw a shift in Castoriadis's understanding of *physis* as a pure 'natural norm' (see for example 1984b and 1984/85), and as such as a completely separate order not amenable to understanding anthropic and, in particular, social-historical modes of being. This reconfiguration was brought about by Castoriadis's increasing interest in the francophone *auto-poesis* debates in the 1980s, a reassessment of objective forms of knowledge, and, in a further wave of immersion in ancient Greek sources, a reconsideration

22 See Castoriadis's paper on *techne* (1984c).
23 This aspect is particularly evocative in his beautiful homage to Merleau-Ponty (1984a[1971]). Over the course of his thought it faded in significance but was not completely erased.

of the creative aspects of Aristotelian *physis*.[24] In all this, Castoriadis's rethinking of 'the living being' emerged as a primary site for the shifting configurations of *nomos* and *physis*.

Although Castoriadis had an enduring interest in 'the living being', it was for a long time marginalized by his overriding concern with 'the social-historical' and 'autonomy', that is to say, with modes of being *nomoi*. He reviewed but did not publish Edgar Morin's 1977 *Nature de la nature*, and was the first scholar to review *Principles of Biological Autonomy* (1980) by Francisco Varela, with whom he had a discussion over many years. This shift was articulated most clearly in his essay '*Physis* and Autonomy', which unmistakably elucidates both the emergence of a broader understanding of the ontological significance of creative *physis* – especially *vis-à-vis* 'the living being' – and its limitations–particularly as Varela's notion of 'biological autonomy' is concerned. In responding to the question of 'biological autonomy', Castoriadis distinguishes between human and non-human modes of being, and maintains the notion of 'autonomy' for the human realm. He prefers speaking of the *teleonomy* (as opposed to teleology) of 'the living being' and the self-constitution of its own world, which Castoriadis elaborates as an ontological creation of 'form'. Thus, although Varela's idea of biological autonomy collapses *nomos* into *physis*, Castoriadis clearly wants to distinguish between the two orders. But there is a further twist to this issue.

First, a quick detour: Castoriadis's elucidation of 'the living being' went through three stages. The first phase includes *The Imaginary Institution of Society* (1987[1975]) and the slightly earlier essay, "Modern Science and Philosophical Interrogation" (1984d). Castoriadis's rethinking of 'the living being' becomes visible during the 1980s; this forms the second stage. Although the focus is on a reconceptualisation of 'the living being'

---

24 Castoriadis's shift from socialism to autonomy was part of one of several waves of preoccupation with Greek sources. The next main wave in the early 1980s and resulted in several key essays and several series of seminars at the EHESS which are currently being published in several volumes.

through a rethinking of the *physis* and *nomos* problematic, it emerges as part of a poly-regional ontology of the *for-itself*.[25] The region of the *for-itself* encompasses several levels, four of which Castoriadis articulates as 'real': 'The social-historical', 'the psyche', 'the social individual', and 'the living being'. He understands two further levels as 'virtual': The autonomous subject and autonomous society. Two things are significant here: In the first instance, the initial level of the *for-itself* encompasses both human and non-human modes of being; in the second instance, and from a different angle, the poly-regional ontology can be understood as the dimension of being that encompasses the two ontological orders (that is, it spans some of *physis* and all of *nomos*). Castoriadis's rethinking of the creativity of 'the living being' – and his shift from a regional ontology of *nomos* to a trans-regional ontology of creative *physis* – underscores the radicality of 'the living being's' rupture with 'physical' regions of being: The living being brings forth an entirely new mode of being, which is centrally linked to the creation of its own *world* and concomitant level of (proto)meaning. The final stage is less a 'stage', interrupted as it was by Castoriadis's death, but more a series of further incipient developments in his elaboration of 'the living being', especially in regard to the imagination (see for example, Castoriadis 1997b, 1997c).

Castoriadis's rethinking of 'the living being' was decisive for his elaboration of the *for-itself*, or modes of being *for-itself*. Recall that at the time of the *IIS*, Castoriadis set out to elucidate a regional ontology of *nomos* as the order of human (self)institution. Here he was reactivating Husserlian as well as Aristotelian themes. It was only anthropic modes of being that were defined by the capacity to (self)create ontological form, which in turn was centrally linked to creative imagination. After the *IIS*, Castoriadis began to rethink forms of objective knowledge, as well

---

25 Thus, even though in the 1980s Castoriadis's ontology shifted from a focus on regional *nomos* to a more encompassing general ontology of creative *physis*, he did not collapse the specificity of human nomos into physis, but rather a simultaneous reconfiguration of the *physis/nomos* problematic occurred in his work.

other aspects of Aristotelian *physis* that he had previously neglected. As discussed elsewhere (2007b, 2011a), a more extended ontology emerged in the 1980s in which ontological creation had been expanded from the anthropic regions to include non-human regions as well. Significant in this theoretical development was the emergence of a poly-regional ontology of the *for-itself* in which Castoriadis's rethinking of 'the living being' was the entry point.

For present purposes, what is important here is Castoriadis's understanding of the emergence of *living* being (as a particular mode of 'being') as a rupture with previous strata of being. On Castoriadis's account 'the living being' inaugurates the 'subjective instance', in that the physical strata of 'natural being' are put into meaning (or at least a proto-meaning) through the creation of its *Eigenwelt*, or 'own world proper to its mode of being'. This is an ontological creation of the first magnitude, and central to this development in Castoriadis's thought is the reappearance of the problematic of 'the world', which had been spirited away in his ongoing elaboration of the 'being of social imaginary significations' (*IIS*' final chapter) and the creation of the social-historical world, but now re-emerges at the level of 'the living being'. Importantly, the creation of the world, i.e. the appearance of the world horizon in general, and also at the level of the living being, emerges from the creative imagination. Those familiar with Castoriadis would know him to distinguish between the radical imagination of the psyche and the radical imaginary of the social-historical. But Castoriadis introduces a third *niveau*: The 'corporeal imagination', which is located at the level of the living being. Although this level of the imagination is not 'radical' in the sense that it is not the 'defunctionalized' imagination of the human condition, nonetheless, in that it creates the *Eigenwelt* of the living being it must be considered as part of the field that comprises the creative imagination, and, as well, as a third dimension to meaning, although, like the psyche this, too, must be considered a variety of proto-meaning.[26] In this way, Castoriadis reintroduces lines of continuity between 'the living being' and 'the social-historical'. This reintroduction extends 'the imagination' beyond the notion of anthropological subjectivity, as he suggested in the *IIS* chapter on the psyche, reaching poly-regional varieties of 'the self'. The 'creative imagination' is linked to the co-emergence of 'the world' as an overarching horizon of meaning, which first appears with the mode of the living being. Thus the link between various modes of the *for-itself-for-the-world* is irreducible to modes of either consciousness or rationality and becomes rather *imagining beings*.

Earlier I wrote that 'the psyche' must be considered as more than *physis*, yet not quite *nomos*. This intermediate status is due to the fact that 'the imagination' as the pre-condition of 'the self' has been extended from 'the psyche' to 'the living being'. Can the same be said of 'the living being'? Within the present context, this issue must remain an open question as well as the lines of continuity – co-emergence of 'selfhood', 'worldhood' and 'meaning' with the level of the living being – and discontinuity, the self-constitution of the living being, and corporeal imagination bound to functional closure is not yet the defunctionalisation and capacity for the political project of autonomy characteristic of 'the social-historical'. That being said, interesting lines of thought open up, such as Hesiod's distinction between humans and animals, which was drawn not along the lines of *nomos* (both humans and animals enjoyed forms of *nomos*) but rather along the lines of 'justice as *dike*', i.e. a trait that humans possessed but not animals.

In inaugurating the 'subjective instance', 'the living being' initiates the level of 'existence' as opposed to 'essence'. Broadly understood, it in-

---

26 In point of fact, Castoriadis does actually refer to the imagination of the living being as part of the 'radical imagination'. Yet, insofar as as he tends to refer to 'the psyche' as *the radical imagination* and contrast it with 'the social-historical' as *the radical imaginary* (both of them being aspects of the defunctionalized imagination), then the term 'creative imagination' seems more appropriate in this context (Castoriadis 1997b: 326; see also Castoriadis 1997c).

augurates the realm of 'the self' and of 'subjectivity'. Essential to this is the creation of its world as a world of meaning. This stands in stark contrast to Heidegger's proclamation that:

> The being that exists is the human being. The human being alone exists. Rocks are, but they do not exist. Trees are, but they do not exist. Horses are, but they do not exist [...]. The proposition 'the human being alone exists' does not at all mean that the human being alone is a real being while all other beings are unreal and mere appearances of human representations. The proposition 'the human being exists' means: the human being is that being whose being is distinguished by an open standing that stands in the unconcealedness of being, proceeds from being, in being (Heidegger 2000: 64).

With his rethinking of the mode of the living being, we see the co-emergence of 'life' *qua* 'experience of something' with the 'world *qua* world', that is to say, as a horizon of meaning (or at least, proto-meaning) and not just a surrounding 'environment' that manifests itself first at the level of non-human living beings. The emergence of the level of 'existential' reality is co-emergent with the appearance of the 'world' as a horizon to be encountered and made meaningful. This occurs at the level of the living being, in its own way, not just at the level of the anthropic being. Thus the living being instaurates the appearance of the world as an overarching horizon of meaning within a new level of being – the subjective instance – that ruptures with physical regions of being. In this, as we have seen, Castoriadis goes beyond Heidegger's dismissal of nature, but also beyond Merleau-Ponty's contextualizing of 'the living being' solely within an *environment* (*Umwelt*), rather than acknowledging the living being's worldhood (Merleau-Ponty 2003). The difference for Castoriadis is that, in creating a world, the living being creates what *for it* is information; it does not find it already existing there in the environment.[27] Here, though, in extension of Castoriadis, the living being and all modes of being *for-itself* within the poly-regional ontology must be considered as much being *for-the-world* as being *for-itself*.

In a similar vein, anthropological preconditions cannot be understood wholly within frameworks of zoology or biology, as merely the background upon which the figure of culture appears. The co-emergence of selfhood, worldhood and meaning that have generally been considered the province of human culture has been relativized by Castoriadis. 'The living being' must be thought of as situated at the frontiers of the anthropological field, not just as its precondition. In this, too, Heidegger's '*Lichtung*', which he elaborated along ontological-phenomenological lines and was implicitly reconfigured by Arnason along the lines of a 'cultural clearing', can be seen as part of a broader *phenomenal field*. This field includes not only the manifestation of and encounter with 'the world' as a meaningful horizon that is central to the *human* condition, but also 'the living being' as an emergent form of selfhood and worldhood. The phenomenal field intersects with ontological layers; the magmatic world is illuminated in the ambience of the *chora*, to draw on Plato or, to lean on Merleau-Ponty, the translucence of its flesh.

In conclusion, the problematic of 'the world' appears at different junctures and with different emphasis in Arnason's and Castoriadis's respective works. Arnason's contribution to a phenomenology of the world is significant and not yet fully recognized as such within currents of thought that focus more centrally on phenomenology primarily as a philosophical endeavour. For him, 'the world' may remain enigmatic, yet it is also central to elucidations of cultural – or civilizational – humanity

---

27 Castoriadis speaks of a 'shock' or Fichtean '*Anstoss*' which the living being encounters; this aspect would need to be developed further to make better sense of the living being as not only for-itself but also for-the-world. (For a discussion of the living being and *Anstoss*, see Klooger 2009, Adams 2007b and 2011a). For an interesting discussion of the reception of Uexküll's notion of the 'animal environment' within phenomenological currents, see Buchanan (2008).

as a shared and therefore interpretative horizon. Amongst other things, his articulation of 'culture' as an element of 'the world' is an attempt to provide a culturological response to an ontological question, and thereby to transform the ontological field *tout court*. For Castoriadis, however, 'the world' appears not only as a philosophical problematic but as an insoluble theoretical problem. Ultimately, Castoriadis could not fully reconcile the ontological creativity of the social-historical with the phenomenological insight that we are always already *in-the-world*. But in pursuing reflections on the ontological creativity of the living being, Castoriadis brings new insights into the problematic of the world and the frontiers of anthropology, fleshing out and problematising lacunae in Arnason's phenomenology of the world. By so doing, Castoriadis invites further interrogation concerning the lines of continuity and discontinuity between the human condition, its anthropological preconditions, and the world of the living being.

References

Adams, Suzi, Smith, Karl.E. and Vlahov, G. (Eds) (2011) *Johann P. Arnason: Encounters and Interpretations*, Special Issue, *European Journal of Social Theory* 14:1.

Adams, Suzi (2007a) "Castoriadis and the Permanent Riddle of the World: Changing Configurations of World Alienation and Worldliness", *Thesis Eleven* 90, 44–60.

Adams, Suzi (2007b) "Castoriadis and Autopoiesis", *Thesis Eleven* 88: 76–91.

Adams, Suzi (2009a) "Dimensions of the World: Castoriadis's Homage to Merleau-Ponty", *Chiasmi International: Trilingual Studies on the Thought of Merleau-Ponty*. Paris: Milan; University Park (PA).

Adams, Suzi (2009b) "The Intercultural Horizons of Johann P. Arnason's Phenomenology of the World", *Journal of Intercultural Studies*, 30:3, 249–63.

Adams, Suzi (2011a) *Castoriadis's Ontology: Being and Creation*, New York: Fordham University Press.

Adams, Suzi (2011b) "The Retrieval of the World Problematic in Castoriadis's Thought" in Jollivet, S., Prémat, C. and Rosengren, M. (eds) *Destins d'exilés. Trois philosophes grecs à Paris. Kostas Axelos, Cornélius Castoriadis et Kostas Papaïoannou*. Paris: Editions du Manuscrit, 235–52.

Adams, Suzi (2012) "Arnason and Castoriadis's Unfinished Dialogue: Articulating the World", *European Journal of Social Theory*, 15:3, 313–29.

Alexander, Jeffrey C. and Smith, Philip (Eds) (2005) *The Cambridge Companion to Durkheim*. Cambridge, UK: Cambridge University Press.

Arnason, Johann P. (1976) *Zwischen Natur und Gesellschaft: Studien zu einer kritischen Theorie des Subjekts*. Frankfurt/M: Europäische Verlagsanstalt.

Arnason, Johann P. (1982) "Rationalisation and Modernity: Towards a Culturalist Reading of Max Weber", *Sociology Papers*, No. 9, La Trobe University.

Arnason, Johann P. (1988) *Praxis und Interpretation: Sozialphilosophische Studien*, Frankfurt/M: Suhrkamp.

Arnason, Johann P. (1989a) "The Imaginary Constitution of Modernity" in Busino, Giovanni (ed) *Revue européenne des sciences sociales: Pour une philosophie militante de la démocratie*, XXVII: 86. Geneva: Librairie Droz, 323–37.

Arnason, Johann P. (1989b) "Weltauslegung und Verständigung" in Honneth, Axel, McCarthy, Thomas, Offe, Claus and Wellmer, Albrecht (eds) *Zwischenbetrachtungen: im Prozess der Aufklärung. Jürgen Habermas zum 60. Geburtstag*. Frankfurt/M: Suhrkamp, 66–89.

Arnason, Johann P. (1989c) "Culture and Imaginary Significations", *Thesis Eleven* 22, 25–45.

Arnason, Johann P. (1993) "Merleau-Ponty and Max Weber: An Unfinished Dialogue", *Thesis Eleven* 36: 82–98.

Arnason, Johann P. (1994) "Reason, Imagination, Interpretation" in Robinson, Gillian and Rundell, John (eds) *Rethinking Imagination: Culture and Creativity*. London: Routledge, 55–217.

Arnason, Johann P. (2003) *Civilizations in Dispute: Historical Questions and Theoretical Traditions*. Leiden/Boston: Brill.

Arnason, Johann P. (2006) "Roads Beyond Marx: Rethinking Projects and Traditions", *Chaos a řád v sociologii a ve společnosti* (Chaos and order in sociology and society), ed. Jan Balon and Milan Tuček. Praha, Matfyzpress, (Festschrift for Miloslav Petrusek), 130–44.

Arnason, Johann P. (2013) "Merleau-Ponty and the Meaning of Civilizations" in *Encounters and Interpretations: Essays In Civilizational Analysis*. Leiden: Brill (forthcoming).

Arnason, Johann P. (2011) "Response to Comments and Criticisms", *European Journal of Social Theory*, 14:1, 107–18.

Barbaras, Renaud (2004[1991]) *The Being of the Phenomenon: Merleau-Ponty's Ontology*. Bloomington: Indiana University Press.

Bermes, Christian (2004) *Die Welt als Thema der Philosophie: vom metaphysichen zum natürlichen Weltbegriff*. Hamburg: Meiner Verlag.

Buchanan, Brett (2008) *Onto-Ethologies: The Animal Environments of Uexküll, Heidegger, Merleau-Ponty and Deleuze*. Albany: SUNY Press.

Busino, Giovanni (Ed)(1989) *Revue européenne des sciences sociales: Pour une philosophie militante de la démocratie*, XXVII: 86. Geneva: Librairie Droz.

Castoriadis, Cornelius (1980) "Francisco Varela, *Principles of Biological Autonomy*", *Le débat*, 1, 126–27.

Castoriadis, Cornelius (1984a[1971]) "The Sayable and the Unsayable: Homage to Maurice Merleau-Ponty" in *Crossroads in the Labyrinth*, trans. Kate Soper and Martin H. Ryle. Brighton, UK: Harvester.

Castoriadis, Cornelius (1984b) "Value, Equality, Justice, Politics: From Marx to Aristotle, and from Aristotle to Ourselves" in *Crossroads in the Labyrinth*, trans. Kate Soper and Martin H. Ryle. Brighton, UK: Harvester.

Castoriadis, Cornelius (1984c) "Technique" in *Crossroads in the Labyrinth*, trans. Kate Soper and Martin H. Ryle. Brighton, UK: Harvester.

Castoriadis, Cornelius (1984d) "Modern Science and Philosophical Interrogation", in *Crossroads in the Labyrinth*, trans. Kate Soper and Martin H. Ryle, Brighton, UK: Harvester.

Castoriadis, Cornelius (1984/85) "Remarks on 'Rationality' and 'Development'", *Thesis Eleven*, 10/11:1, 18–36.

Castoriadis, Cornelius (1987[1975]) *The Imaginary Institution of Society*, trans. Kathleen Blamey. Cambridge Mass: MIT Press (*IIS*).

Castoriadis, Cornelius (1989) "Fait et à faire" in Busino, Giovanni (ed.) *Revue européenne des sciences sociales: Pour une philosophie militante de la démocratie*, XXVII: 86, Geneva: Librairie Droz.

Castoriadis, Cornelius (1993) "Institution of Society and Religion", *Thesis Eleven* 35:1, 1–17.

Castoriadis, Cornelius (1997a) "*Physis* and Autonomy" in *World in Fragments*, ed. and trans. David Ames Curtis. Stanford: Stanford University Press.

Castoriadis, Cornelius (1997b[1994]) "Radical Imagination and the Social Instituting

Imaginary" in *The Castoriadis Reader*, ed. and trans. David Ames Curtis. Oxford: Blackwell.

Castoriadis, Cornelius (1997c[1996]) "Psychoanalysis and Philosophy" in *The Castoriadis Reader*, ed. and trans. David Ames Curtis. Oxford: Blackwell.

Castoriadis, Cornelius (2007) *Figures of the Thinkable*, trans. Helen Arnold. Stanford: Stanford University Press (*FT*).

Durkheim, Emile (1995[1912]) *Elementary Forms of Religious Life*, trans. Karen E. Fields. New York: Free Press.

Heidegger, Martin (1996[1927]) *Being and Time*, trans. Joan Stambaugh. Albany: SUNY Press.

(1998[1946]) "Letter on Humanism" in *Pathmarks*, ed. William Mc Neil. Cambridge, UK: Cambridge University Press.

(2000) "Introduction", in *Introduction to Metaphysics*, trans. Gregory Fried and Richard Polt, New Haven: Yale University Press.

Joas, Hans (2002) "On Articulation", *Constellations* 9:4, 506–15.

Klooger, Jeff (2009) *Castoriadis: Psyche, Society, Autonomy*. Leiden: Brill.

Knöbl, Wolfgang (2000) "In Praise of Philosophy: Johann P. Arnason's Long but Successful Journey Towards a Theory of Modernity", *Thesis Eleven* 61:1, 1–23.

Merleau-Ponty, Maurice (2003[1995]) *Nature: Course Notes from the Collège de France*, Compiled and with notes by Dominique Séglard, trans. Robert Vallier. Evanston: Northwestern University Press.

Richir, Marc (1993) "The Meaning of Phenomenology in *The Visible and the Invisible*", *Thesis Eleven* 36:1, 60–81.

Rockhill, Gabriel (2011) "Eros of Inquiry: An Aperçu of Castoriadis's Life and Work" in Rockhill, G. (ed) *Postscript on Insignificance: Dialogues with Cornelius Castoriadis*, trans. John V. Garner and Gabriel Rockhill, ix–xxxix. London: Continuum.

Smith, Jeremy (2009) "Civilisational Analysis and Intercultural Modes of American Societies", *Journal of Intercultural Studies*, 30: 3, 233–48.

Smith, Karl E. (2010) *Meaning, Subjectivity and Society: Making Sense of Modernity*, Leiden: Brill.

Taylor, Nik (2007) "Human-Animal Studies: A Challenge to Social Boundaries?", *PROTEUS* 24:1, 1–5.

Thesis Eleven (2000) *Johann P. Arnason: Modern Constellations, Civilizational Horizons*, Special Issue, *Thesis Eleven* 61.

Part II

Rationality

Odd Bedfellows: Cornelius Castoriadis on Capitalism and Freedom[1]

Giorgio Baruchello

Introduction

Capitalism and Freedom is not only the title of an influential book by Milton Friedman (1962) that played a major role in spreading the neoliberal paradigm worldwide.[2] It is also the slogan that leading statesmen, politicians and opinion-makers have been heralding in recent decades to justify, amongst other things, the privatisation of public services, the slashing of welfare states, the liberalisation of international capital trade, and the military invasion of Iraq. In this context, 'capitalism' evoked Karl Marx's 19th-century critique and has therefore been rephrased typically as 'free trade' or 'free market', so as to strengthen an 18th-century-born conceptual connection between the pursuit of profit on invested capital and the broader notion of human freedom.[3]

---

1 This book chapter stems from a previous essay of mine on Castoriadis (Baruchello 2008a).

2 I discuss in detail the key-tenets of this paradigm in a previous essay of mine (Baruchello 2008b).

3 Galbraith (2004) offers a non-Marxist reason to prefer 'capitalism' to 'free market' or any analogous terminology: whereas the latter entails either uncritically or hypocritically that a competitive, meritocratic market mechanism is effectively present, the former reminds us of the economy's actual subjection to age-defining concentrations of power that, historically, have always succeeded in establishing monopolies, oligopolies, cartels, self-remunerations schemes irrespective of performance and other conspicuous barriers to competition, merit and trade (e.g. 17th-century great merchants, 18th-century chartered companies, 19th-century trusts, 20th-

As such, it has been easier to couple 'capitalism' with 'democracy', the latter term denoting the political system that is believed to best entrench and promote freedom or, as Castoriadis would often dub it, autonomy. Capitalism and democracy have even been described as the two sides of one and the same project for human emancipation, informing the ideology and the agenda of governments, both left and right of the political spectrum, thus showing how deeply neoliberal beliefs have become part of the dominant public mindset. Bill Clinton, for one, asserts:[4]

> Fair trade among free markets does more than simply enrich America; it enriches all partners to each transaction. It raises consumer demand for our products worldwide; encourages investment & growth; lifts people out of poverty & ignorance; increases understanding; and helps dispel long-held hatreds. That's why we have worked so hard to help build free-market institutions in Eastern Europe, Russia, and the former Soviet republics. That's why we have supported commercial liberalization in China-the world's fastest-growing market. Just as democracy helps make the world safe for commerce, commerce helps make the world safe for democracy. It's a two-way street (Clinton 1996: 36).

I shall address the thought of Cornelius Castoriadis, for it tackles and elucidates how capitalism and democracy have different historical-geographical origins and, more profoundly, different orientations of value or defining aims. By stressing these two points, which Castoriadis discusses conjointly, I wish to highlight a fundamental contradiction between capitalism and freedom. This contradiction was denounced

---

century corporate managers, 21st-century financial managers).

4 I choose a political representative from the left, for neoliberal views and policies are commonly associated with right-wing parties and politicians (e.g. Margaret Thatcher and Ronald Reagan). Yet, during the 1990s, neoliberal views and policies became quite simply the conventional wisdom.

in the past under many guises, two of which will be recalled hereby. However, I shall focus primarily upon Castoriadis's own denunciation and its unique, original blend of political, economic, philosophical and psychoanalytic notions.

A First Lesson in History, Geography, and Axiology

Castoriadis (*ASA*: 72) writes that the earliest forms of democracy recorded in the West were the creative product of a variety of Greek city-states, Athens *in primis*, and of other communities in pre-Christian antiquity. As vastly substantiated by archaeologists and historians (cf. Guldager Bilde and Stolba 2006), democratic regimes, including communistic ones, appeared not solely in the urban centres of the Hellenic peninsula, and most famously in Athens, but also in rural and colonial settlements in Southern Italy and the Black Sea region. Further experiments took place in Continental Europe:

> [A]t the end of the Middle Ages, in the interstices of the feudal universe, communities that aspired to be self-governed collectivities began to be constituted … the new towns or free boroughs, in which a protobourgeoisie (long before capitalism was even an idea, not to speak of a reality!) created the first seeds of modern movements for emancipation and democracy (Castoriadis, *FT*: 97).

Historical research (cf. Griswold 1948, Hanson 1995) suggests that risk-averse family farmers were behind democratic and republican regimes in ancient Greece and ancient Southern Italy, rather than protobourgeois merchants, as in Medieval Europe. As Castoriadis points out in his essay "Imaginary and Imagination at the Crossroads", all these experiments in democratic self-rule were meant to shield the citizen's liberty from tyranny and allow them to pursue safer lives, the direction of which they could determine to a higher extent (*FT*: 75). All such experiments wcre aimed at establishing societies in which at least some groups of individuals enjoyed "the possibility and the ability to call established institutions and significations into question" (*FT*: 75). This was no small feat, for such an openness to critical self-scrutiny and reconfiguration has represented, according to Castoriadis, "a minute number in the history of humanity" (*FT*: 75).

On its part, capitalism, though too anticipated in late-medieval southern Europe, flourished truly and only in modern northern Europe, particularly in Britain. This modern economic structure is such that: "[A]ll human activities and all of their effects", hence politics as well, "come to be more or less viewed as economic activities and products, or at the least, their economic dimension is viewed as their essential, most *valuable* feature. Needless to say, this *valuation* is formulated in purely monetary terms" (*FT*: 50). As a consequence of this value-orientation, capitalism selects for/against that which is monetarily valuable/dis-valuable and, *a fortiori*, it responds to/overlooks that which is/is not computable in monetary terms. Democracy, quite obviously, is not:

> [Capitalist] societies include a strong democratic component. But the latter has not been engendered by human nature or granted by capitalism or necessarily entailed by capitalism's development. It is there as residual result, as sedimentation of struggles and of a history that have gone on for several centuries (Castoriadis 2003: 53).

Were we even to concede that, in its expansion in modern times, the capitalist axiological shift was accompanied throughout by an affirmation of democratic forms of government, this rather unlikely hypothetical *datum* would not diminish or contradict the fact that the attribution and active pursuit of monetary value is not the same thing as, nor is logically implied by, "the possibility and the ability to call established institutions and significations into question", i.e. that of which Castoriadis (*FT*: 75) conceives as the core of autonomy, hence of any actual democracy.

Not only the "rights and liberties" celebrated in the liberal, democratic constitutions, "did not arise with capitalism, nor were they granted by the latter" (Castoriadis 1997b: 12). Also, their defining orientation of value has been too divergent to be necessitated by capitalism. Whereas democracy aims at human autonomy, which entails the creative ability to reconfigure economic structures, capitalism aims at "increas[ing] output while reducing costs" (*FT*: 53), that is to say, at money-making: "Capitalism as such has nothing to do with democracy" (Castoriadis 1995a: 102). The following paragraphs will further substantiate this point.

A Previous Denunciation: Adam Smith

The geographically located historicity of capitalism is not a new theme or realisation. Castoriadis (*FT*: 50) cites Saint-Simon and Comte as enthusiastic supporters of the industrial revolution, who were aware of the utter novelty of the economic system that they commended and recommended. For that matter, Adam Smith (2001: §§ I.11.95ff) himself, the prime intellectual ambassador of modern capitalism, had already observed and studied the particular and unique "events" – his choice of words – making it possible for the new economic system to develop. In his "Digression concerning the Variations in the Value of Silver during the Course of the Four last Centuries", Smith (2001: §§ I.11.96ff) divides the history of modern Europe in three periods, explaining how "the market of Europe has become gradually more and more extensive" and why "since the discovery of America, the greater part of Europe has been much improved."

Concerning the different fundamental axiology of capitalism and democracy, Adam Smith does not suggest that free trade would translate necessarily into democratic regimes – in which, to be true to his thought, he does not place his trust wholeheartedly. Adam Smith is an 18th-

century liberal, not a republican. And to understand what the process of 'liberalisation' may have in store today, it is advisable to be familiar with the past of 'liberalism'. For the 18th-century Scottish liberal Adam Smith (2001: §§ I.11.261–63), all that "democracy" could ever mean was to enlarge slightly the franchise for political participation amongst the "order of proprietors". In other words, the race or order of "those who live by rent" would be joined by the race or order of "those who live by profit" in making laws and wielding political power. At the same time, the "race of labourers", namely the vast majority of the population, should be left in a state of subjection. This state of subjection being such that:

> In civilized society it is only among the inferior ranks of people that the scantiness of subsistence can set limits to the further multiplication of the human species; and it can do so in no other way than by destroying a great part of the children which their fruitful marriages produce (Smith, 2001: § I.8.38).

Furthermore, whenever the "real wealth of society becomes stationary" and eventually "declines ... there is no order that suffers so cruelly from its decline ... than that of labourers" (Smith 2001: § I.11.263).

Life-destructive as it may be, Smith sees no alternative to this state of affairs, upon which relied the whole economic system unfolding in Britain in his lifetime and, *a fortiori*, British society at large. After all, according to Smith, the pursuit of private profit may prevent the real wealth of society from declining, if left unhindered by the State, since it is guided by God's invisible hand.[5]

This is no cheap metaphor, but God's Providential plan *in acto* (cf. Clark 1992, Denis 2005, Evensky 1993, Werhane 1991).[6] Adam Smith

5 Smith (2001: § IV.2.43) regarded the full establishment of "the freedom of trade" even in as advanced a modern economy as Great Britain as "an Oceana or Utopia", for rich entrepreneurs would try to avoid actual competition and they would lobby politicians so as to enjoy special protections and monopolies.
6 It is perplexing, to say the least, that even the scholars at the British Adam Smith Institute

(2001: § IV.2.9) does claim that the individual pursuing "only his own gain ... *is* in this, as in many other cases, *led* by an invisible hand to promote an end which was no part of his intention" (emphasis added).

In this divinely ordained context, which 'Panglossianly' defies and pre-empts any falsifying scientific and historical evidence, the "race of labourers" should not aspire to actual political participation:

> But though the interest of the labourer is strictly connected with that of the society, he is incapable either of comprehending that interest, or of understanding its connection with his own. His condition leaves him no time to receive the necessary information, and his education and habits are commonly such as to render him unfit to judge even though he was fully informed. In the public deliberations, therefore, his voice is little heard and less regarded, except upon some particular occasions, when his clamour is animated, set on, and supported by his employers, not for his, but their own particular purposes (Smith 2001: § I.11.263).

Much more bluntly than most of today's nominal followers of his doctrine, Smith admits that "Civil government, so far as it is instituted for the security of property, is in reality instituted for the defence of the rich against the poor, or of those who have some property against those who have none at all" (Smith 2001: § V.1.55). What is more, one can easily infer that Adam Smith was not planning or promoting any major

---

(2008: "Adam Smith") fail to acknowledge this important aspect of Smith's worldview. On their official website, Smith's claim is explained such that the pursuit of individual self-interest benefits society at large "as if guided by" an invisible hand. This is a misrepresentation of Smith's stance, which is of crucial importance, because it explains: (A) the inability of liberal and neoliberal economics to perceive and consider counterevidence to the presupposed ability of free markets to self-regulate, if given enough time; and (B) the plethora of pseudo-scientific, *ad hoc* explanations of market failures, such as national character (e.g. the post-Soviet meltdowns of the 1990s), crony capitalism (e.g. the South-East Asian meltdowns of the 1990s), and State legislation (e.g. the US-UK financial collapse of 2007–8).

change in these matters, for neither the private pursuit of profit nor the public defence of private property *via* the institution of civil government are ever criticised by him.

Adam Smith and many later heirs of his, such as Friedrich August von Hayek (2005) or Ayn Rand (1964), do possess some good reasons to argue that certain civil and political freedoms are related to economic freedom. Individual self-affirmation, for example, can express itself through entrepreneurial activity, whilst the interconnected global world of 'free trade' may create opportunities for self-expression previously not available to the individual. Also, successful entrepreneurial activity implies certain forms of freedom, such as: degrees of unhindered intellectual research and circulation of technical or scientific-technological information; reliable and possibly capillary transportation networks; given opportunities for independent judgment and autonomous activity. Moreover, two parallel insights characterise political liberalism and economic capitalism: (A) the individual, political as well as economic, knows best what should be done in order to pursue her self-interest (this better knowledge being however an empirical question, not an *a priori* given); (B) a society in which successful enterprises flourish is likely to be a prosperous society, and so is a society that allows its members to pursue their life-plans unimpeded (this too being an empirical question).

Nevertheless, despite these possibly good reasons, there appears to be no necessary link between the democratic aspirations of political liberalism and liberal or 'classical' economics. History has shown repeatedly why and how this can be the case, in Latin America, Europe and Asia, whenever illiberal regimes have had no difficulty in promoting 'free trade'. Moreover, political liberalism, though democratic to some extent, is not the only form of democracy possible, nor does it guarantee *a priori* a high degree of autonomous self-determination, which Castoriadis takes as the defining element of any actual democracy (cf. Straume 2008). Insofar as modern democracy shoots its roots in the liberal tradition and relies upon capitalism, it can even work against autonomy: whenever profitability is at issue, "capitalism has need not of autonomy but of conformism" (Castoriadis 2003: 149).

Another Previous Denunciation: Karl Marx

I have dwelled on the case of Adam Smith because it is extremely significant. Adam Smith is a major point of reference for today's neoliberals. His denunciation of capitalism's geographically located historicity and undemocratic axiology should result much more thought-provoking than Karl Marx's. On balance, Marx's denunciation finds a direct and patent echo in Castoriadis's own activities as a Trotskyite partisan, an engaged social scientist, a critical philosopher, and an alienation-fighting psychoanalyst.

Stern at times, appreciative at others, Castoriadis (*ASA*: 11ff) abandoned Marxism in the early 1960s, yet he owes much to Marx nonetheless and cannot but retrieve in his thought "the acute awareness of the historicity of the phenomenon," i.e. of the historical affirmation of capitalism (*FT*: 50). Such a simple historical fact has been regularly, dishonestly, and "soon eclipsed by apologists of the new regime, recruited mostly among economists" (*FT*: 50). In other words, as soon as the feudal world started to wane, the "denial of the historicity of capitalism" made its appearance as a disingenuous reconstruction of events (*FT*: 51). Deaf to criticism and blind to evidence:

> [this denial] has prevailed among economists, from Ricardo to the present. Political economy and its object have been glorified as the investigation of "the pure logic of choice" or as a study of "the allocation of limited means for the achievement of unlimited objectives" (*FT*: 51).

This pseudo-scientific hagiography has abstracted the historical, socio-cultural, and geographical reality of the actual economies and of the living persons observable in the world. On the contrary, it has turned all of these into impalpable fictions within formalised "situations of 'optimization'", thus losing more and more touch with reality (*FT*: 61).[7]

In his lifetime, Karl Marx witnessed phenomena analogous to those studied by Adam Smith, yet on a much larger scale. In the 19th century, the capitalist machinery described in the latter's 1776 *Wealth of Nations* was affirming itself worldwide, no longer solely in Great Britain and its colonial empire, and with a much more intensive deployment of institutional and technological components. Nevertheless, Marx too regards the discovery of the Americas as a unique, crucial event, which made it possible for the process of "primitive accumulation" to be ignited (*FT*: 52). This process is geographically and historically specific and, as Castoriadis (*FT*: 52) writes, "conditioned by factors (especially extortion, fraud, and private and state-led violence) that are in no way 'economic' and owe nothing to 'the market.'"

Aware of these factors, Marx (1976, Marx and Engels 1998) desires ardently to achieve a new social order whereby to grant all citizens freedom to the fullest extent, quantitative as well as qualitative – a goal that Castoriadis, unlike Smith, shared with Marx throughout his adult life. Not only does Marx (1976, Marx and Engels 1998) aspire to establishing a society in which all citizens would be free from despotic control, whether due to *de iure* legal-political oligarchic rule or by *de facto* oligarchic control of the available means of life. Marx wishes also to establish a society in which each citizen would be free to explore and cultivate her inclinations, interests, and abilities.[8]

For Castoriadis (*FT*: 75), similarly to Marx, "the possibility and the ability to call established institutions and significations into question"

---

7 This unreality expresses itself grotesquely in contemporary economics' alleged value-neutrality and the discipline's regular use of value-laden yet life-blind terms such as 'goods' (Baruchello 2009).

8 As Oscar Wilde (2001) interprets it in his 1891 essay "The Soul of Man under Socialism", the realisation of socialism is the precondition for the actual realisation of political liberalism.

means the departure from an economic reality condemning the majority of the world's population to: (i) *de facto* legal subjection (e.g. the inability to afford adequate legal counsel); (ii) precariousness of livelihood (e.g. today's starving unemployed in "free market" Western Africa); and (iii) utter political impotence (e.g. national parliaments controlled by corporate lobbies).

As known, Marx (1976, Marx and Engels 1998) tackles critically that element which Smith himself claims to be at the centre of the human-made arrangements causing the vast majority of the world's population to depend on wages for their survival: private property. Contrary to widespread belief, Marx's criticism of private property is not meant to do away with it in all of its forms. Rather, it is meant to find ways to control and select forms of private property, so as to serve human life without privilege of class:

> Capital is a collective product, and only by the united action of many members, nay, in the last resort, only by the united action of all members of society, can it be set in motion ... We by no means intend to abolish [the] personal appropriation of the products of labour, an appropriation that is made for the maintenance and reproduction of human life, and that leaves no surplus wherewith to command the labour of others. All that we want to do away with is the miserable character of this appropriation, under which the labourer lives merely to increase capital, and is allowed to live only in so far as the interest of the ruling class requires it (Marx and Engels 1998: 53),

Committed to changing the forms of appropriation of the products of human labour within existing society, Karl Marx (and Engels 1998) argues confidently that capitalism is digging its own grave by producing revolutions that it cannot control. Indeed, one of these revolutions – the proletarians' – is bound to burst the entire system asunder, paving the path to the full realisation of a socialist, classless society. On this point, Castoriadis agrees with Marx, but to a limited extent, as the following section is going to show.

The Freedom to be Free from Capitalism

Castoriadis believes that two fundamental conditions for the continued existence of capitalism are being destroyed by capitalism in its neo-liberal manifestation. On the one hand, the worldwide affirmation of the neoliberal agenda has been weakening trade unions, left-wing parties, and workers' associations, i.e. the main source of those "social struggles" (Castoriadis 1995a: 102) that have reined in capitalism's self-destructive quest for omnipotence (e.g. the ominous post-1929 Great Depression) and brought about some mitigating, corrective mechanisms (e.g. Christian- and social-democracy, Keynesian countercyclical State intervention, regulation of international currency flows, middle-class-enhancing wages and living standards). On the other hand, the consumerist society promoted by the same agenda has been erasing the pre-capitalist "series of anthropological types [that capitalism] did not create and could not itself have created: incorruptible judges, honest Weberian-style civil servants, teachers devoted to their vocation, workers with at least a minimum of conscientiousness about their work, and so on" (Castoriadis 1995a: 102). What is more, the astounding growth of the short-term-focussed virtual economy beyond the real economy has been demolishing even the one and only original anthropological type created by capitalism, i.e. "Schumpeter's entre-preneurial type" (*FT*: 55).

In lieu of these anthropological types, contemporary capitalism has been substituting the eternal teenager, whether active (e.g. the marketing yuppie) or passive (e.g. the fashion-addict consumer) or both, conditioned if not stupefied by endless adverts since early childhood, and focused upon money and the exclusive satisfaction of her media-nurtured selfish, shallow impulses, for that alone is deemed 'rational' in economic terms. Ethical, responsible, or simply ideally committed individuals who, say, may "prefer a beautiful mathematical demonstration to high pay" or become "conscientious workers, honest judges, Weberian bureaucrats" are "crackpots … But how long can a system count exclusively on systemic anomalies to reproduce itself?" (*FT*: 147).

Even so, the "suicide" of capitalism is up to human communities. According to Castoriadis, what lies ahead is creative freedom, which can be either constructive or destructive:

> No immanent tendency pushes human societies toward all-out 'rationalization' of production to the detriment of all else, or toward political regimes that accept certain overt forms of intestine conflict while securing certain liberties. Historical creations, these two forms [capitalism and democracy] have nothing fated about them (Castoriadis 2003: 51–52).

That event which Marx claims to be the inevitable terminus of a law-like progress – by virtue of historical necessity that apologists of capitalism have replicated in their own "fatal" way – is described by Castoriadis as a possible horizon amongst many, some of which we have not even begun to fathom. The "fragile existing world disorder" (Castoriadis 1995b: 113) in which contemporary nations wander is yet another chaos from which many a possible future can emerge, depending on human collective agency.

A Second Lesson in History, Geography, and Axiology

Whether Marx's attempt was successful or not, it is too complex an issue to be discussed here. Probably, it would bring us back to Soviet Russia, which Castoriadis criticises mercilessly as totalitarian bureaucratic capitalism (*FT*). Similarly, I am not interested in discussing the differences between Marx's top-down, State-centred communism and Castoriadis's bottom-up, self-managing system of social ownership, which he obviously prefers.[9] Rather, I shall discuss how Castoriadis criticises the neoliberal mantra stating – much more vocally than ever after the fall of the Berlin Wall – that "[c]apitalist society" has "proved its excellence – its superiority – by a Darwinian selection process" (*FT*: 51).

According to Castoriadis, any serious historical study would show the pointlessness of applying such a simplistic and extra-social notion as "Darwinian selection" in order to make sense of the development of capitalism. To this end, Castoriadis (*FT*: 52) mentions several authoritative intellectuals whose work substantiates his critical remark: "Max Weber, Werner Sombart, Richard Tawney ... Karl Polanyi". Still, this issue concerns Castoriadis because the Darwinist justification of capitalism would attain a threefold rhetorical goal that is rife with disastrous consequences for freedom:

> Along a line recalling the Marxist one, the Darwinist justification of capitalism would attribute some sort of historical necessity to the advent of capitalism, thus emptying whatever value autonomous human creativity may have in economic matters.
>
> It would state this historical necessity in seemingly rational, scientific terms, thus casting the shade of irrationality and 'unscientificity' to alternative economic systems, including those that may better entrench human autonomy.
>
> It would imply an overall positive evolutional evaluation of the same phenomenon, thus accusing any alternative economic system to be contrary, whether intentionally or not, to the very survival of the human species, whilst it is in fact capitalism that is threatening it today.

---

9 In his maturity, Castoriadis became positive to the prospect of a well-regulated, humane capitalist economy, though he remained harshly critical of the existing "planetary casino" due to "the absolute freedom to transfer capital" (*FT*: 47).

For Castoriadis, *contra* the neoliberals, "applying Darwin's conception to the history of social forms" constitutes an "absurdity … and the repetition of the classic fallacy (the survival of the fittest is the survival of those fittest to survive…)." (*FT*: 51) All that such an application would reveal, as Castoriadis contends, is that:

> [T]he fact that capitalism prevails simply shows that it is the strongest, at the limit in the coarsest, most brutal sense of the term, not that it is the best or most "rational" – Hayek, the "antimetaphysician," turns out to be the most vulgar kind of Hegelian here (*FT*: 51).

If we were to accept the gross application of Darwinian selection to the history of human societies, then the next Genghis Khan, Stalin or Osama bin Laden that were resolute, lucky, and merciless enough as to reshape the face of the planet according to his gory plans, would prove 'scientifically' the superiority of his nightmarish New Order. And that is more or less what the history of capitalism reveals:

> What took place in the sixteenth, seventeenth, and eighteenth centuries was not a competition among an indefinite number of regimes, with capitalism as a winner, but the enigmatic synergy between a multitude of factors all tending toward the same outcome. There is nothing mysterious about the fact that a society based on a highly sophisticated technology was then able to demonstrate its superiority by exterminating American Indian nations and tribes, as well as Aboriginal Tasmanians and Australians, and subjugating many others (*FT*: 51–52).

The relentless and cruel pursuit of wealth displayed by capitalism is, in itself, *nihil novum sub sole*: "Wealth is amassed in many historical societies, and we also know that latifundist landowners used slave labor in their attempts at large-scale farming (in particular, not so distantly, in the Roman Empire)" (*FT*: 53). What is specific to the capitalist type of accumulation is "the ongoing transformation of the process of production in order to increase output while reducing costs" (*FT*: 53). In its current form, capitalism aims at maximising profit by increasing revenues and reducing costs in as many and as thorough ways as possible – what is regarded nowadays as the standard itself for the individual's rational behaviour under the textbook economic formula of self-maximisation. According to Castoriadis:

> Here we have the fundamental feature of what Max Weber would later call "rationalization" and about which he noted, correctly, that under capitalism it tends to take over every sphere of social life, especially by expanding the realm of calculability … the reification of all social life by capitalism (*FT*: 53).

In this process, "Capitalism [becomes] a regime that cuts off virtually every relationship between the institution and an extrasocial instance of authority. The sole instance of authority it invokes is Reason, to which it gives a quite peculiar content" (Castoriadis 2003: 274). Anything that contradicts this peculiar form of rational imperialism is obliterated from view. Nothing is sacred. Nothing is spared. No alternative form of reason is possible, whether Plato's or Aquinas's; only options that are labelled and dismissed as irrational, sentimental, utopian, out of date, standing in the way of progress or, if insistent, threats to law and order (cf. McMurtry 1999, 2002). Capitalism embodies "one of the most deep-seated traits of the singular psyche – the desire to be omnipotent" (*FT*: 53). Consistently, 20th-century:

> [T]otalitarianism is only the most extreme point of … the demented capitalist project of an unlimited expansion of pseudorational pseudo-

mastery ... which, moreover, is inverted into its own contradiction, since in it even the restrained, instrumental rationality of classical capitalism becomes irrationality and absurdity, as Stalinism and Nazism have shown (Castoriadis 2003: 135).

"This drive, this thrust toward mastery," as Castoriadis (*FT*: 53) emphasises, is not "exclusively specific to capitalism." Rather, with capitalism, "this thrust toward mastery is not simply oriented toward 'foreign' conquest, but is aimed just as much, or more, at society as a whole... education, law, politics, and so on" (*FT*: 53).

Behind the waves of privatisations unleashed by the so-called 'reforms' and 'liberalisations' of the past few decades lies a dream of totalitarian omnipotence. Pervasive and decisive, the value-orientation of capitalism pushes it to attempt to control every aspect of human life, so as to increase efficiency of output – in its myopic pecuniary understanding of reality. Thus, whereas democracy has typically implied pluralism and indeterminacy of ends within a basic constitutional framework, capitalism cannot support such pluralism and openness, for there can be only one economic system, driven by the paramount goal of maximising profit. If there is anything sacred left, then, that is profit.[10]

The Contingent, Instrumental Marriage of Capitalism and Freedom

Castoriadis (*FT*: 54–56) argues that, in the modern age, capitalism's "thrust toward mastery adopts new means for its accomplishment, and those means are of a special, 'rational' – that is to say 'economic' – nature", which include: [i] "the outburst of scientific activity",[ii] "technoscience", [iii] "the birth and consolidation of the modern State

---

10 Significantly, today's corporate executives are said to have a 'fiduciary duty' to this end. Such is the etymological *reductio* of religious faith (Lat. *fides*) and human morality (i.e. our mutual duties and obligations). On their part, liberal constitutions had spoken in the past of the 'sanctity' of property.

... [and] modern nations", [iv] "[the mindset of] *homo oeconomius*" and [v] the "the questioning of the established order".

This peculiar mindset was noticed as early as the 18th century. According to Edmund Burke, in the feudalism-abandoning Europe "all the decent drapery of life is to be rudely torn off" *in lieu* of a novel age "of sophisters, economists, and calculators" that is bound to annihilate "that generous loyalty to rank and sex, that proud submission, that dignified obedience, that subordination of the heart, which kept alive, even in servitude itself, the spirit of an exalted freedom" (Burke 1953: §§ 126, 128, 134).

It is not relevant to assess whether Burke's depictions of the Middle Ages, its diffuse sense of fealty, and its peaks of civil gentlemanship and religious piety are accurate or not. What matters here is that it too sheds light on the *homo novus* of the capitalist age, long before and analogously to Marx, Weber and Castoriadis, who addresses as well the quintessentially capitalist *homo computans*. This novel human being, back in the 18th century, calculated that it could be good for business to challenge the existing legal and political institutions in the name of democracy, as the Frenchmen dreaded by Burke had done with ample shedding of blood. It is only in this axiological perspective, i.e. as an *instrumental* attribution of value, that capitalism chose – in addition to science, statehood and nationhood – "the resumption ... of the ancient movement for autonomy" (*FT*: 55).

Constrained by the pre-existing feudal institutions, this resumption of emancipatory projects "first took the form of a movement in which the protobourgeoisie strove to gain freedom for the boroughs" (*FT*: 55). Only at a later stage did this early movement evolve into a properly bourgeois movement, which was capable of calling into question the existing political and legal structures and of reshaping them so as to suit its own ends.

However, as a self-aware expression of human creative freedom capable of critical activity, democracy can be no longer appreciated by capitalism, once capitalism is firmly established. As soon as this happens, the memory and the possibility of any creative human freedom that may mould alternative economic systems must be erased, so that "capitalism's domination of the modern era does not appear then as what it is – namely, arbitrary creation of a particular humanity – but as fated phase of all historical movement, at once fated and welcome" (Castoriadis 2003: 48). Yet, despite all *a posteriori* claims of inevitability, capitalism and democracy arose together in modern times contingently and instrumentally: the former exploiting the latter (cf. Foucault, 2008).

First of all, as I have already emphasised, "the adoption of capitalism does not entail a liberal political regime – as Japan shows us ... from 1860 to 1945, or South Korea after the war" (Castoriadis 2003: 52). The tyrannies of Mussolini's Italy, Hitler's Germany, Chicago-boys-advised Pinochet's Chile and 'two-system' human-rights-violating China could be added to the lot (cf. Hobsbawm 1994, 2000). Not only have there been democratic experiments prior to capitalism, but the latter has made use of the former if and only if instrumental to the achievement of its goals, within certain historical contexts.

Secondly, even in those historical contexts, as soon as capitalist goals were achieved, democracy turned into a secondary matter, if not even a nuisance, an impediment, a menace to further profits. One must simply recall the fierce resistance that 19th- and 20th-century liberal States showed against "the resumption of the ancient movement toward autonomy ... in the form of the democratic and working-class movement" (*FT*: 55).[11] Paupers, women, and various ethnic 'minorities' had to fight long and hard for the recognition of even just those basic civil and legal rights that the liberal bourgeoisie extorted from the ruling class of the *ancien régime* one or even two centuries before them. Indeed, the very same liberal bourgeoisie often formed alliances with the former aristocratic rulers, in order to prevent further enlargement of the legal-political franchise

---

11 In my native country, to name one case, this resistance meant Mussolini's fascist regime.

(cf. Mayer 1981). Typically, what all the excluded groups fighting for recognition have had in common was not to own significant shares of private property and the aspiration to find ways to secure the satisfaction of their life needs (cf. Noonan 2006).

Thirdly, the result of these prolonged struggles has not been full-fledged autonomy or actual democracy, but, as the liberal economist Vilfredo Pareto (1935) himself had already observed long ago, "regimes of *liberal oligarchy* ... [i.e.] the compromise our societies have reached between capitalism properly speaking and the emancipatory struggles that have attempted to transform or liberalize capitalism" (Castoriadis 1997a: 115; emphasis added). Such regimes foster autonomy in strict proportion to its ability to serve capitalism, hence "the liberal-oligarchic regime" is only "fallaciously called democracy" (Castoriadis 2003: 51; emphasis removed).

The intrinsic character of capitalism is not scientific, State-centred, national, or democratic: it is profit-centred. Were the circumstances to change, then the attribution of value to science, statehood, nationhood and democracy could change – and, as a matter of historical fact, it has changed. Keen observers of contemporary capitalism (cf. Hobsbawm 2000, McMurtry 1999, 2002) have registered its regular opposition to:

- unprofitable science and forms of knowledge (e.g. early versions of electric cars, research suggesting the dangerousness of GMOs, the teaching of humanities inside universities),

- modern States (e.g. *via* global free movement of financial capital and currency speculation, subtraction of public revenues by siphoning private revenues to fiscal havens, blackmailing governments by off-sourcing threats),

- nationhood (e.g. by marketing internationally standardised goods and behavioural codes, promoting English as the world's *lingua franca*, exerting continued pressure for international economic integration), and

– democracy (e.g. by enmity to tax-centred egalitarian redistribution of wealth, political lobbying for destabilisation of countries owning publicly profitable resources, superseding popular representation and locally based regulatory legislation by supranational trade agreements).

As Castoriadis eloquently writes:

> In the effectively actual social-historical reality of contemporary capitalism, these [democratic] liberties function more and more as the mere instrumental complement of the mechanisms that maximize individual 'enjoyments' [*jouissances*]. And these 'enjoyments' are the sole substantive content of the 'individualism' being pounded into our heads these days (Castoriadis 1995a: 97).

The relationship between capitalism and democracy is extrinsic, instrumental. Democracy and the little individual autonomy that it secures in its current dominant form are primarily, if not even merely, cogs in the larger, much more crucial capitalist machinery, the end-product of which is to be profit.

Human Alienation in Consumerist Societies

As a practicing psychotherapist, Castoriadis is worried by the alienating effects of capitalism upon people's life-plans and mental health: "almost all of human history has taken place in regimes for which economic 'efficiency,' the maximization of outputs, and so on were absolutely not central to social activities" (*FT*: 52). Even if there may have been nearly always a merchant class, some degree of financial activity, and various forms of private accumulation of wealth: "Those sectors of social activity were subordinated to and integrated in others viewed, in each case, as embodying the main goals of human life, and above all, they were not separated as 'production' or 'the economy'" (*FT*: 52).

Today, the anthropological assumptions of capitalism do seem to depict the motivations and the aspirations of a conspicuous part of the world's population. Rappers walking out of fancy SUVs and celebrating money may well be taken as their popular manifestation. Contemporary female rhythm & blues band *Pussycat Dolls* sing far less sarcastically an old song by the Beatles: "The best things in life are free / But you can keep'em for the birds and bees / Money / That's what I want". Twenty years earlier, Madonna extolled the "virtues" of the "material girl". One can even step back to Marilyn Monroe's un-Aristotelian claim that "diamonds are a girl's best friend". Nonetheless, according to Castoriadis, not even the popularity of greed or self-maximisation constitutes a valid substantiation of the neoliberal assumption of their naturalness:

> [T]he justification is circular. In "'affluent'" countries, people "'want'" the goods because they are reared from earliest infancy to want them (a visit to one of today's nursery schools is enlightening), and because the regime prevents them in a thousand and one ways from wanting anything else (*FT*: 66).

The tyrannical 'free market' conditions the subject from cradle to grave, as any market expert would state candidly and shamelessly, causing people to mistake artificially instilled cravings for actual needs (cf. Rifkin 2000).[12] Then these people are set 'free' in the realm of consumer

---

12 Praising fashion designer Giorgio Armani, Amy M. Spindler (2007) reveals the unnatural nature of this process: "selling fashion means creating new needs, and most men do not need another classic jacket. Armani is an expert at creating new needs."

sovereignty, where they are trained to measure their worth by what they appear to be able to afford to buy.

John Kenneth Galbraith (2007) commented on this perplexing issue back in the late 1960s, while a pervasive means of indoctrination already exploited by Mussolini and Stalin was finding an analogue in capitalist societies. This analogue was the sophisticated bamboozling by scientifically crafted advertising and omni-pervasive media technologies seeking the "management" of "consumer demand" and corporate "control over behaviour" (*FT*: 6). This bamboozling runs deep, as Galbraith and others have observed (cf. Baudrillard 1970), instilling the desire to conform/distinguish oneself *qua* perceived need, whether for the enjoyment of the purchased good *per se* or of the status that it supposedly guarantees. As irrational as it sounds and it is, utility – absolute as well as marginal – can thus be ascribed to utterly superfluous priced goods and services conferring status to those who own them and making those who do not own them either contemptible or pitiable, along the lines of Veblen's (1994) pecuniary standard of decency.

Adding madness to irrationality, the masses, whether seeking higher status or simply prevention from suffering public humiliation, participate in a consumer economy that is no longer able to generate happiness (cf. Galeano 1998, Frey and Stutzer 2002, Heath and Potter 2005). Amidst humbled lower classes, frustrated middle classes, and self-conscious upper classes, the media strategies of bamboozlement seem to be at least as powerful as the tyrants of old, if not more: "This is true everywhere," as Castoriadis writes, "because if capitalism has not invented *ab ovo* what we call the demonstration effect [i.e. causing conditions such that the *demostrandum* is demonstrated], it has taken it to previously unknown heights" (*FT*: 66).

Mechanisms for social distinction and exclusion have always existed, and very painful ones too, but never before the age of television was the propagation of the dominant mindset so pervasive and uninterrupted.

The reader might want to pause and ponder seriously upon the fact that the average US child is exposed today to 40,000 TV commercials a year, not to mention billboards and vicarious advertising (cf. Clark 2007). Besides, this media bamboozling is present also in less affluent countries, as Castoriadis acknowledges: "Televisions, too, rank among these gifts [from Europe] ... allowing ... [the] sergeant ... [that] seize[s] power and proclaim[s] a socialist people's revolution while massacring a fair proportion of his compatriots ... to go about stupefying the population" (2003: 51).

Although Castoriadis (2003: 172) does not assert that "televisual" propaganda annihilates critical thought and free will *in toto*, he endorses the notion that it does numb its target audience to a noticeable extent, thus reducing the opportunities for autonomous self-creation. Stupefied and atomised, the individual can be controlled – in fact bought and sold – by the bourgeoisie that operates the media. This is what he calls "the privatization of individuals in the societies of modern capitalism." (Castoriadis 2003: 172) Additionally, on this point, Castoriadis observes:

> The atomization of individuals is not autonomy. When an individual buys a fridge or a car, he does what forty million other [French] individuals do; there is here neither individuality nor autonomy. This is, as a matter of fact, one of the mystifications of contemporary advertising: 'Personalize yourself, buy Brand X laundry detergent.' And millions of individuals go out and 'personalize' (!) themselves by buying the same detergent (2003: 148–49).

On top of the media-pumped brainwashing, one should add then the active destruction of non-capitalist economies and forms of social life by other means, including the threat or the actual use of military force and large-scale financial usury. Televisions and consumer glitter may not always be enough, according to Castoriadis (*ASA*: 174–75):

A society that worships consumerism and zapping on TV cannot erode the anthropological hold of the Koran or of Hinduism. People who are at a loss in the modern world and adhere tensely to their religious identity can't find any example worth imitating or any incitement to think for themselves in those apathetic citizens, huddled up in their petty private worlds, who leave their government to the political, economic, and cultural oligarchies, to the party apparatuses and the mass media.

What all this reveals, in essence, is that capitalism's empire is open to any instrument that may serve its sovereign end, i.e. the pursuit of profit, including, as we have seen, nationhood, democracy, autonomy – and their destruction.

Concluding Remarks

In the previous section of this chapter I have emphasised the non-naturalness of capitalism because this realisation sheds further light upon the axiological contradiction that exists between capitalism and human freedom. Yet, an additional contradiction is spotted by Castoriadis, to which I wish to bring some attention, even if very hastily, in these concluding remarks of mine:

> For the time being, [capitalism] is still capable of delivering the goods, more or less. This necessarily puts an end to the discussion: the situation will not change as long as people want all that accumulation of junk, which growing numbers of people today are increasingly less sure of getting, and with which they may or may not be fed up some day (*FT*: 66).

This passage about 'junk' highlights a fairly simple but most important matter: certain goods are 'bads', in a way that the *homines oeconomici* do not often, if ever, grasp. The 'goods' that they want, produce, advertise, trade and exchange most profitably can be bad for the environment, bad for the many non-human life-forms inhabiting the same environment, bad for people's health, bad for people's children, and bad for their children's children. This divergence of defining values is visible to most intelligent observers but neoliberals, whose agenda still dominates institutional decision-making. Jurist Aulis Aarnio, whilst talking about interpretation of statutes in the Finnish legal system, states plainly: "Environmental values and economic values often clash, as in the protection of the forests and waterways. Almost without exception, the values that have prevailed have been economic" (Aarnio 1991: 131).

The aims of capitalism are not those of biological life, which, instead, actual democracy is meant to serve by granting people the ability to shape and reshape societies in which they and their descendants may live healthily, if not even happily (Baruchello 2008b). This is important with respect to Castoriadis's hopes for human emancipation, for he believes that "capitalism … based on the continuous, rapid growth of production and consumption" has caused such a havoc upon "the environment" (*ASA*: 197) that it provides better reasons for its radical critique than "Marx" and his positive assessment of "capitalist technology and its products as an integral part of the process of human development" (*ASA*: 200). The future of emancipation, according to Castoriadis, is green, not red – a large, intriguing theme that cannot be explored in this chapter.[13]

---

13 Castoriadis (1981) provides the first as well as one of the most eloquent analyses of his on this theme.

References

Aarnio, Aulis (1991) "Statutory Interpretation in Finland", in MacCormick, D. Neil and Summers, Robert S. (eds.) *Interpreting Statutes. A Comparative Study*, 123–70, Aldershot, Dartmouth.

Adam Smith Institute (2008) "Adam Smith". Available at: http://www.adamsmith.org/adam-smith/ (last accessed: 18 December 2009).

Baruchello, Giorgio (2008a) "Capitalism and Freedom: The Core of a Contradiction. An Essay on Cornelius Castoriadis and John McMurtry" *Nordicum-Mediterraneum* 3(2). Available at: http://nome.unak.is/nome2/issues/vol3_2/baruchello.html

Baruchello, Giorgio (2008b) "Deadly Economics: Reflections on the Neoclassical Paradigm", in Tandy, Charles (ed.) *Death and Anti-Death Volume 5: Thirty Years After Loren Eiseley*, 65–132. Palo Alto: Ria University Press.

Baruchello, Giorgio (2009) "Good and Bad Capitalism: Re-thinking Value, Human Needs, and the Aims of Economic Activity", *Economics, Management, and Financial Markets* 4(3), 125–69.

Baudrillard, Jean (1970) *La Société de consummation*. Paris: Éditions Denoël.

Burke, Edmund (1953[1790]) *Reflections on the French Revolution*. London: Everyman's Library.

Castoriadis, Cornelius (1981) "From Ecology to Autonomy" *Thesis Eleven* 3(1), 8–22.

Castoriadis, Cornelius (1995a) "The Dilapidation of the West" *Thesis Eleven* 41(1), 94–111.

Castoriadis, Cornelius (1995b) "Postscript" *Thesis Eleven* 41(1), 111–14.

Castoriadis, Cornelius (1997a) "Anthropology, Philosophy, Politics" *Thesis Eleven* 49(1), 99–116.

Castoriadis, Cornelius (1997b) "Democracy as Procedure and Democracy as Regime" *Constellations* 4(1), 1–18.

Castoriadis, Cornelius (2003) *The Rising Tide of Insignificancy (The Big Sleep)*, translated from the French and edited anonymously as a public service. Available at: www.notbored.org

Castoriadis, Cornelius "Third World, Third Worldism, Democracy", 46–56.

Castoriadis, Cornelius "The Rising Tide of Insignificancy", 124–54.

Castoriadis, Cornelius "The *Coordinations* in France", 165–76.

Castoriadis, Cornelius "Unending Interrogation", 259–87.

Castoriadis, Cornelius (2007) *Figures of the Thinkable*, trans. Helen Arnold. Stanford CA: Stanford University Press (*FT*):

Castoriadis, Cornelius "The 'Rationality' of Capitalism", 47–70.

Castoriadis, Cornelius "Imaginary and Imagination at the Crossroads", 71–90.

Castoriadis, Cornelius "Primal Institution of Society and Second-Order Institutions", 91–101.

Castoriadis, Cornelius "What Democracy?", 118–50.

Castoriadis, Cornelius (2010) *A Society Adrift. Interviews and Debates, 1974–1997*, trans. Helen Arnold. New York: Fordham University Press (*ASA*):

Castoriadis, Cornelius "Why I Am No Longer a Marxist", 11–44.

Castoriadis, Cornelius "Response to Richard Rorty", 69–82.

Castoriadis, Cornelius "The Gulf War: Setting Things Straight", 171–75.

Castoriadis, Cornelius "The Revolutionary Potency of Ecology", 197–205.

Clark, Charles (1992) *Economic Theory and Natural Philosophy: The Search for the Natural Laws of the Economy*. Hants: Edward Elgar.

Clark, Eric (2007) *The Real Toy Story: Inside the Ruthless Battle for America's Youngest Consumers*. New York: Free Press.

Clinton, Bill (1996) *Between Hope and History*. New York: Random House.

Denis, Andy (2005) "The Invisible Hand of God in Adam Smith" *Research in the History of Economic Thought* 23(A), 1–33.

Evensky, Jerry (1993) "Ethics and the Invisible Hand" *Journal of Economic Perspectives* 7(2): 197–205.

Foucault, Michel (2008[2004]) *The Birth of Biopolitics. Lectures at the Collège de France 1978–1979*, trans. Graham Burchell. Houndmills: Palgrave MacMillan.

Frey, Bruno and Stutzer, Alois (2002) *Happiness and Economics*. Princeton: Princeton University Press.

Friedman, Milton (1962) *Capitalism and Freedom*. Chicago: University of Chicago Press.

Galbraith, John Kenneth (2004) *The Economics of Innocent Fraud: Truth for Our Time*. Boston: Houghton Mifflin.

Galbraith, John Kenneth (2007[1967]) *The New Industrial State. With a New Foreword by James K. Galbraith*. Princeton: Princeton University Press.

Galeano, Eduardo (1998) *Upside Down: A Primer for the Looking-Glass World*, trans. Mark Fried. New York: Picador.

Griswold, Alfred W. (1948) *Farming and Democracy*. New Haven: Yale University Press.

Guldager Bilde, Pia and Stolba, Vladimir F. (2006; eds.) *Surveying the Greek Chora. The Black Sea Region in a Comparative Perspective*. Aarhus: Aarhus University Press.

Hanson, Victor D. (1995) *The Other Greeks: The Family Farm and the Agrarian Roots of Western Civilization*. New York: The Free Press.

Hayek, Friedrich A. (2005[1944]) *The Road to Serfdom* London: Routledge.

Heath, Joseph and Potter, Andrew (2005) *The Rebel Sell. How the Counterculture Became Consumer Culture*. Southern Gate Chichester: Capstone.

Hobsbawm, Eric (1994) *Age of Extremes: The Short Twentieth Century: 1914–1991*. London: Michael Joseph.

Hobsbawm, Eric (2000[1999]) *The New Century. In Conversation with Antonio Polito*, trans. Allan Cameron. London: Abacus.

Marx, Karl (1976[1867–94]) *Capital*, trans. David Fernbach. Harmondsworth: Penguin.

Marx, Karl and Engels, Friedrich (1998[1848]) *The Communist Manifesto*. London: Verso. [1888 English translation].

Mayer, Arno J. (1981) *The Persistence of the Old Regime*. New York: Pantheon Books.

McMurtry, John (1999) *The Cancer Stage of Capitalism*. London: Pluto Press.

McMurtry, John (2002) *Value Wars: The Global Market Versus the Life Economy*. London: Pluto Press.

Noonan, Jeff (2006) *Democratic Society and Human Needs*. Montreal & Kingston: McGill-Queen's University Press.

Pareto, Vilfredo (1935[1916]) *The Mind and Society*, trans. Andrew Bongiorno and Arthur Livingston. London: Jonathan Cape.

Rand, Ayn (1964) *The Virtue of Selfishness: A New Concept of Egoism*. New York: Signet.

Rifkin, Jeremy (2000) *The Age of Access: the New Culture of Hypercapitalism Where All of Life Is a Paid-for Experience*. New York: Tarcher/Putnam.

Smith, Adam (2001[1776]) *An Inquiry into the Nature and Causes of the Wealth of Nations*. Available at: http://www.econlib.org/library/Smith/smWN.html

Spindler, A.M. (1993, July 1st) "Review/Fashion; In Milan, Bold Visions And a Softer Silhouette". Available at: www.nytimes.com

Straume, Ingerid (2008) "Freedom and the Collective" *Nordicum-Mediterraneum* 3(2). Available at: http://nome.unak.is/nome2/issues/vol3_2/straume.html

Veblen, Thorstein (1994[1899]) *Theory of the Leisure Class: An Economic Study in the Evolution of Institutions*. London: Penguin.

Werhane, Patricia (1991) *Adam Smith and his Legacy for Modern Capitalism*. Oxford: Oxford University Press.

Wilde, Oscar (2001[1891]) *The Soul of Man Under Socialism and Selected Critical Prose*. London: Penguin.

From Modernity to Neoliberalism: What Human Subject?[1]

Sophie Klimis

Introduction

'What democracy?' is the provocative title Castoriadis had chosen for a paper he presented at Cerisy-la-Salle in 1990 (*FT*: 118–50). Whilst the planetary triumph of democracy was celebrated in the mass media as well as by many intellectuals, Castoriadis was questioning its mere possibility. To him, democracy should tie in its etymological sense: democracy is the power (*kratos*) of the people (*demos*). To put it in other words, democracy is the regime of autonomy. A democratic collectivity institutes itself by creating its own laws (*auto-nomos*), values, social institutions and collective aims, without any reference to any kind of transcendence. This autonomous and democratic collectivity is also characterized by self-limitation: the people are totally responsible for themselves and must create their own principles of limitation, as nothing is limiting their power from the outside. As democracy is autonomous, self-instituted and self-governed (based on the direct participation and self-organization of the people), a representative democracy is not

1 I am indebted to Helen Arnold and the editors for carefully reading my paper. I thank them very much for their help with my English. I would also like to thank all the participants of the Nordic Summer University's summer session of July 2009 (and especially Isabelle Delcroix, Olivier Fressard and Stathis Gourgouris) as well as Alice Pechriggl for our friendly discussions and their constructive remarks about my paper.

democratic for Castoriadis. Does this mean that the only democracy that has ever existed was the Athenian polis? The answer is no. The Athenians *invented* democracy, but Castoriadis has stressed several times the fact that the Athenian *polis* is not a model but a germ (*WIF*: 267–89 and Castoriadis 2004: 35–64). Democracy understood as a dynamic project of autonomy has been revived several times by the Moderns: in the 11th and 12th centuries in Western Europe, and thereafter especially in periods such as the Enlightenment, the American and the French revolutions, the Paris Commune, the working class' struggles in the 19th and 20th centuries, or May 68.

However, Castoriadis's diagnosis of the contemporary situation is very pessimistic. According to him, the so-called 'democracies' in contemporary Western capitalist societies are in fact liberal oligarchies: they are "oligarchies because they are dominated by a specific stratum of people, liberal because that stratum consents a number of negative or defensive liberties to citizens" (*FT*: 126). "Generalized conformism" is the only content of those 'opened' societies, characterized by the reproduction of the same in the economy, politics as well as in culture (*FT*: 126). This reproduction of the same is due to the general application of two norms: "one is the hierarchical-bureaucratic norm within those huge organizations of all sorts (be they productive, administrative, educational or cultural) in which most people spend their lives. The other is the norm of money, wherever today's pseudo-marketplace setups prevail" (*FT*: 126–27). The liberal societies are therefore "fragmented bureaucratic capitalist societies" (*FT*: 127), in which the project of autonomy keeps disappearing. Castoriadis gives several reasons for that 'eclipse', but I would like to emphasize one of them: the collective project of autonomy is diseappering because autonomy is no longer *desired* by the contemporary capitalist individuals.

'What human subject?' is therefore the question I have chosen to explore in the present paper, echoing Castoriadis's question about democracy. Indeed, the democratic project of autonomy connects inextricably the individuals and the collective: "one cannot want autonomy without wanting it for everyone and its realization cannot be conceived of in its full scope except as a collective enterprise" (*IIS*: 107). This Castoriadian statement could sound like a vicious circle: an autonomous society presupposes autonomous individuals and autonomous individuals can only appear in societies that promote autonomy. But for Castoriadis, the circle is fruitful: individuals create themselves as autonomous while struggling for the creation of an autonomous society. In the *Imaginary Institution of Society*, Castoriadis calls this autonomous individual a *subject*: "but just what is this subject? ... It is certainly not the point-like ego of the 'I think'. It is not the subject as pure activity, possessing no constraints, no inertia, this will o' the wisp of subjectivist philosophers ..." (*IIS*: 105). The autonomous 'subject' Castoriadis has in mind is obviously not the Cartesian ego.

But what is its positive definition? What are the essential differences but also the possible connections between the 'true' autonomous subject, the classical Cartesian *ego* and the capitalist individual? If contemporary capitalist societies are not autonomous anymore, what could revive the capitalist individual's desire for self-transforming into an autonomous subject?

These are the three issues that I propose to consider in this paper. In its first part, I will present Castoriadis' critique of the Cartesian *ego*, in order to show how he defines the 'true' autonomous subject. Secondly, I will examine if modernity, capitalism and neoliberalism have to be considered as three different types of society, or as one and the same society altering itself through time.[2] Indeed, we must first consider the collective level, if

---

2 From now on, I will call contemporary capitalism 'neoliberalism', in order to distinguish it from the first phase of capitalism.

135

we want to understand the specific links and the differences between the Cartesian *ego*, the neoliberal individual and the autonomous subject. In the third and last part of this paper, I will extend Castoriadis'analysis of the Cartesian *ego* and of the contemporary individual to its paradoxical consequences. As a conclusion, I will bring out the antinomy of desire for money and desire for autonomy, with the help of Aristotle's analysis of money.

1. *Ego cogitans* is *homo computans*

From Castoriadis's point of view, the Cartesian *ego* is not true subjectivity but only its 'ghost' because of four reasons: its artificial solipsism; the narrowness of its so-called rationality, in fact limited to instrumental rationality; its lack of self-reflexivity, in fact limited to self-referentiality; and its unawareness of the fact that its ideal of pure rationality is a product of the imagination.

Let us consider first the charge of artificial solipsism: Forgetting that he is in the world with others, the Cartesian *cogito* is presented by Castoriadis as " ... a pure gaze, the naked capacity for evoking something, setting it at a distance, a spark outside of time ... " (*IIS*: 105). On the contrary, Castoriadis states that the fundamental truth, forgotten by all subjectivist philosophies, is that "in the subject as subject, we find the non-subject":

> In the subject there is, to be sure, as one of its moments 'that which can never become an object', inalienable freedom, the always present possibility of redirecting the gaze, of abstracting from any particular content, of bracketing everything, including oneself, except inasmuch as the self is this capacity that springs forth as presence and absolute proximity at the very moment it places itself at a distance from itself. However, this moment is abstract, empty; it never has and never will

produce anything other than the silent and useless self-evidence of the *cogito sum*, the immediate certainty of existing as a thinking substance, which cannot legitimately express itself through language. For once even unpronounced speech makes a first opening, the world and others infiltrate from every direction … (*IIS*: 105–06).

In the 'content' of the thought, others are always present, because of the impossibility of thinking outside of language, which for Castoriadis is the first and most fundamental social institution. Furthermore, the support of this union of the subject and the non-subject within the subject, of this articulation of the self and the others is the body:

> It is because it 'forgets' this concrete structure of the subject that traditional philosophy, the narcissism of consciousness fascinated by its own naked forms, reduces to the level of the conditions of servitude both the other and corporeality. And it is because it wants to base itself on the pure freedom of a fictive subject that it condemns itself to rediscover the alienation of the actual subject as an insoluble problem (*IIS*: 106).

Therefore the 'true' subject is not the abstract, absolute and monadic subjectivity created by modern philosophy, but "the actual subject traversed through and through by the world and by others" (*IIS*: 106). This 'true' embodied subject is also characterized as the active and lucid instance constantly organizing the contents of its activity of thinking, with the help of those contents.

We may now turn to the second Castoriadian charge against the Cartesian *ego*. Whereas the Moderns are proud of their supposedly extremely developed rationality and rationalization of all fields of life and being, Castoriadis considers modern rationality to be limited, in fact, to instrumental rationality. The rationality in which modern societies have placed their trust is "…simply a matter of *form*, externally necessary connections, the perpetual dominance of the syllogism" (*IIS*: 156). In Castoriadis's view, this kind of instrumental 'rationality' may be attributed even to a bacterium and more generally to any living being: "the living being discriminates, separates, chooses, identifies, works with classes, properties and relations … there is recognition of forms, there is always the 'if … then' syllogistic schema" (Castoriadis 2002: 91). As a result, the living being shapes the world as 'its' world, that is to say as a world in which it can live, preserving itself (*CR*: 306–07). Castoriadis therefore calls the living being a '*pour soi*' (for-itself), and states four levels of *pour soi*: the living being, the psyche, the social individual and society (Castoriadis 2002: 57). Each is characterized by the ability to calculate and perform instrumental reasoning of the 'if…then' type.

As each *pour soi* is characterized by self-finality, it is important to stress, with Castoriadis, that this implies self-referentiality (2002: 104). Self-referentiality is therefore not the same as self-reflexivity, and is not specific of human subjectivity. Castoriadis takes the example of the immune system of an organism (2002: 104):

> There is constantly the essential presence of reckoning, of calculation, of computation. But there is also self-referentiality: the immune system is able to distinguish the self from the non-self and to act consequently. Because this system cannot exist without this capacity, some diseases, called precisely auto-immune, appear when this capacity collapses and when the cells of the immune system attack the self, not recognizing it anymore. More generally, if any system is endowed with the property of self-finality, self-referentiality is necessary implied.[3]

While increasing the scope of *pour soi* even to bacteria and stating that rationality and calculation are not specific of human beings, Castoriadis

---

3 All translations of Castoriadis's texts that have not yet been translated into English are mine.

challenges the whole philosophical tradition of modernity, including Freud himself:

> Freudian consciousness is first characterized by reasoning and calculation [...] This definition of reason or subjectivity has very ancient philosophical legitimacy: for Hegel, even apart from considering the subjectivity, 'reason is operation in accordance with a goal'.[4] It is thus teleological logic. Hobbes had already defined reasoning as reckoning and in his *Ars Combinatoria*, Leibniz praised Hobbes for having seen that the activity of the reasoning subject is nothing else than reckoning .... This confusion is to be avoided because calculating supposes ensidical operations ... and is to be found wherever *pour soi* is involved (Castoriadis 2002: 103–04).

I would like to emphasize this third point in Castoriadis's criticism of the modern subject. Self-finality and self-preservation through calculating rationality exist for all living beings. The only specific human characteristic is *self-reflexivity understood as self-transformation*. In order to fully understand this statement, we must turn to the fourth and last Castoriadian charge against the Cartesian *ego*. In its perfect, mathematised and mechanized world, the Modern *ego* does not see that "...in the syllogisms of modern life, the premises borrow their contents from the imaginary..." (*IIS*: 156). Moreover, the ideal of rationality is in fact an 'obsession with rationality'. Castoriadis speaks therefore of a "pseudo-rationality" (*IIS*: 156): "...arbitrary in its ultimate ends to the extent that these ends themselves stem from no reason, and it is arbitrary when it posits itself as an end, intending nothing but a formal and empty 'rationalization'. In this aspect of its existence, the modern world is in the throes of a systematic delirium ..." (*IIS*: 156). The autonomization and development of technique for itself, no longer 'in the service' of any

4   Castoriadis 2002: 104. Footnote 3 says Castoriadis is quoting the *Preface* of Hegel's *Phenomenology of Spirit*, translated by Jean Hippolyte (1941: 20).

other ascribable aim (such as greater happiness or education or free time for all mankind), is for Castoriadis its most immediately perceptible and most directly threatening form. Modern rationality therefore seems not only to be criticised by Castoriadis, but unmasked as an insane – that is, exceeding certain limits – product of the imagination.

To put an end to this first section, we could of course 'critique the critique'. In many ways, Castoriadis's portrait of the Cartesian *ego* seems exaggerated, if not caricatural. Many scholars have studied the importance (even paradoxical) of the body, others and madness in Descartes' works. Moreover, the critique of Modern rationality (of its intrinsic irrationalism and violence) is due to Horkheimer and Adorno, whose work has influenced Castoriadis. However, it seems to me that Castoriadis's views are original and thought-provoking for the following reasons.

Firstly, his critique of the Modern subject challenges the commonplace according to which the subject is a Modern invention and did not exist in the Ancient world. Indeed, the 'true' subject is for Castoriadis the autonomous one, inherited from the Greeks, as the Moderns have inherited the Greek inventions of philosophy – defined as never-ending questioning – and democracy – defined as a society supported by itself, responsible for the invention of its own institutions. Castoriadis considers therefore the project of autonomy as a specific characteristic not of Modernity but of the Greek-Western world. The autonomous subject he praises is a self-reflecting one, capable of transforming himself by thinking and acting deliberately. The 'true' subject is never done, but 'to be done'. It is self-creating as a reflexive and deliberate subjectivity, because challenging the laws of its own existence (the laws of Nature as well as the laws of Society). For instance, from a Castoriadian point of view, Socrates and his interlocutors, as well as the contemporary psychoanalyst and the analysand, may be viewed as subjects, because they have undertaken the project of transforming themselves, which is never-ending.

Secondly, Castoriadis's caricature of the Modern subject seems to aim at emphasizing the ambivalent power of imagination in the constitution of the subject. On the one hand, Castoriadis considers Descartes as a typical representative of what he calls "inherited ontology": the whole philosophical tradition since Plato has missed the comprehension of imagination as *vis formandi*, creation *ex nihilo* of new forms of being, i.e. the capacity of creating a form which was not there before (*FT*: 72). Indeed, in his *Metaphysical Meditations*, Descartes explicitly reduces imagination to the recombination of pre-existing elements and contrasts the clarity of reason with the deceptive power of imagination. In his correspondence with Mersenne, Descartes also writes that only two things are conceived without the use of imagination: the certitude of the *cogito* and of the idea of God. For those reasons, it is important for Castoriadis to show that the *cogito* and the general ideal of a pure reason are *creations of a theoretical imaginary*, as all major philosophical concepts (Castoriadis 1984: xx-xxiii). The irony of the Castoriadian critique therefore aims at showing that the so-called self-reflexive *cogito* is unable to reflect on its true foundation. This seems to me to deepen and to increase the critique of Modern rationality made by the Frankfurt School.

On the other hand, what characterizes the human being is to be a "mad animal" says Castoriadis, ironically inverting the Aristotelian definition of human as a "rational animal" (*IIS*: 299). This 'lunacy' refers to the defunctionalized processes of the *psyche* in relation to their biological substratum: the *psyche* of a human being does not function essentially to protect the body and to reproduce the species. Human beings can neglect their biological needs to death, as the extreme examples of the *infans'* anorexia or the philosopher's lucid suicide demonstrate (Castoriadis 2002: 86). Instead of shouting to call the breast, the *infans* can phantasize it and be satisfied with that phantasm. Socrates preferred to die rather than to disobey the laws of Athens, in order to maintain the coherence and unity of his life and philosophical principles. This human 'lunacy' is due to the over-development of the human imagination, which originates in the first state of the psyche, which Castoriadis calls the "monadic core of primal subject". This monadic core is characterised as a continuous and unending flow of representations where the *infans* and the world, 'its' representation, desire, affect and intention are one and the same (*IIS*: 294–300). This monadic core will be transformed into a social individual by the action of society (socialization by the mother). Nevertherless, a rest of this monadic core will continue to act in the depths of the psyche. Moreover, it will be partly responsible for all the most complex productions of the human mind: it is the nostalgia for the primitive unity of this core, that will secretly guide the philosophers' or the scientists' desire for a unified and totally coherent system. Therefore Castoriadis emphasizes the fact that "the sperm of reason is also contained in the complete madness of the initial autism. […] [R]ather than being faithful to reason one betrays it, if one refuses to see in it something other than, of course, but *also* an avatar of the madness of unification" (*IIS*: 299).

As a consequence of this specificity, the self-creation of the true subject originates in the imagination, as imagination is the condition of possibility of both reflexivity and deliberate action. Indeed, reflexivity is the result of an imaginative internal split: "the possibility of making the self's own activity its explicit object, apart from any functionality" (Castoriadis 2002: 106–7). Deliberate action is "the possibility for a human being to put the results of his process of reflection into the relays conditioning his acts … or in other words: will or deliberate activity is the reflexive dimension of what we are as imaginative beings" (2002: 113).

2. Modernity, capitalism, neoliberalism: one and the same *eidos*?

Now that we have described Castoriadis's criticism of 'modern subjectivity', and what is 'true subjectivity' for him, we may go on with the question of the relationship between these two representations of subjectivity and the Castoriadian analysis of the capitalist and neoliberal individuals. As announced in the introduction, this presupposes to wonder whether modernity, capitalism and neoliberalism may be considered as one and the same society self-transforming through time. When talking about 'modernity', 'capitalism' and 'neoliberalism' from a Castoriadian point of view, we are talking about a specific mode of being, which is the *social-historical* one. Criticizing what he calls "inherited ontology", Castoriadis created this expression to signify that, in the field of human affairs (Aristotle's *ta anthrôpina*), history is not merely a dimension of society: history *is* the self-deployment of society within time

> It is ... impossible to maintain an intrinsic distinction between the social and the historical [...] The social *is* this very thing – self-alteration, and it is nothing if it is not this. The social makes itself and can make itself only as history; the social makes itself as temporality ... [and] it is instituted implicitly as a singular quality of temporality. In the same way, it is not that history 'presupposes' society .... The historical *is* this very thing – the self-alteration of this specific mode of 'coexistence' that is the social as such .... The historical makes itself and can do so only as social; the historical is ... the emergence of the institution and the emergence of *another* institution (*IIS*: 215).

More precisely, history is the self-alteration of society in a process of creation and destruction of forms. These forms Castoriadis calls *eidè*. This is not an innocent terminological choice: from the point of view of the inherited ontology, creation and destruction of an *eidos* is impossible, unthinkable (*FT*: 225). As the *eidos* provides specificity – in the sense of what is proper and common to all individuals of the same species – it is supposed to be eternal (uncreated and immortal). Furthermore, inherited ontology conceives "being as being-determined, beingness as determinacy" (*IIS*: 221). This interpretation of being is coextensive with inherited logic, which Castoriadis calls "identitary logic and also ... set-theoretical logic" (*IIS*: 221). Acknowledged since Plato and Aristotle (as principles of identity and non-contradiction), this logic is based on two main operations: "*legein*: distinguish-choose-posit-assemble-count-speak" (*IIS*: 223) and "*teukhein*: assembling-adjusting-fabricating-constructing" (*IIS*: 260). According to Castoriadis, this inherited logic does not make creation thinkable at all, because it restricts processes of creation and destruction to recomposition and decomposition of pre-existing elements.

In opposition to this static 'inherited' conception of being, Castoriadis highlights that the social-historical mode of being is *essentially dynamic*. He is there referring to the creation of a primary *eidos* – the fact that society creates itself as society – which patterns itself in specific modes for each society, creating and articulating secondary *eidè*: a magma of social-imaginary significations, specific institutions, social aims, and also specific affects (*FT*: 73–87 and Klimis 2010). One of the most original aspects of Castoriadis's analysis of societies as social-historical forms (*eidè*) is his demonstration of the importance of the social imaginary significations (*IIS*: 135–64). According to Castoriadis, a society is not reducible to a functional role. In order to aim at perpetuating itself, a society must first define what is meaningful for itself. Creating and instituting its own imaginary significations, "Thus, each social-historical form is truly and genuinely singular; it possesses an essential, not numerical or combinatorial, singularity ..." (*FT*: 225). Those significations are not created by individuals, but by an anonymous and collective imaginary. These imaginary significations (such as God, Nation, the Market, etc.) provide the true foundation of each society.[5] They materialise in political institutions, guide the social ends and give

---

5 Castoriadis challenges Marx, contending that the imaginary significations are the true substructures of society, rather than the modes of production.

rise to specific affects in order to support them.

This singular dynamics of a social-historical *eidos* seems to me to be considered as its *rhythm*, just as Castoriadis (*FT*: 75) speaks about *tempi*, "pulsating processes" in which phases of creation of forms alternate with phases of destruction of forms (without any hidden principle of progress, nor decadence). When talking about 'rhythm', I am more precisely referring to the pre-Platonic meaning of the Greek term *ruthmos*: self-deployment of a moving form, which is synonymous to self-creation of an *eidos*.[6] This, I postulate, helps us to perceive the radicality of the Castoriadian idea of creation – irreducible to the laws of causation. With 'rhythmicity', we do not speak of a combination of pre-existing and static elements, but of modulations that *are* the process of self-transforming of the social-historical *eidos*. Therefore, talking about the rhythmicity of the *eidos* of modernity allows us to consider the question of its singularity, through the main *eidetic modulations* of Enlightenment, capitalism and neoliberalism.

The most accurate way is to pay closer attention to the relationship between what Castoriadis considers to be the two main imaginary significations of modernity: the unlimited expansion of "so-called rationality" (the so-called rational mastery of everything), and the " revival of the project of autonomy" (the challenging of the established order) (*IIS*: 156–64, 1996b: 129–31).

Within a first rhythmic modulation, it seems that something like a 'swinging harmony', or even a 'discordant harmony'[7] is attained through the interaction of those two contradictory imaginary significations. For centuries and especially during the Enlightenment, one could say

---

6 See Benvéniste's (1966) pioneering study on the Greek notion of *ruthmos*, followed by Meschonnic (1982 and 1995), showing the political-poetical *continuum* within rhythm. Pascal Michon (2007) has applied this concept of rhythm to the analysis of societies in a very thought-provoking way.
7 I am thinking of the *palintropos harmoniè* in Heraclitus's fragment 51 (Diels), discussed in Castoriadis 2004: 235. Heraclitus is referring to the movement in two opposite directions when one is using a bow or a lyre. Castoriadis translates this expression as '*harmonie oscillante*'.

that the imaginary signification of autonomy guided the expansion of instrumental rationality. For example, according to both Descartes' enthusiastic account of medical progress in the *Discours de la Méthode* and Diderot's *Encyclopedia*, more technical progress would lead to more freedom and happiness for all human beings. What has often been called 'the first phase of capitalism' also fits into this dynamic. Castoriadis stresses the fact that the workers'struggle for emancipation enabled the expansion of capitalism: the tendency for capitalism, during the first half of the 19th century, was toward impoverishment and overproduction (*FT*: 68). The struggles of the working class thwarted these tendencies, "… imposing wage increments and shorter working hours, creating enormous domestic consumer markets, and preventing capitalism from drowning in its own wares" (*FT*: 68). Castoriadis also describes the Schumpeterian 'entrepreneur', whom he considers as the only human type created by capitalism, in a rather positive way: "a person having a passion for creating this new historical institution, the enterprise, and for constantly expanding it, introducing new technical complexes and new methods in an attempt to penetrate the market" (Castoriadis 1996a: 68). So we could see the Schumpeterian 'entrepreneur' as a variation on modern subjectivity, stressing instrumental rationality but not totally apart from the project of autonomy: this 'entrepreneur' was searching for and wanting more and more progress in science and knowledge, that is to say, somehow, more freedom for himself and for others.

But little by little, within a second rhythmic modulation, the expanding rational mastery spread to 'everything', nature as well as human beings. Unlimited expansion of technology became an aim in itself, to the detriment of the project of autonomy. Castoriadis therefore notes the disappearance of the ideal and vision of 'progress', leaving only the empty form of "more and more for its own sake" (*FT*: 149). Belief in the progress of 'technoscience' for its own sake resembles the ancient religious beliefs: nobody seems able to question it. New 'opium of the masses', the expansion of 'technoscience' is furthermore a mere pretext for the vacuity of the whole system (*FT*: 149). Castoriadis notes the limitations of this type of rationality, that will never be more than the rationality of a system of means, aiming at the unlimited expansion of production, itself necessarily subordinated to the unlimited expansion of consumption. Therefore, the unlimited expansion of consumption seems to be the final aim of capitalism, which is absurd: "everything that may be invented is invented, everything that may be produced is produced, the corresponding 'needs' will be invented afterwards" (Castoriadis 1996a: 71). So neoliberal society has without any doubt become a heteronomous one, subordinate to imaginary significations such as 'market' or 'economic growth'. Castoriadis's diagnosis is therefore that Western societies are not democratic, but, rather, masked oligarchies. Furthermore, in Castoriadis's view, these 'oligarchies' are about much more than a few men's will to power. It is about the general denial of mortality in our civilization (1996a: 71 and *FT*: 149–50).

3. The neoliberal individual: the *oxymoron* of a social monadic psyche?

We still have to make a step forward to end our reasoning. We have to bring out the specificity of the relationship between the 'individual' and 'society' in contemporary neoliberalism. Following Castoriadis's analyses in different texts, it is possible to reconstruct the portrait of a new anthropological type, whose characteristics seem to be as follows. His general identificatory model is "the individual who earns as much as possible and enjoys himself as much as possible. Earning money is disconnected from any social function and even from any legitimization within the system: you don't earn money because of your worth: rather, you have worth because you earn money" (Castoriadis 1996b: 131). So enjoying oneself becomes the only criterion for a successful life, which means that everybody is trying to avoid any kind of frustration. This leads to a strange kind of 'education'. In neoliberal societies, parents seem not to educate their children anymore: *they do not give them any sense of limitation, which means that they do not socialize them.* From a concrete example, the fact of giving presents to every child at a birthday party, Castoriadis shows how parents are constantly trying to deny frustration (1996b: 133). This also means that parents invalidate the *devenir signifiant* of the present and the pleasure which characterizes it. Without any frustration, there is no more fantasizing ('phantasmatisation') of the absent object, no imaginary compensation for its absence. Therefore, there is also no more sublimation, no more investment in collective significations, nor any possibility of developing any autonomous and singular creation. The message these parents implicitly convey to their children is: "enjoy yourself, the rest is not important" (1996b: 133).

For Castoriadis, this paradoxical 'education' is the sign of the denial of death: in neoliberal societies, there can be no more bereavement nor mourning rituals. The accumulation of gadgets and presents at every minute is a way of masking the horror of death (*FT*: 149), which is no longer symbolically elaborated in rituals, tales, etc. And this tendency continues in adult life: doing a job which is most of the time not invested as socially useful, only wanting to earn as much money as possible, trying to enjoy oneself as much as possible, wanting to stay young and fit forever, jogging to forget that death is near (1996b: 134).

Castoriadis does not say so explicitly, but these characteristics of the neoliberal individual remind us remarkably of his descriptions of the monadic core of the primal subject: self-centered, all-powerful, asocial and antisocial, always searching for pleasure and satisfaction, trying to destroy or incorporate within itself everything from the outside world (*IIS*: 294–300 and Klimis 2007). But on the other hand, the most important characteristic of this monadic core, unlimited activity of the imagination, seems to be missing. So we are led to a crucial question: does the neoliberal society create individuals that are social *analoga* of the monadic psyche? This sounds paradoxical: how could a 'society' possibly be made up of monadic psyches, disconnected from each other, self-centered, orientated only towards their own pleasure? That would mean that instead of creating individuals assuring their own reproduction, this society creates individuals who are logically going to try to destroy the social institution itself. And yet, that is what neoliberal society is actually doing!

Has this society produced a kind of individual that resembles the monadic psyche, but which, *being a social creation*, is not able to reactivate the imaginative potential of that monad? Does this mean that our society does not provide for its individuals socialization but dehumanization? We must remember that Castoriadis describes the monadic psyche as a little 'monster' that becomes human only through education and through the limits imposed on its unlimited imaginative activity by the parents, representing society (*IIS*: 297–308). As time goes by, the 'monster' becomes a 'social individual' while accepting those social limitations: "But hate of the ego goes on living in the psychical depths, almost silently"; hatred for this 'social individual' which the monadic nucleus sees a dangerous stranger (*FT*: 156). According to Castoriadis, hatred is therefore the most original affect of the human *psyche*, because hatred is the reactivation of the all-powerful state of the monadic psyche. Hatred is the innate tendency of the monad to destroy everything that prevents it from enjoying itself. Therefore, if society raises its individuals as 'social-monadic' ones, this can only encourage hatred. And this cannot lead to anything but social self-destruction.

I therefore propose to consider the power that accompanies the unlimited expansion of instrumental rationality as the expression of the triumph of the monadic psyche, which has succeeded in subverting the process of socialization from within. This would be the last, tragic characteristic of the ambivalent power of the human beings' imaginary: instead of aiming at creating imaginary significations, their defunctionalized imagination would lead them to adore the nonsense. Instead of aiming at reproducing themselves like all other living beings, their defunctionalized imagination would lead them to construct societies that aim at destroying themselves. Castoriadis gives us evidence for this thesis, saying that the capitalist system has survived only because of anthropological types inherited from other phases of society: 'the honest judge', 'the devoted teacher', 'the conscientious worker' (Castoriadis 1996a: 68). Because they believed in values such as honesty, integrity, responsibility, state service etc., those 'types' did their jobs well, and helped capitalist society to stay well. But when the only value is money, Castoriadis asks, what prevents a judge from putting up his judgement for auction? (1996a: 68). The conclusion is: individuals living for money, which is the only capitalist value and aim, will not be able to keep their society alive for very long. Furthermore, for the first time in human history, a society, capitalist society, has produced a type of individuals that may lead not only to the destruction of *their* society, but of *any form of society*: capitalism has developed itself by irremediably depleting the planet's natural resources as well as the historical heritage created by previous ages and that it cannot reproduce (*FT*: 146).

4. Desire for autonomy and desire for money

To complete our development, we must consider our last question: if the neoliberal society is not autonomous anymore, what is likely to revive its individuals' desire for autonomy? In comparison with the Greeks, the most striking point of the *eidos* of the Western type society is the disappearance of the idea of 'self-limitation'. This is certainly one of the main reasons why the project of autonomy has almost disappeared in neoliberal societies. In order to understand why there is a necessary link between autonomy and self-limitation for Castoriadis, let us first focus on the meaning of the Greek notion of *peras*. *Peras* is that which provides a limit, sketches a form, therefore it is that which enables the construction of an *eidos*, that which makes things *thinkable*. On the contrary, *a-peiron* is that which is without limits. Therefore, it is that which can neither be apprehended, nor defined: *apeiron* is the indeterminate, beyond, or beneath, human comprehension. In his seminar course on ancient Greece at EHESS,[8] Castoriadis carefully studied the poetical and philosophical representations of *peras* and *apeiron*, *khaos* and *kosmos* (Castoriadis 2004: 171–201). He emphazised the fact that one of the 'truths' contained in the Greek myths is to represent *kosmos* emerging from *khaos* and forever grounded on *khaos*, as in Hesiod's *Theogony*. Anaximander inherited this poetical representation, stating that *apeiron* was the first principle and origin of the *kosmos*. For Castoriadis, this means that the Greeks were conscious of this fundamental and universal truth: all significations are grounded on nonsense, and, insofar as they are imaginary creations, they are somehow nonsensical themselves (2004: 167–69). The tragic dimension of the human condition will be constantly to confront *khaos*, *apeiron* and nonsense, in an endless quest to create an orderly and meaningful world (*kosmos, peras*).

Whenever he mentions the Athenian *polis*, Castoriadis emphazises the importance of self-limitation for the self-creation and self-institution of democracy (*CR*: 282–86, 2008: 125–31). The Athenians had to limit themselves in order to be able to face their absolute power to invent their own laws, rules and institutions. That is the reason why they invented two main institutions of collective self-limitation: the 'accusation of unlawfulness' (*graphè paranomôn*) and tragedy. As every citizen could make a law proposal at the Assembly (*ekklesia*), every citizen could bring another before the court, accusing him of inducing people to vote for an unlawful law. The accused citizen was judged by a jury of citizens and he was acquitted or convicted. In the latter case, the law was annulled (*CR*: 283). Athenian tragedy had the function to give to all citizens to see that Being is Chaos (*CR*: 284). Tragedy also showed that *hubris* was essentially due

---

8 École des hautes études en sciences sociales.

to the inhability to self-limit: *hubris* is the transgression of a limit that was not pregiven. *Hubris* is the error and failure of practical wisdom (*phronèsis*). Therefore, the tragic imaginary representations revealed the necessary connection between individual and collective self-limitation. According to Castoriadis, self-limitation was therefore one of the main conditions of possibility of political freedom and autonomy for the Athenians.

In contrast, from a modern point of view, any form of limitation is seen as an unbearable restriction or even as an attack on individual freedom. Therefore, the expansion of so-called 'technological progress' as well as the expansion of the desire for money, show how dangerous these imaginary significations are, *because they destroy the meaning of limitation and promote what is without any limits* (endless 'progress', 'endless' consumption). More precisely, the promotion of *apeiron* for itself, through these neoliberal imaginary significations, appear to be self-destructive of what Castoriadis has called 'human self-creation'.[9]

For a better understanding, let us go back to Aristotle's interpretation of the invention of money. In *Politics*, Aristotle distinguishes between two sorts of 'goods'. The natural goods, for example products from hunting or agriculture, are the ones providing true wealth "because the quantity of such goods sufficient for a happy life *is not unlimited*" (1256b30–32, my emphasis). On the contrary, "another type of acquisition exists which is called chrematistic, because there seems to be *no limit* to the wealth and the possession of such goods" (1256b41–1257a1). Natural goods allow the satisfaction of natural needs. Therefore they enable the perpetuation of life (*zèn*), understood in a biological sense, and also of what Castoriadis calls the ensemblist-identitary dimension of society. But those natural goods also lead to the good life (*euzèn*), that is: the true life of a human being actualizing his reason (*logos*) and his intellect

---

9 By 'human self-creation', Castoriadis means that human beings do not have any pregiven 'essence'. Their essence is to create themselves as human beings in creating what being human means to them (*FT*: 16).

(*noûs*), because those goods are subordinated to a measure, which is a 'right measure'. Necessarily limited, the possession of such goods is a mere means, subordinated to the superior aim of the good life: an active life of deliberating, judging and deciding about political things; or a contemplative life, trying to understand the principles and causes in every sphere of being.

On the contrary, 'chrematistic' acquisition (money) alienates: it makes people desire 'the unlimited' (*apeiron*), because money becomes the final and only aim in human life, subverting all virtues: "but the aim of courage is not to make money but to make people brave, the aim of medicine is not to make money but to make people healthy again" (1258a10–14). For Aristotle, money is "against nature" in the strongest sense: "mere convention, absolutely unnatural" (1257b10–11); money is a symbolic substitute aimed at complexifying exchanges, while establishing an equivalence between things which are not naturally commensurable (the product of a shoe-maker's work and the product of an architect's work, for instance).

Therefore, I think we may consider money as an invention *ex nihilo*, the invention of a measure which is a pure human creation. The invention of 'money' is part of the process of the human self-creation. But, paradoxically, money makes human beings revert to an *analogon* of their most 'biological' life and move away from their 'human' and good life. If money triggers the desire for what has no limits, it is because "men are intent upon living only (*zèn*), and not upon living well (*euzèn*); and, as their desires upon living are unlimited they also desire that the means of gratifying them should be without limit" (1257b40–1258a2). "Putting the finishing touches to what nature has created", in a very weird way, the technical and symbolic invention of money, as *specifically human*, is nevertheless what makes human beings behave *as if*[10] they

---

10 I refer here to the Kantian *als ob*, precisely to show the contemporary subversion of this creation of modern rationality and criticism.

were purely natural beings such as bacteria.

To sum it up, money is *at the same time* a human invention *ex nihilo* which contributes to the human self-creation, *and* that which may take human beings back to a most primary stage of living, artificially reconstructed (not even the animal one, but the microbian). *As endless,* the desire for money is a regression. It is also contradictory to 'true' humanity, because human self-creation is based on self-limitation. Therefore, if we are living 'the tragedy of money' in real life today and not watching it at the theatre, that is because, as Aristotle had already understood, *money is, in its essence, tragic.*[11]

Conclusion

Modern rationality has produced a society – the society we are now living in – which seems to aim at its own destruction, for the first time in human history. This is so for two reasons: first, if the final goal of this civilization is unlimited consumption, it would imply the destruction of Earth's natural resources, which are *not* unlimited, and therefore the destruction of our planet itself. Second, because for the first time in history the education of neoliberal society produces individuals who do not aim at the perpetuation of society: nowadays, modern rationality has come to raise social *analogues* of monadic psyches. However, the 'social individual' implies precisely a radical transformation of the monadic psyche, through the action of society (i.e. socialisation). As a paradoxical result of the modern confusion between *ego cogitans* and *homo computans*, contemporary neoliberalism has done something far worse than teaching its individuals to return to their monadic status. It has created, from its collective imaginary, a monstrous kind of social individuals whose living root – imagination – has been drained off, and who resembles a kind of self-centred ghost. In a way, we may say that

11 'Tragic' meaning here capable of bearing contradictory significations such as the famous Sophoclean *deinotès* which characterizes human beings as 'extraordinary and marvelous' but at the same time 'terrible and dreadful' creatures. See Castoriadis (2007a) and also Klimis (2004).

what Freud called the 'death instinct' now makes our society go round.

But since human affairs are not ruled by Fate, and because Freedom is our will, *this ought to be different.* When speaking about 'The' neoliberal society, I fall of course myself into the trap of metaphysical desire for unity and its monolithic kind of holism. Several rhythmical modulations work within our societies in contradictory directions. New values and new aims appear, calling for a sense of responsibility extending, like never before, to the entire Earth. We are challenged to invent new and creative ways of collective self-limitation. This involves inventing a new concept of 'good life' for all human beings, extended to all living beings, where technological progress must be submitted to cosmo-political aims. The current financial crisis may be a chance, but only if we take it as an opportunity to deliberately modulate the *eidos* of our society in a new direction. All of this implies that we are still capable of both criticism and imagination. All of this implies that the project of a personal and collective autonomy is still in function.

Therefore, the social-monadic *psyche* itself is an ideal type, in the Weberian sense, or more precisely, what could be called a 'theoretical fiction'.[12] No social-monadic *psyche* exists as such in real life. When designing it, my purpose was to fix the dynamics of a social and psychic tendency, in order to be able to reflect upon it. In neocapitalist societies, we can observe the true and effective power of this tendency in individuals to be self-centred, all-mighty, searching always more instinctual satisfactions and pleasures, living only for the present moment. This means that society somehow fails to limit the desires of the monadic core that still remains in the depth of each psyche. More exactly, the failure of neoliberal societies is not simply to refrain from limiting those desires, but on the contrary to encourage them. Neoliberal societies do not provide any compensatory satisfaction to help the psyche to invest in collective significations, as the unlimited desire for 'money' is their only

---

12 See Klimis (2007) on Castoriadian monadic psyche seen as a theoretical myth.

significance, aim, value, institution and even affect. So, as Castoriadis said, we are at a cross-road: we have to decide in which direction we want to investigate the abyssal complexity of human self-creation.

References

Aristotelis (1957) *Politica*, W.D. Ross (ed.). New York: Oxford University Press.

Benvéniste, Emile (1966) "La notion de rythme dans son expression linguistique", in *Problèmes de linguistique générale*, I, 327–35. Paris: Gallimard.

Castoriadis, Cornelius (1984) *Crossroads in the Labyrinth*, trans. Kate Soper and Martin H. Ryle. Brighton, UK: Harvester.

Castoriadis, Cornelius (1986) "Psychanalyse et société I", in *Domaines de l'Homme. Les carrefours du labyrinthe, II*, 35–49 Paris: Seuil.

Castoriadis, Cornelius (1987) *The Imaginary Institution of Society*, trans. Kathleen Blamey. Cambridge, Mass.: MIT Press.

Castoriadis, Cornelius (1996a) "Le délabrement de l'Occident", in *La montée de l'insignifiance. Les carrefours du labyrinthe, IV,* 58–81. Paris: Seuil.

Castoriadis, Cornelius (1996b) "La crise du processus identificatoire", in *La montée de l'insignifiance. Les carrefours du labyrinthe, IV*, 125–39. Paris: Seuil.

Castoriadis, Cornelius (1997a) "The Greek *Polis* and the Creation of Democracy", in *The Castoriadis Reader*, ed. and trans. David Ames Curtis, 267–89. Oxford: Blackwell.

Castoriadis, Cornelius (1997b), "The logic of Magmas and the Question of Autonomy", in *The Castoriadis Reader*, ed. and trans. David Ames Curtis, 290–318. Oxford: Blackwell.

Castoriadis, Cornelius (2002) *Sujet et vérité dans le monde social-historique. Séminaires 1986-1987, La création humaine, I*. Paris: Seuil.

Castoriadis, Cornelius (2004) *Ce qui fait la Grèce. 1. D'Homère à Héraclite, Séminaires 1982-1983, La création humaine, II*. Paris: Seuil.

Castoriadis, Cornelius (2007a) "Aeschylean Anthropogony and Sophoclean Self-Creation", in *Figures of the Thinkable*, trans. Helen Arnold, , 1–20. Stanford: Stanford University Press.

Castoriadis, Cornelius (2007b) "The 'Rationality" of Capitalism", in *Figures of the Thinkable,* trans. Helen Arnold, 47–70. Stanford: Stanford University Press.

Castoriadis, Cornelius ([1999] 2007c) "Imaginary and Imagination at the Crossroads", in *Figures of the Thinkable*, trans. Helen Arnold, 71–90. Stanford: Stanford University Press.

Castoriadis, Cornelius (2007d) "What Democracy?", in *Figures of the Thinkable*, trans. Helen Arnold, 118–50. Stanford: Stanford University Press.

Castoriadis, Cornelius (2007e) "The Psychical and Social Roots of Hate", in *Figures of the Thinkable,* trans. Helen Arnold, 153–64. Stanford: Stanford University Press.

Castoriadis, Cornelius (2007f) "The Social-Historical: Mode of Being, Problems of Knowledge", in *Figures of the Thinkable*, trans. Helen Arnold, 223–35. Stanford: Stanford University Press.

Castoriadis, Cornelius (2008) *Ce qui fait la Grèce. 2. La cité et les lois, Séminaires 1983–1984, La création humaine, III.* Paris: Seuil.

Hegel, Georg Wilhelm Friedrich ([1807] 1941) *La Phénoménologie de l'Esprit*, trans. Jean Hippolyte. Paris: Aubier.

Klimis, Sophie (2003) *Archéologie du sujet tragique*. Paris: Kimé.

Klimis, Sophie (2004) "Antigone et Créon à la lumière du terrifiant/extraordinaire (*deinotès*) de l'humanité tragique", in François Ost and Lambros Couloubaritsis (eds.) *Antigone et la résistance civile*, 63–102. Bruxelles: Ousia.

Klimis, Sophie (2006) "Explorer le labyrinthe imaginaire de la création grecque: un projet en travail ... ", in Sophie Klimis and Laurent Van Eynde (eds.) *L'imaginaire selon Castoriadis. Thèmes et enjeux, Cahiers Castoriadis*, 1, 9–46. Bruxelles: Publications des Facultés Universitaires Saint Louis.

Klimis, Sophie (2007) "Décrire l'irreprésentable ou comment dire l'indicible originaire", in Sophie Klimis and Laurent Van Eynde (eds.) *Psyché. De la monade psychique au sujet autonome, Cahiers Castoriadis*, 3, 25–54. Bruxelles: Publications des Facultés Universitaires Saint-Louis.

Klimis, Sophie (2010) "Créer un *eidos* du social-historique selon Castoriadis", in Raphaël Gély and Laurent Van Eynde (eds.) *Affectivité, Imaginaire, Création Sociale*, 13–42. Bruxelles: Publications des Facultés Universitaires Saint-Louis.

Meschonnic, Henri (1982) *Critique du rythme. Anthropologie historique du langage.* Paris: Verdier.

Meschonnic, Henri (1995) *Politique du rythme, politique du sujet.* Paris: Verdier.

Michon, Pascal (2007) *Les rythmes du politique. Démocratie et capitalisme mondialisé.* Paris: Les Prairies Ordinaires.

Artistic Critique?
Socialisme ou Barbarie's and Castoriadis's Concept of Revolutionary Work Research[1]

Andrea Gabler

There is a broad spectrum of different views of Socialisme ou Barbarie (below: S. ou B.), the French political group, which was co-founded by Castoriadis in 1948. Interpretations reach from rather absurd allegations (the group as precursor of Holocaust deniers, cf. Bourseiller 2003) to interpretations in the tradition of Bourdieu (cf. Gottraux 1997). Many adorn themselves with membership of or closeness to S. ou B. While the influence of the group on the anti-authoritarian movements of the 1960's is undisputed, the narratives about the group's life vary considerably. At the same time statements on the group often prove to be misinterpretations, political appropriations, or display rather rudimental knowledge of it.

This contribution deals with the analysis of work done by the group, which represents an important part of the history of S. ou. B., and describes its main concepts, experiences and results. The concept of

1 This contribution is based upon two lectures held at the NSU Winter Symposium "The Adventure of Modernity: Castoriadis Beyond Post-Modernism And Neo-Modernism", held in Akureyri (Iceland) on March 7th 2008 and at the NSU Summer Symposium "The Modern Problématique – tensions and transformations – openings and closures", held in Tyrifjord (Norway) on July 21st 2009. Unless otherwise noted, translations of French and German quotations are by the author.

revolutionary work research will be introduced as an attempt to analyse daily work and work experiences and to search for the hidden traces of self-organisation. Castoriadis draws a good deal of his theoretical inspiration from the work analysis of S. ou B. (1). In light of this account I shall critically discuss another classification of S. ou B. and Castoriadis as agents of an 'artistic critique' by Boltanski and Chiapello (2). The text concludes with a suggestion to reorient a future analysis and critique of capitalism with regard to the general argument by Castoriadis based on the work analysis of S. ou B. (3).

1. The analysis of work by Socialisme ou Barbarie

At least until the mid-1960s Castoriadis developed his ideas by reflecting on the discussions and activities of S. ou B. Repelled by the perversions of Marxist theory and experiences, especially those of Stalinist bureaucracy, the group referred instead to an undogmatic interpretation of Marxism, focusing on all open and hidden forms of class struggle and aiming at council-communist objectives. Thus the group came to develop a new conception of the analysis of work (cf. Gabler 2009).

Claude Lefort, co-founder of S. ou B., elaborated in his essay "L'éxperience prolétarienne" (Lefort 1952) a programme for a revolutionary analysis of work. Claiming with Marx that the working class is more than a mere economic category, Lefort points out that the history of the proletariat means experience, and that this experience should be seen as a progressing self-organisation. By thinking of class struggle as a pure expression of an objective economic process and the executor of laws of historical development, party-based Marxism had become counter-revolutionary. Therefore it was necessary to rethink the revolutionary perspectives. The objective analyses should be subordinated to concrete analyses, because not conditions but men alone are revolutionary, Lefort says. The basic question is to know how people appropriate their situations and change them in a spontaneous way.

Instead of analysing the situation and the development of the proletariat from the top down, one should try to reconstruct proletarian attitudes towards work and society from an inside perspective. Lefort claims that the culture of working people is a kind of special power to organise things and to adopt technical development. At least it is a kind of special attitude towards social relationships. It is the proletariat's special creativity and ability for social organisation appearing in everyday life.

The analysis of everyday life has to be done by *témoignages* (Eng. testimonies), i.e. written reports on personal experiences. It is important that working people should regard this writing as part of their own experience. This could be a way to intensify and reflect upon insights which until now were apprehended in an unconscious and fragmentary way. This kind of analysis should allow the authors to think about their experiences themselves, Lefort says. An important point – differing from traditional scientific methods – is that workers should not only write but interpret their *témoignages* themselves. Ideally there should be no separation between subject and object of research. Though real limitations exist, we could imagine this as a process of merging the roles of subject and object and of an increasing self-activity, ending in a condition of autonomy.

Lefort refers to two examples of *témoignages*, (cf. Albert 1952, Romano and Stone 1947)[2] and suggests basic questions which the *témoignages* of S. ou B. should deal with: How does the subject acquire work under modern industrial conditions? Are there specific social relations between workers? How do workers see themselves in society? Are there expressions of collective experiences, which could be a historical power? Is there really a progress in self-organisation and in which form does this progress appear?

---

2 Romano's report first was published in 1947 by the American "Johnson-Forest-Tendency", a political group close to S. ou B. at that time. S. ou B. translated and published it in the first five issues of their journal.

As subjects for the *témoignages*, Lefort suggests: relations amongst worker, work and factory; relations to co-workers and other social groups in the production plant; social life outside the factory and knowledge of the development of society; and attitudes towards proletarian tradition and history. All these aspects should help to make the culture of struggles and of collective solidarity on the shop floor visible, and become a possible starting point for revolutionary transformation. Lefort formulates a very demanding programme with a clear phenomenological approach.[3] He recognises some problems and limitations of his approach, but nevertheless calls upon writing, collecting and publishing *témoignages*.

Following Lefort's demand, four members of S. ou B. published impressing, often long reports of their daily working life experiences in the journal Socialisme ou Barbarie. The first one was Georges Vivier (real name: Georges Dupont), a co-founder of S. ou B., who was employed at the Chausson bus factory. His *témoignages*, published between 1952 and 1955, describe work as a relationship of subordination and humiliation (cf. Vivier 1952, 1953, 1954a, 1954b, 1955). Class relations clearly define themselves in daily situations at work, e.g.: entering the factory every morning; the ceremony of getting hired and getting a contract of employment; the moment of getting paid; situations of monotony and adaptation. Even the 'unpolitical' worker is conscious of always being exploited and therefore it is important for him/her to reduce the degree of exploitation. Social relations between workers and (the lower) management are characterised as an 'armed peace'; every change that comes from the top (e.g. management's interventions, technical changes) risks to provoke an open war. The relationships between the workers themselves are described as conflictual, based on competition and limited by a system of professional and wage hierarchies. Solidarity among workers is mostly reduced to the team or the working group.

---

3 This approach could be traced back to the influence of his teacher and friend Maurice Merleau-Ponty (cf. Hastings-King 1998: 175–80).

Vivier, concerned with semi-skilled labour in automobile production, shows the strong tendencies of the Fordist system to 'inferiorise' and to 'roboterise' semi-skilled workers – but even here rebellion against monotony and alienation at work appears to exist in various forms. One example among many is the active labourer working for private affairs, which appears interestingly also in 'real socialism' (cf. Haraszti 1977). Besides, there is the permanent feeling of waging war. The workers have to defend their living conditions at work, and their discussion about work organisation is a kind of daily practice. They embody a kind of practical critique of the organisation of the production process. Inside the factory as well as outside it, a strong desire for dignity and respect appears, as Vivier points out. Vivier's orientation toward Lefort's question is obvious. He shows the ambivalence of a working day – the experience of being a cog in a superior system of exploitation and power, as well as the experience of individual and collective self-management and resistance.

Another of S. ou B.'s co-founders, Philippe Guillaume (real name: Cyril de Beauplan), a former white-collar worker, became a semi-skilled worker at Renault-Billancourt. "The factory is exactly the opposite of freedom" (Guillaume 1961: 83) – that is the conclusion of his experience as a semi-skilled worker on piece-rate (cf. Guillaume 1960, 1961). "Everything that gets in touch with the factory is as if it was contaminated. When you quit it you'll want something new, something of your own, some cheap trinkets, you want movement, noise, violence ..." (Guillaume 1961: 81). Adopting an idea of Marx, Guillaume describes a totalitarian factory system whose function is to produce human characters assimilated to factory work. The factory absorbs people arranging them in human poles of execution and management comparable to the tense relation between anode and cathode. Almost absent in these articles is the promising reference to emancipatory potentials of proletarian self-organisation in the bureaucratic-capitalist production process. He focuses on the superior coercive character of employment contracts and the nearly perfect interaction of society's production and reproduction in an almost closed system. Max Weber's dictum of modern bureaucracy as the 'iron cage of serfdom' is clearly visible; Fordist mass workers seem to be the modern fellahs in a totalitarian factory order. There are also parallels to Marx's words about factory despotism. The innermost restlessness of work relations seems to come to a complete standstill. In modern production freedom does not appear, but, as Guillaume points out, the opposite. The totalitarianism of the factory goes hand-in-hand with the totalitarianism of society. The latter expresses itself as modern morals and a consumerist world – an "air-conditioned nightmare" (Castoriadis) with generalised exploitation, heteronomy and proletarianisation.

Henri Simon, another important member of S. ou B., was a white-collar worker at an insurance company, Assecurances Générales Vie, and his *témoignages* from 1956 deal with the transformation of white-collar work at the time. He describes non-simultaneous processes of rationalisation differing from department to department, as well as the increase in new forms of control and management strategies causing resistance, struggle and opposition even in the world of the seemingly conformist white-collar worker. On the one hand Simon sees a convergence towards the class of blue-collar workers, the distress of traditional individual behaviours, and the raising of a new class consciousness. On the other hand the white-collar worker's behaviour and consciousness remain ambivalent: hierarchies are not criticised automatically. Simon, just like the other *témoignages*, describes struggles on the shop floor – "every working white-collar worker is a struggling white-collar worker" (Simon 1956: 31) – but he also points out differences between blue- and white-collar milieus. In white-collar workplaces similar developments to industrial work take place with the same inherent contradictions. White-collar workers, too, are reduced to the role of executers, their work gets more and more senseless and unsatisfying, and there are daily guerrilla battles on concrete arrangements of work organisation. Simon describes how the employee's ability to invent little tricks reaches an unexpected level. Sometimes these struggles are sources of conscious critique, but often not even the involved persons perceive them as extraordinary. In spite of the heterogeneous composition of white-collar workers at the time, their ambivalent mentality and their slowly progressing consciousness, Simon writes about possibilities of autonomous organisation, especially the "Conseil" (Eng. council), a successful organisation of an independent, grassroots staff association.

I shall conclude these short descriptions of exemplary *témoignages* with Daniel Mothé (real name: Jacques Gautrat), a skilled worker at Renault-Billancourt at the time, who became an industrial sociologist in the 1970s. His *témoignages* published between 1953 and 1965 are the most extensive and continuing reports on work and self-organisation, as well as on factory politics and workers' consciousness, immigrant workers, young and old workers, workers and culture. In his essay "L'usine et gestion ouvrière" (Mothé 1957) Mothé summarises his experiences on the shop floor focusing on germs of autonomy, and stimulates decisively Castoriadis's theory.

Mothé destroys the common picture of rational work organisation in modern capitalist factories. In reality nothing is left of it. Mothé writes that workers see "... something totally different. (...) [O]n our level we can hardly talk about rationality; what we see is even the negotiation of any organised plan, in other words, something that we call 'a pigsty'" (Mothé 1957: 78). The organisational schemes of the management try everything to avoid communication and contact between workers while they are working. Mothé writes that even shaking hands with a colleague means a violation of the "holy factory law" (Mothé 1957: 83): Though the worker's collective really exists, the order of the factory tries to isolate individuals through a complex system of surveillance. Engineering draughtsmen, engineers, storekeepers, foremen, gaffers, transport workers, inspectors, super-inspectors, timekeepers, safety experts, union delegates:

"All of them, including the cleaner sweeping our workplace, all of them are concerned with us, so that we have to do only one thing: to keep the machine running and not to care about the rest" (Mothé 1957: 84). This system restricts more and more the worker's initiative, their variety of tasks and responsibility – this goes for semi-skilled workers on the assembly line as well as for skilled workers, like Mothé himself. The worker should not know anything about production processes and work organisation. He should stick blindly to the rules, produce automatically, care nothing about colleagues and their problems, and in case of doubt always ask his superiors and do nothing else. The workers should be ignoramuses, who are not allowed to know what they do every day.

But on the whole these Fordist principles of bureaucratic management of production are in conflict with the real necessities of production. Production only works thanks to the worker's initiatives that are not allowed to exist and are systematically obstructed by the management. Mothé mentions a lot of examples of such permanent divergences from the official plan. Knowledge and ignorance, rationality and irrationality are not distributed as they should be, following the prevailing role descriptions. Workers overtake tasks and adopt other qualifications. Semi-skilled workers do the work of skilled workers (without getting paid as such) – formal and official qualifications and professional hierarchy do not matter much in the face of production's necessities. To learn how to work, Mothé says, is only possible in a community of workers, where you can participate in your co-workers experience and techniques.

The workers' informal self-organization, which appears in different forms, derives from their refusal of being reduced to mere executors and obey to these irrational structures. Mothé reports on toolmakers that do not care about the rules and produce user-friendly tools instead of spending a lot of energy to fetch unsuitable tools from the depot. Workers themselves arrange their machines, overtake 'expert' tasks to get on faster, and keep hidden depots for themselves. It is a sort of constructive infringement of the rules, which workers think are necessary and appropriate to solve problems at work and to keep the production running. To follow only the official rules of work organisation would lead to an immediate collapse of production – remember 'work to rule' being a form of strike. "One more time we have short-circuited factory organisation, but that's only the price for being able to work" (Mothé 1957: 90).

The workers' self-management consists in gaining control over their own work and to cooperate tacitly with their colleagues. This kind of opposition exists on every level. It is required not only to compensate for insufficient processes, but also to fight against working conditions, especially against timekeepers and production speed. Forms of collective socialisation and of tacit moral counter-norms arise from this informal field. The pressure of the counter-moral prevents workers from adopting dominating norms too much, assuring and stabilising unity among them: if one talks too long to the gaffer, one risks being booed by co-workers. If one squeals openly, one could immediately leave for another department. Worker's counter-norms enable opposition and resistance. Mothé describes this as a social separation between management and workers, between planning/controlling work and 'real' work with no real cooperation between the two. The management has no access to the reality of production; its knowledge remains abstract and theoretical. But the pressure of this blind hierarchy paralyses the whole organisation and is the main reason for chaos, inefficiency and the permanent crisis on the shop floor.

All authors of the *témoignages* notice that the crux of work organisation is the separation between directors and executants – with different accentuations. With Henri Simon, this separation becomes virulent mainly as disinformation of the employees. Simon describes the situation and the inconsistent consciousness of the white-collar workers and also their successful experiment of an independent, grassroots staff association. Georges Vivier locates the separation between management and producers within the traditional Marxist view of class struggle. He describes the experience of being a cog in a superior system of exploitation and power as well as the experience of individual and collective self-organisation and resistance. Philippe Guillaume compares the totalitarian system of the factory to the electro-chemical antagonism and the reactions between cathode and anode. 'Factory despotism' (Marx) goes hand-in-hand with the totalitarianism of society, expressed as modern morals and consumer's world (an "air-conditioned nightmare" in the words of Castoriadis) with generalised exploitation, heteronomy and proletarianisation. Daniel Mothé deconstructs the common fiction of rationality, order and efficiency in modern capitalist factories. Based on his experiences on the shop floor, he develops a model of a production liberated from dominating hierarchical constraints, in which continuous informal self-organisation is the basis of future production and economy.

The *témoignages* project of S. ou B. was not successful in the long run: It did not go as far as the group wanted for the main reason that only a few workers could be motivated to express themselves through writing. But some important results should be recorded: As reports from the shop floor, the *témoignages* give insights from the inside. All of them – at least nearly 400 pages out of about 4500 pages in their journal – are thick descriptions of the daily work life in French Fordism at a time when concrete experiences of work were at best a subject of American-inspired industrial sociology focusing on the aspect of socio-psychological deviation. S. ou B.'s project remains a unique source of information on the effects of implementation of Fordism in France that ended in the 1960s. They show the almighty bureaucratic rationalisation on different shop floors as well as the changes in the behaviour and consciousness of the working class, the dissolving of proletarian milieus, processes of individualisation and changing values – the 'silent revolution' (cf. Inglehart 1977) –, the depoliticisation of the former revolutionary class and its integration in bourgeois society. The former figure of the proud producer becomes a confused, unhappy figure through technical change and social and organisational consequences – e.g. the changes in old social milieus and new forms of training. Hence S. ou B.'s concept is fundamental for a counter-history of Fordism because of its insistence on the experience of daily work as a central point and because of its radical conception.

S. ou B.'s *témoignages* answer Lefort's question in a positive way: yes, there is a process of progressive experience of emancipation; yes, an informal autonomy of working people, their creativity and originality, can be found. The double life of the factory is described as an interplay of heteronomy and autonomy. Workers are excluded from managing their work themselves and *at the same time* they have to be included to guarantee the running of the production process. Having exposed this simultaneity of exclusion and inclusion is one of the most important results of the *témoignages*. This simultaneous movement can be seen at all levels of the hierarchy, it even pervades individuals, and it is the source of contradictory interests and contradictory behaviour in situations of conflict. S. ou B. saw these germs of tacit self-organization as a political potential for changing society. The group tried to support these germs when they were focusing on a model of direct democracy through assemblies and councils that should liberate people from hierarchies and install self-organisation at all levels, individual as well as collective, at work as well as in society at large.

S. ou B.'s *témoignages* and the group's own history describe processes of modernisation. The 'self-modernisation' of S. ou B. is linked directly to their observations. At the end of the group's revolutionary work research, revolution is an option not only for the until then 'privileged' working class, but also for all movements seeking autonomy – at that time especially the new movements like the women's liberation, the student's movement, or the civil rights movement in the USA. The later fundamental breach of Castoriadis with traditional Marxism at the end of the 1950s can be seen as a further result of this 'self-modernisation'. But what makes the *témoignages* particularly interesting is the way they are theorised by Castoriadis. It raises them above similar attempts of participatory research or literary narrations. Particularly Mothé's contributions possess a remarkably close, nearly symbiotic relationship to the theoretical ideas developed by Castoriadis.

Above all, in his three-piece essay "Sur le contenu du socialisme" (Castoriadis 1955, 1957 and 1958) Castoriadis uses the *témoignages* as empirical material and deconstructs the fiction of rationality, order and efficiency in capitalist enterprises. The Fordist organisation of work is not only contradictory and bureaucratic – a point of view which is shared by many Marxists –, but it is bureaucratic because it requires the subject's participation and exclusion at the same time. The irrationality of this process is not only shown by waste (of materials, time and possibilities) or by 'bureaucratic dysfunction', but through the permanence of this dichotomy, constantly kept alive by economic expansion and technological upheaval. The crisis of the whole capitalist society follows the same logic.

> It [the crisis] consists in the fact that the social organisation can attain the ends it sets for itself only by setting forth means that contradict these ends, by creating demands it cannot satisfy, by posing criteria it is incapable of applying, norms it is obliged to transgress (*IIS*: 170 [1964]).

The simultaneity of inclusion and exclusion produces a double reality and an extremely conflictual society. So bureaucratisation finds expression on every level of society. At work it expresses itself through a bottom-up, everlasting resistance against the existing institution of work as such.

Castoriadis continues – as seen above in the *témoignages* – to describe the contradiction between inclusion and exclusion as the most important social source for the revolutionary project. This contradiction can be observed as an informal self-activity, the raising of self-consciousness and, occasionally, as openly revolutionary situations. All these phenomena show that the conflict is not centred on quantities (e.g. of working hours or wages) but on qualities (e.g. on the content and organisation of work). From here Castoriadis derives his concrete Utopia of autonomy at work and in society. Even later on, when S. ou B. and Castoriadis were to analyse the social "integration" of the working class, Castoriadis would insist on the fundamental possibility of people to create autonomy and a radical transformation of society.

2. S. ou B. and Castoriadis as part of an 'artistic critique'?

S. ou B.'s analysis of work is part of their rich theory and praxis, which still inspires many people. As mentioned above, there is a broad spectrum of interpretations of S. ou B.'s and Castoriadis's work and influence and recently another classification has been added to it. In their book *L'ésprit nouvel du capitalisme* (1999),[4] Luc Boltanski and Ève Chiapello (hereafter: B/C) understand S. ou B. and Castoriadis as part of an "artistic critique" of capitalism. The authors provide an important contribution to the debate on capitalism, capitalist ideology, the problem of change in capitalism, and its capacity to adjust and adapt everything new. Accordingly, their book was received in an open-minded and even enthusiastic way and hailed as a 'new classic' of sociology, translated into a number of languages and reprinted several times (cf. e.g. Budgen 2000).

Nevertheless, their classification of S. ou B. and Castoriadis as agents of an 'artistic critique' seems to be a misleading and at least incomplete interpretation if the real history, the projects, experiences, and theories of

---

4 English edition: *The New Spirit of Capitalism*, London: Verso, 2007. Below, quotations will be from this edition.

the group are considered. The following remarks do not intend to discuss the approach of B/C in total, but to critically review their categories and their reception of S. ou B. and Castoriadis. B/C focus on capitalism as a system of social order which motivates human beings to continually participate in the process of accumulation and to sustain it by normative persuasion, justification and legitimisation. Different historical periods of capitalism generate a specific variety of legitimisation models – a 'spirit' that legitimises the capitalist order of society. Capitalism depends on these so-called '*Poleis*' (Fr. *Cités*) – the authors observe six different forms – because it historically creates its own critique. Critique is seen by B/C as the determining factor of the dynamics of change. It attacks capitalism's structures of normative legitimisation and forces it to apply modifications, adjustments and corrections. The sources, the focus and the social agents of this critique may vary. Historically, B/C differentiate mainly between two forms of critical discourse: on the one side, social critique, formulated by parties and organisations of the workers' movement; on the other side, artistic critique, brought forward by intellectuals and artists.

Social critique attacks capitalism as a source of poverty, inequality, injustice and exploitation. Inspired by Christian as well as by socialist and Marxist ideas, it demands equality, solidarity, and security; it criticises the egoism of private interests rejecting individualism and 'the egoism' of artists.

Artistic critique, the second form of critique, regards capitalism as an obstacle of individual freedom, creativity, and authenticity. Its hierarchical system of factories and offices, its uniformisation and product fetishism, generate alienation and reification. Thus, the capitalist order becomes an impediment to self-realisation, freedom and originality. The artistic critique, rooted in the 'bohemian lifestyle' of artists and intellectuals, criticizes the loss of meaning and sense, the standardisation, generalised commodification and alienation in bourgeois–capitalist society. "To this it counterposes the freedom of artists, their rejection of any contamination of aesthetics by ethics, their refusal of any form of subjection in time and space and, in its extreme forms, of any kind of work" (Boltanski and Chiapello 2007a: 38).

B/C concede a great deal of significance to their categories of social critique and artistic critique. The categories are the measuring bar in the analysis of the discourses of different agents – like employers, unions, and politics and so the whole book is structured around the dichotomy of social critique and artistic critique. (cf. Boltanski and Chiapello 2007b: 169) Both forms of critique contain modernistic and anti-modernistic elements and possess an inherent ambivalence, as they always share their normative frame with the capitalist social system. However, capitalist 'logic' is more fundamentally criticised by artistic critique than by social critique (e.g. different attitudes towards 'progress'). It is an important aspect that both forms of critique may – exceptionally – form alliances, like in 1968, but in principle, they are incompatible. It is true; both of them can be connected to form a combination of critique of domination and the demand for liberation. The socially disadvantaged and the "new intellectual wage-earners" (Boltanski and Chiapello 2007a: 401) could meet on a common denominator. But in B/C's book, this possibility of a connection only flares up; it constitutes only an exception, which is not followed up systematically. Even though artistic critique has penetrated the world of thought of some unions, and even though it would be desirable to take the best out of both forms of critique 'regulating' each other, according to B/C, the fundamental dichotomy cannot be overcome.

Today's agents of artistic critique are seen as mainly higher educated, flexible and mobile persons in the upper strata of the socio-cultural hierarchy. As agents of a more 'aristocratic', non-egalitarian critique of capitalism they are less interested in ordinary working people (cf. Boltanski and Chiapello 2007b: 174f). This comparably negative view of the agents of artistic critique can be traced back to the changed relation between capitalism and the critique of capitalism since the 1960s. With the remake and mass distribution of artistic critique around 1968, the dynamic interdependencies between capitalism and its critique, which was partly absorbed by it, enters a new period. Subsequently, by accepting artistic critique, capitalism not only pushes social critique to the background, but also changes its complete order and, above all, its system of values. This is the central point of B/C: A 'new spirit of capitalism' emerges (as different from the 'old' one, which was described by Max Weber). Capitalism enters a new, third period of its existence. Its most visible appearances are modified strategies of management, newly structured worlds of work, generally a 'project based *polis*'. In this flexible, networked new society there is no place for solidarity, security, and equality.

B/C name S. ou B. and Castoriadis as agents of the artistic critique. Initially, they describe them and the *Internationale Situationniste* as small avant-garde groups of the 1950s, which transported the outdated artistic critique of the 19th century into the 20th century and modernised it by their critique of alienation and domination. They argue that through this, both groups played the role of important mediators, and enhanced and updated the artistic critique, so that, with 1968, it could disseminate further. Already in their "General Introduction" B/C approvingly paraphrase the assumption of Castoriadis, which describes the main contradiction of capitalism as dual movement of participation and exclusion at the same time:

> The concept of spirit of Capitalism is grounded in this contradiction, in the sense that it involves mobilizing initiative for a process that it cannot mobilize by itself. And capitalism is permanently tempted to destroy the spirit that serves it, since it can serve it only by curbing it (Boltanski and Chiapello 2007a: 53).

As seen above, this dynamic simultaneity of control and self-determination is a main figure in Castoriadis's texts. Especially in the realm of work it becomes clear that self-organisation of the executants is unrequested, but at the same time necessary to make the system function. Consequently, the new central social conflict line consists in the separation between those who have the knowledge and those who have not, between decision makers and those excluded. (cf. Castoriadis [1964] *IIS*: 80 and 16) In generalised terms, Castoriadis's description expresses a "central implication of the (...) capitalist 'Imaginary'" (Wolf 2008: 219). As stated by Wolf:

> In the text quoted by Boltanski/Chiapello as well as in other works ..., Castoriadis, in the final analysis, attributes this contradictory dual tendency of exclusion and participation to the basic fact, that in modern capitalism, rational *dominance* of the social and natural world *and* the limitless *expansion* of this rational dominance are at stake (Wolf 2008: 221).

It is remarkable that B/C basically agree with the main thesis of Castoriadis and see it as the fundament of the concept of the 'capitalist spirit' based on the inconsistency described above. But their subsumption of Castoriadis and S. ou B. under the category of artistic critique remains irritating, as it does not take into account the genesis of Castoriadis's texts. Castoriadis's theory is based upon the experiences and discussions in S. ou B., that is to say, the political praxis of the group. Especially when it comes to the analysis of the simultaneous movement of participation and exclusion in bureaucratic capitalism, the genetic context is clearly 'non-artistic'. As seen above, Castoriadis referred explicitly and extensively to empirical and material experiences of the working members of S. ou B.. Therefore, the cliché of an 'egocentric' intellectual (or artist) in his ivory tower, which is at the core of B/C's category of artistic critique, does not fit. In this case, the category of artistic critique suppresses the fact that real experiences are the basis of a critique of capitalism as well; experiences which, according to the characterisations of B/C, would rather be expected in social critique.

Another objection against B/C's categorisation can be drawn from the self-perception of S. ou B. and Castoriadis. Even if they were very critical towards the organisation and the parties of the workers' movement, S. ou B. always regarded itself as a (revolutionary) part of this movement. In its self-concept, its organisation and its programmes, S. ou B. was part of a leftist-socialist wing, which remained a minority in the workers' movement, but nevertheless, in its various forms, such as anarchism, council communism, and libertarian movements, it provided important impulses for the movement as a whole. In many cases, such minority movements distinguish themselves from orthodox Marxism – embodied in parties and unions – by centering on grassroots policy.

S. ou B. originally saw themselves as a group of revolutionary Marxists. Different from other organisations, they wanted to listen to the workers, take them seriously, and initiate and support their self-organisation. The group always despised a separation between intellectuals and manual workers. S. ou B. claimed to have developed their theory as a "... result of a thorough examination and systematisation of work experiences" (*Socialisme ou Barbarie* 1959: 85).

These references show that it would be misleading to simply add S. ou B. and Castoriadis to the "artists" and force them into a contradiction with the workers' movement. In their eclectic classification, B/C deny the whole context of critique of capitalism. As a consequence, a "strange reception gap" (Wolf 2008: 221) occurs. One may speculate about the causes of this – again – biased understanding of S. ou B..[5] But to me,

---

5 In my opinion, both French monographs on S. ou B. by Gottraux (Philippe Gottraux: *Socialisme ou Barbarie. Un engagement intellectuel dans la France de l'après-guerre,* Lausanne 1997) and Raflin (Marie-France Raflin: *Socialisme ou Barbarie. Du vrai communisme à la radicalité,* Paris 2005) insinuate that the group was a breeding place for intellectuals who became famous later on.

it seems more important to discuss the question of whether a future critique of capitalism should take up the categories of 'artistic critique' and 'social critique'.

3. Future Critique of Capitalism – open questions

The 'case' of S. ou B. and Castoriadis shows that a strict separation of artistic and social critique does not take into account the many hybrid forms and interferences, which can also be found in the workers' movement. In generalised terms, the categories of B/C reflect a wrong dichotomisation of liberty and equality, autonomy and security (cf. Lazzarato 2007: 191).

Furthermore, unanswered questions regarding the formulation of a future critique of capitalism remain. Does this categorisation consider changed, new forms of work? Studies on the working conditions of the precariously and temporarily employed in the creative and academic areas cause some doubt. Especially here, social and artistic critique often merge together. It is no coincidence that in the protest movement of artists and technicians in the French cultural industry, which began in 2004, a main slogan said: *"Pas de culture sans droits sociaux!"* (Eng.: No culture without social rights! Cf. Lazzarato 2007: 191-93). Other authors – often in the line of thought of Hardt and Negri (cf. Hardt and Negri 2000) – point to the dissolution of strict boundaries in new forms of 'immaterial work'. The term of 'immaterial work' may be blurred and clouding – nevertheless, it remains up to discussion if B/C's dichotomy does not miss the core of today's employment.

The academic discussions and research dealing with the new organization of work mostly see it as a pendulum movement, dominated sometimes by tendencies to heteronomy (organization from the outside, rational power) and sometimes by tendencies to participation. These motions oscillate between 'chances' and 'risks': The positive chance to bring in creativity and to enlarge the individual's room for manoeuvre, is the opposite of the negative risk of the highly flexible employee, who is submitted to the imperatives of exploitation in a subtler way, but even more extensively, and whose personal resources are to be used more efficiently. Opposing this perspective, S. ou B. and Castoriadis point out that inclusion and exclusion are necessary, and both necessarily exist at the same time. That is why reality is ambiguous and contradictory. The view of a pendulum movement between these poles risks to underestimate this contradictory simultaneity, going through all phenomena and every person. In generalising the subject of inclusion and exclusion, it can be stated that modern society always remains Janus-faced. It is difficult, confusing; sometimes nearly impossible to separate the simultaneous movement of inclusion and exclusion that exists at every level of society. Here, S. ou B. and Castoriadis can provide us with useful considerations for a further analysis of post-Fordistic society.

Do we find simultaneous movements with alternating accents on participation and exclusion in work as well as in other fields of capitalist society?[6] What about inclusion and exclusion in today's work, 'modernised' in the last decades through changing organisation, new concepts of management, and the flexibilisation of work and life? New management strategies like job enlargement, job enrichment and job rotation are forms of rationalisation as well as a kind of reaction to the worker's critique of work organisation as dehumanising. The new work organisation is characterised by qualitative and quantitative flexibility and is described as a form of processing interactive rationality. The factory rationalises itself, production seems to be integrated and unified, and even controlling and leading functions are dissolved in the working process (cf. v. Heydebrandt 1989; cf. Womack and Jones and Roos 1990). These features of a post-Fordist organisation of work seem to dissolve

---

6 It would be interesting to have further research in this perspective, e.g. on gender relations – including women and excluding them from real power in society at the same time – or on representative 'democracy' – including people by elections and excluding them from real decision-making.

former bureaucratic structures based on the antagonism of capital and labour. In this way S. ou B.'s critique of the bureaucratic-capitalist power seems to become pointless.

B/C take the same line, when they say that capitalism arrived at incorporating the 'artistic critique', the critique of bureaucratic heteronomy, hierarchy and alienation *via* offers of participation and strategies of flexibilisation. They postulate that the demands and hopes for self-organisation by the leftist anti-authoritarian movement have been incorporated into the new concepts of management, that the topics of the left have been reinterpreted and made compatible with the new norms of management. They stress that they do not mean to 'rescue' an artistic critique that has contributed to make capitalism more functional and demand to base a new formulation of critique of today's 'project-based' capitalism much more on the 'old' social critique.

But obviously they do not take into account that many aspects of artistic critique – in any case, as formulated by S. ou B. and Castoriadis – are not compatible with capitalism. Above all, the question arises whether partial observations have not been generalised prematurely. Perhaps the capitalist misappropriation of artistic critique is only superficial, as the content is completely different. And is it not only a very limited misappropriation, which may be revoked in order to hide the immanent contradictions of capitalist organisation temporarily? Concerning the sphere of production, the new developments are to be expressed more unambiguously as "subaltern democracy"(Coriat 1992) and "managed participation" (Linhart 1986: 276), thus reflecting that relations of power at work are modernised, but not abolished. Castoriadis questions the content of participation, too:

> But self-management and self-government of what? Would it be a matter of the self-management of prisons by the prisoners, of assembly lines by compartmentalized workers? [Would the object

of self-organization be simply the decoration of the factories?] Self-organization, self-management has no meaning except when it comes to grips with the instituted conditions of heteronomy (*CR*: 313).

The critique of capitalism should be aimed at capitalism itself. Hence, it is worthwhile to draw upon the general arguments of S. ou B. and Castoriadis in order to reorient future analyses and critiques of capitalism onto their proper target.

References:

Albert, Eric (1952) "La vie dans une usine", *Les Temps Modernes* 81, 95–130.

Boltanski, Luc and Chiapello, Ève (2007a) *The New Spirit of Capitalism*, trans. Gregory Elliott. London: Verso.

Boltanski, Luc and Chiapello, Ève (2007b) "Für eine Erneuerung der Sozialkritik. Luc Boltanski und Ève Chiapello im Gespräch mit Yann Moulier Boutang", in Gerald Raunig and Ulf Wuggenig (eds) *Kritik der Kreativität*. Wien: Turia + Kant, 167–80.

Bourseiller, Christophe (2003) Histoire général de „l'ultra-gauche", Paris: Denoël.

Budgen, Sebastian (2000) "A New 'Spirit of Capitalism'", *New Left Review* 1, 149–56.

Castoriadis, Cornelius (1955) "Sur le contenu du socialisme (I)", *Socialisme ou Barbarie* 17, 1–25.

Castoriadis, Cornelius (1957) "Sur le contenu du socialisme (II)", *Socialisme ou Barbarie* 22, 1–74.

Castoriadis, Cornelius (1958) "Sur le contenu du socialisme (III)", *Socialisme ou Barbarie* 23, 1–20.

Castoriadis, Cornelius ([1964] 1998) "Marxism and Revolutionary Theory", in Castoriadis, Cornelius *The Imaginary Institution of Society*, trans. Kathleen Blamey. Cambridge: Polity, 7–164

Castoriadis, Cornelius (1997) "The Logic of Magmas and the Question of Autonomy", in Castoriadis, Cornelius *The Castoriadis Reader*, trans. and ed. David Ames Curtis. Oxford: Blackwell, 290–318.

Coriat, Benjamin (1992): *Penser à l'envers. Travail et organisation dans l'entreprise japonaise*, Paris: Bourgois.

Gabler, Andrea (2009) *Antizipierte Autonomie. Zur Theorie und Praxis der Gruppe "Socialisme ou Barbarie"*. Hannover: Offizin Verlag.

Gottraux, Philippe (1997) *"Socialisme ou Barbarie". Un engagement politique et intellectuel dans la France de l'après-guerre*, Lausanne: Editions Payot.

Guillaume, Philippe (1960) "Dix semaines en usine (I)", *Socialisme ou Barbarie* 31: 33–50.

Guillaume, Philippe (1961) "Dix semaines en usine (II)", *Socialisme ou Barbarie* 32: 73–83.

Haraszti, Miklos (1977) *A Worker in A Worker's State: Piece-Rates in Hungary*, trans. Michael Wright. Harmondsworth: Penguin.

Hardt, Michael and Negri, Antonio (2000) *Empire*. Cambridge, Mass.: Harvard University Press.

Hastings-King, Stephen (1998) *Fordism And the Marxist Revolutionary Project: A History of Socialisme ou Barbarie*, Part I. Dissertation Cornell University.

Heydebrandt, Wolf von (1989) "New Organizational Forms, Work and Occupations", *Work and Occupations* 16(3), 323–57.

Inglehart, Ronald (1977) *The Silent Revolution. Changing Values and Political Styles Among Western Politics*. Princeton: Princeton University Press.

Lazzarato, Maurizio (2007) "Die Missgeschicke der „Künstlerkritik" und der kulturellen Beschäftigung", in Gerald Raunig and Ulf Wuggenig (eds) *Kritik der Kreativität*. Wien: Turia + Kant, 190–204

Lefort, Claude (1952) "L'expérience prolétarienne", *Socialisme ou Barbarie* 11, 1-19.

Linhart, Danièle (1986) "Ein japanisches Modell à la française oder ein französisches Modell à la 'japoinaise'", in Leo Kißler (ed) *Toyotismus in Europa. Schlanke Produktion und Gruppenarbeit in der deutschen und französischen Automobilindustrie*. Frankfurt/New York: Campus Verlag, 265–79.

Mothé, Daniel (1957) "L'usine et la gestion ouvrière", *Socialisme ou Barbarie* 22, 75–111.

Romano, Paul and Stone, Ria (1972 [1947]) *The American Worker*. Detroit: Bewick Editions.

Socialisme ou Barbarie (1959) "Comment Mallet juge Mothé", *Socialisme ou Barbarie* 28, 83–85.

Vivier, Georges (1952): „La vie en usine (I)", *Socialisme ou Barbarie* 11, 48–54.

Vivier, Georges (1953): „La vie en usine (II)", *Socialisme ou Barbarie* 12, 31–47.

Vivier, Georges (1954A): „La vie en usine (III)", *Socialisme ou Barbarie* 14, 51–61.

Vivier, Georges (1954B): „La vie en usine (IV)", *Socialisme ou Barbarie* 15-16, 44–59.

Vivier, Georges (1955): „La vie en usine (V)", *Socialisme ou Barbarie* 17, 49–60.

Womack, James P., Jones, Daniel T. and Roos, Daniel (1991) *The machine that changed the world. The story of Lean Production*. New York: Harper Perennial.

Wolf, Harald (2008) "Die duale Institution der Arbeit und der neue(ste) Geist des Kapitalismus. Einige Anmerkungen zu einer Anmerkung", in Gabriele Wagner and Philipp Hessinger (eds): *Ein neuer Geist des Kapitalismus? Paradoxien und Ambivalenzen der Netzwerkökonomie*. Wiesbaden: VS Verlag für Sozialwissenschaften, 219–231.

Part III

Autonomy

The Power of the Imaginary

Harald Wolf

Castoriadis developed his project of an elucidation of the social-historical – grounded in *The Imaginary Institution of Society* – in his later works, in the direction of a concept of power, not least in the programmatic text from 1988, "Power, Politics, Autonomy" (*PPA*: 143–74), which will be discussed in my contribution. In a first step, my paper deals with this conception of power and its specifics (1). This conception of power refers to the ground-power of society, which can 'transform' the 'a-social' (e.g. the psyche) into something social. On a secondary level, we have to deal with explicit power: this is the realm of the political. Politics would be the effort to open up as far as possible the work of the imaginary social 'ground-' or 'infra-power' to our reflection and to a conscious collective shaping/forming by all. Then – in a second step – I want to highlight some crucial differences of this concept of power compared with other approaches dealing with power theoretically (2). I want to point out, very briefly, some features of the concepts of power by Foucault, Nietzsche, Heidegger, and Bourdieu, all of which, in a sense, deal, like Castoriadis, with the 'semantics' of power. Yet, eventually, it seems as if all the mentioned theorists cannot transcend too narrow a view of power as pseudo-natural, i.e. heteronomous. Something like the 'power of autonomy', practised by politics, seems beyond their conceptions. Finally,

I try to connect these points with some of the 'time-diagnostic' theses and speculations of Castoriadis (i.e., the 'rising tide of insignificancy' or 'big sleep' theme) whereby some open political questions immediately come to mind (3). What are today's chances for the powers of autonomy? Are they more and more 'imaginary' (in a 'bad', pre-Castoriadean sense)?[1]

1. The imaginary and the power of Castoriadis

'Power to the imagination', *l'imagination au pouvoir*, was one of the emphatic slogans of May 68 in France. It referred to the imagination of an overall new beginning, the imagination of individual and collective emancipation. This seizure of power failed, as it is well known. For Castoriadis, however, – certainly not this imagination, but nevertheless – imagination is always already in power, in the sense of the power of the imaginary. The imaginary is – as radical imagination of the psyche and as radical imaginary of society and its institutions – the centre of the thinking of Castoriadis. Radical imagination means at first the fundamental creative element in the domain of the psychical. Apart from philosophy, which obscured this crucial element again and again, in the end psychoanalysis also evades the problematic of the radical imagination as the core of the psychical monad. Especially when, following Lacan, one takes the notion of the 'imaginary' for the fictive, for that which *is not*, as in the example of the mirror image. For Castoriadis,

> ... instead the 'mirror' itself and its possibility, and the other as mirror, are the works of the imaginary, which is *creation ex nihilo* [...]. The imaginary of which I am speaking is not an image *of*. It is the unceasing and essentially undetermined [...] creation of figures/forms/images, on the basis of which alone there can ever be the question *of* something. What we call 'reality' and 'rationality' are its works (*IIS*: 3).

---

1 I would like to thank Anders Ramsay for his helpful proposals for improvements of an earlier version, almost all of which could be used in the revision of this article.

Like the psychical, the domain of the social-historical is for Castoriadis also a mode of being, which is mostly misconceived. It is neither appropriately conceivable – with the usual means of the inherited discourse – as 'subject', nor as 'thing', nor as 'concept'. The self-creating, self-instituting, emerging society – in each case in specific institutions – is, as he calls it, radical imaginary: the basic capacity of implementing imaginary significations by and in the anonymous collective, and of implementing institutions, which bear/carry these significations and keep them alive – thus the founding source of a certain society, of its identity, and of a certain type of individuals, who reproduce this society.

Here, too, we have to consider the specific characteristics of Castoriadis's s imaginary. It is not as if it were the total sum of social representations or another word for ideology: what *diverts* and *misleads* the actors. In Castoriadis the term aims at what answers the question '*Who are* these actors, what shapes them, what forms the conditions of their being as such (*So-sein*)?' The imaginary significations that embody such answers – a religious set of beliefs with or without holy war, the holy market, the drive for truth and autonomy – must be created by the anonymous collective and must be socially embodied, instituted, in order to enable these actors to act. A socially unconditioned actor-subject is a fiction - a fiction, which is certainly revived in contemporary 'liberalism' and 'individualism', but, in addition, is effective in the 'egology' of traditional philosophical thinking. *Ego* and *Alter* remain however chimeras, if they are cut off from the social-historical field and the social imaginary, which in reverse make both the *Ego* and the *Alter* possible in the first place, by lending them their specific significations.

Which conclusions does Castoriadis derive from this concept of the imaginary for the concept of power? And what are the differences from traditional conceptions of power? First: Concerning the concept of power, a complete ambiguity prevails. A good proportion of the power of power, as Luhmann says, consists of the fact that one does not exactly know what it actually is about. Despite this ambiguity, however, a lot what is commonly said about power, can be reduced to a simple formula, which designates a causal relationship between *Ego* and *Alter*:

> The power of *Ego* is the cause, which causes a certain behaviour of *Alter* against his/her will. It enables *Ego* to enforce his/her decisions without having to consider *Alter*. Thus *Ego*'s power limits *Alter*'s freedom. *Alter* suffers *Ego*'s will as something alien to him/her (Han 2005: 9).[2]

Remember, for example, Weber's definition of power. He defines it as "each chance/ability within a social relationship to enforce one's own will even on the face of conflict or resistance, no matter on what this chance is based" (Weber 1972: 28). Power becomes the superordinate concept of socially relevant superiority. Power appears as the superior scope of disposal of one part of society, which exerts inevitable influence against another, inferior part of society. Power becomes domination (*Herrschaft*) by legitimation and institutionalization (in Weber), it appears as coercion and violence, when it includes the impairment, in extreme cases the destruction of the inferior. Thereby a specific society is always presupposed already – whose 'parts' exercise power over other 'parts' of it, or which use power as varying stakes in a game – no matter what the chances in this game are based on, or what its rules consist in. But, of course, the specific character of the game, its fundamental rules, which define and distribute its possibilities and restrictions, also exercise power over the players. Only the fundamental rule-creating and rule-setting power determines *who Ego* and *Alter are*, *which* those relevant 'parts' of society *are* that are able to appear only in this given horizon as superior and inferior. It is this power that Castoriadis wants to elucidate.

He begins the discussion – in "Power, politics, autonomy" – with the following consideration:

---

2 Translations by the author, here and below.

If we define *power* as the capacity for a personal or impersonal instance ... to bring someone to do [...] that which, left to him/herself, s/he would not necessarily have done ... it is immediately obvious that the greatest conceivable power lies in the possibility of preforming someone in such a way that, *of his/her own accord*, s/he does what one wants him/her to do, without any need for *domination* (*Herrschaft*) or of *explicit power* (*Macht/Gewalt*) to bring him/her to... [...]. Equally obvious, a being subject to such shaping will present at the same time the appearances of the fullest possible spontaneity, and the reality of a total heteronomy. Compared to this absolute power, any explicit power and any form of domination can be seen as deficient, for they betray the markings of an irreparable failure (*PPA*: 149–50).

Castoriadis is concerned with the fundamental power of society to make the a-social social – as far as possible – particularly regarding the psyche. Here the imaginary 'acts' as a framing, forming, imprinting power and force, which frames and forms the subjects (*Einbildungskraft/ Bildung* in German; to 'form' here in a double sense). Castoriadis again and again describes this procedure of socialisation as a process of power execution and coercion. At the same time this process concerns the most difficult and most powerful form of mediation: the mediation between psychic and social imaginary. The subject has – so to speak – on the one hand to be impregnated with power and on the other hand at the same time to absorb (to imbibe) power from its infancy (as with the mother's milk):

From the psychical point of view, the social fabrication of the individual is the historical process by means of which the psyche is coerced (smoothly or brutally; in fact, the process always entails violence against the proper nature of the psyche) into giving up its initial objects and its initial world (this renunciation is never total, but almost always sufficient to fulfill social requirements) and into investing (cathecting) socially instituted objects, rules, and the world. This is the true meaning of the process of sublimation. The minimal requirement for the process to unfold is that the institution provide the psyche with *meaning* – another type of meaning than the protomeaning of the psychical monad. The social individual is thus constituted by means of the internalization of the world and the imaginary significations created by society ... (*PPA*: 148–49).

Before any open exercise of power and before any form of domination, the institution of society thereby exerts – as Castoriadis calls it – a 'radical infra-power' or 'ground-power' on all individuals (*PPA*: 150). This infra-power – an expression of the instituting power of the radical imaginary – cannot be localized anywhere. It is never the power of a certain individual or of any identifiable instance – it almost bundles the forces of the instituting imaginary, the instituted society and its entire past history. "Ultimately, therefore, [Castoriadis says] we are dealing with the power of the social-historical field itself, the power of *outis*, of Nobody" (*PPA*: 150).

If that were all, then this infra-power or ground-power would have to be absolute and form the individuals in such a way that they would eternally reproduce the system which brought them into being. That may be the tendency of the institutions. Its realization, however, would end and exclude all history. But the instituted society never succeeds – as we know – to exercise its ground-power in such an absolute way, historicity is always at work. Be it that external nature causes change or that internal nature, the psyche, transcends limits in unpredictable ways; be it that the confrontation with other societies forces change. For Castoriadis, in the end, the most important reason is the radical imaginary itself, covered under the established order of things, "beneath which its insurmountable historicity continues to work imperceptibly and over very long periods. Seen as absolute and total, the ground-power of the instituted society [...] is therefore, sooner or later, bound to fail" (*PPA*: 151).

At this point, where the instituted society is most vulnerable – that is: society's own instituting imaginary – the strongest mechanism of defence against change is established: the denial and the covering up of the instituting dimension of society by the fact that the origins and the basis of the institution are attributed to an extra-social source. For Castoriadis, this is the main characteristic of social heteronomy: imaginary signification's taking on a life of their own, their predominance over society creating them as pseudo-nature.

But 'disorder' can and will always result from these factors. Therefore, there is always a dimension of the social institution, which deals with the re-establishment of the given order, the protection of society, of its mere existence and more or less regulated functioning. This is *one* of the reasons for *explicit power*, as Castoriadis calls it. Above all, however, the following has to be added: unawareness and uncertainty concerning the future do not permit a comprehensive determination of decisions taking place in advance, even in the most stable traditional society. Thus, explicit power derives from the necessity to make decisions about what to do and what to let be. A judging and/or governing power must always be explicitly present, as soon as there is a society. "The question of *nomos* ... may be covered up by a society; but this cannot be done as regards *dike* – the judiciary – and *telos* – the governmental" (*PPA*: 155).

This dimension of explicit power of society Castoriadis calls the dimension of the *political* – for which it is unimportant whether the corresponding instances are embodied in a whole tribe, the elder, the warriors, a king, the *demos*, a bureaucratic apparatus or whatever else. Conceived that way, the political cannot be limited to the state, but neither can it be expanded so far – as it sometimes happens – until it covers nearly all activities and the whole institution of society. And *this* political was not – as it is sometimes stated – invented by the Greeks. They, however, in Castoriadis's nomenclature, invented *politics*. Politics is defined by him apart from the always existing dimension of the political; as:

> ... the explicit collective activity which aims at being lucid (reflective and deliberate) and whose object is the institution of society as such. It is, therefore, a *coming into light*, though certainly partial, of the instituting in person; a dramatic, though by no means exclusive, illustration of this is presented by the moments of revolution. The creation of politics takes place when the established institution of society is put into question as such and in its various aspects and dimensions ..., that is to say, when *another relation*, previously unknown, is created between the instituting and the instituted (*PPA*: 160).

In other words: Politics is the project of autonomy in its collective dimension, which aims straight on at the institution of society; simply formulated: If we want to be free to make, we must make our own *nomos*. The radicality of this Greek creation 'politics' consists for Castoriadis in the following:

> 1. A part of the instituting power has been made explicit and has been formalized: this is the part concerning legislation properly speaking [...].
> 2. Specific institutions were created in order to render the explicit part of power [...] *open to participation*. This led to the equal participation of the body politic in the determination of nomos, of dike and of telos – of legislation, of jurisdiction, and of government (*PPA*: 168–169).

Therefore, politics would be the attempt of a conscious appropriation of the social infra-power – as far as possible – to turn it into explicit power, available in an egalitarian way: "*Create the institutions, which, by being internalized by individuals, most facilitate their accession to their individual autonomy and their effective participation in all forms of explicit power existing in society*" (*ibid*: 173, emphasis in the original).

Let us come back again to the notion of infra-power: *infra* means below, underneath (the limits of perception, for example; think of the infra-red radiation, not perceptible to our eye). Perhaps an analogy is permitted: The so-called cosmological background radiation, as predicted consequence of the Big Bang, is interpreted by physicists as proof of the Big Bang theory. This means that out of all directions of the sky a photon flux is coming that is interpreted as a kind of image of the early universe. In a similar way one could speak of a kind of *social* background radiation – of the radical, instituting imaginary. As soon as we have discovered it, we perceive an image of the social creation, the *creatio ex nihilo* of this, our society. As long as the original image of the social institution remains, however, underneath/below our perception limit, we stick to a heteronomous state. Then we remain subject to its power. We must raise it beyond the social perception threshold – open it to reflection and the appropriating, transforming praxis. The autonomy project implies this raising beyond those limits.

"We must and we ought to ...". My mode of speaking refers to the fact that elements - to remain in the image: a part of the spectrum - of this background radiation must permit, even demand us to think and act in this perspective: to become autonomous. That means that it must already include and potentiate the quiet and gentle power of autonomy.

2. Heteronomous semantics of power

There are also other attempts in the philosophical and sociological tradition, similar to Castoriadis's, addressing the constitution or creation of meaning through power - at least some authors can be interpreted in such a direction. Byung-Chul Han, whose stimulating study *Was ist Macht?* (2005) I already quoted once, does this under the chapter heading "Semantics of power". In the following, I will pick some well-known authors – Nietzsche, Foucault, Bourdieu, Heidegger – in a completely cursory manner, following the guideline of Han's argument. In doing so, instructive parallels and differences will result. Particularly Nietzsche enunciated vividly the connection between power and the constitution of meaning. Meaning *is* power. Nietzsche understands name-giving as a master's (*Herren*) right, and name-giving is at the same time a sense-giving: power thus founds (*stiftet*) sense. Each word is a call to order. Only the ruling power determines the sense, the where and wherefore of things. For the ruling power this continuum of meaning would be simultaneously a continuum of its sameness, in which it reflects itself. And this power is even '*dichterisch*' (poetic) in Nietzsche: It always creates new forms, new perspectives. In this sense it is not a despotic rule, which sets one perspective absolutely. With Nietzsche all phenomena of meaning are power phenomena.

Foucault on several occasions criticizes the wrong yet prevailing tendency to acknowledge power only in the negative form of prohibition. Actually, repression represents for him only a specific, poorly mediated or non-mediated form of power. Power, however, is not based on repression. "What makes power hold good, what makes it accepted, is simply the fact that it doesn't only weigh on us as a force that says no, but that it traverses and produces things, it induces pleasure, forms knowledge, produces discourse. It needs to be considered as a productive network which runs through the whole social body, much more than as a negative instance whose function is repression" (Foucault 1980: 118–19). One finds such an emphasis on the productivity of power more frequently in Foucault's later writings. Earlier, he had oriented his power analysis more towards enforcement/disciplining practices or the paradigm of struggle.

In *Discipline and Punish* Foucault speaks of three technologies of power (Han 2005: 48–51). The first is the well-known power of the 'sword'. The second technology of power, the power of the civil law book, i.e. of norms and the institution, operates with a system of signs. It does not want to act by terror, but by reason. The 'stylus', which fixes this system of signs, bases power on a more solid ground than the sword, because it does not act from the outside, but from within, without coercion from outside. In it, freedom and subjection seemingly coincide. The power of the stylus works continuously, by composing a continuum of ideas and representations, which penetrates a given society. The power of spirit is that of the law, which as a system of signifiers is circulated and updated again and again. The disciplinary power as the third technology of power – Foucault's main interest - penetrates the subject more deeply than norms or representations. It almost penetrates the body interior, leaves its traces, and produces thereby automatisms of habit. It acts just as inconspicuously and subtly as the power of the law book, but more directly, namely without any detour *via* representations. The disciplinary power works with reflexes rather than reflection

Bourdieu's *habitus* has a similar structure; it refers, however, more to the symbolic level, while Foucault to a large extent remains fixed onto the body. Here also, coercion *via* incorporation is experienced as freedom and as quasi-nature at the same time. Power unfolds its operations by inscribing itself into a public horizon of meaning and thus produces normalization effects, "reflexes of meaning, requiring no reflection" (Han 2005: 61). *Habitus* designates the sum of dispositions or habits of a social group. Power, which establishes or stabilizes itself *via* the *habitus*, operates on the symbolic level. It reaches its effectiveness not on the level of physical strength, but on that of meaning and of recognition. It makes use of signs and of meaning structures. What has to be established is a certain worldview or a certain value system, which legitimizes the domination of a group.

Looked at from the viewpoint of *habitus*, sociological light may also be shed on Heidegger's analysis of the everyday (*Alltäglichkeit*) (*ibid*: 59–61). In his phenomenology of everyday life Heidegger speaks about the "public expoundedness" (*öffentliche Ausgelegtheit*), which determines the average understanding, namely the *normal* perception, the *normal* view of the world. It dominates all interpretations of the world and of being and always maintains its point. It functions as a continuum or a horizon of meaning which effects that things and actions are understood this way and not that way. The finding of an interpreted world, a 'truth' of that kind, which is unquestionable (*unhinterfragbar*), performs - as Heidegger very characteristically puts it – a relief of being (*Seinsentlastung*): "And because the everyone (*das Man*) constantly accommodates the respective existence (*Dasein*) with the relief of being, it holds and solidifies its persistent domination" (Heidegger, cited after Han 2005: 60). The semantic "dictatorship of the everyone (*Diktatur des Man*)" does not operate by repression or prohibitions. It rather takes on the shape of the habitual. It is a dictatorship of the self-evident.

This normalizing power of the everyone does not dominate *over* everyday life. It works rather *from* it, or from *within*. Its character of immanence provides it with great stability. It works by determining the view, by prescribing the understanding of everyday life. Instead of the sovereign, who would be a special somebody, nobody performs: "The everybody, with whom the question about the *who* of the everyday existence is answered, is the nobody, to whom all existence in the mutuality/to be among one another (*Untereinandersein*) already gave up itself." (Heidegger, cited after Han 2005: 62). "Power becomes so to say indestructible, where it is perceived as nobody's power, that means not perceived in itself (at all)" (*ibid*).

The fact that Heidegger speaks in this way of "relief of being", when he speaks of the "dictatorship of the everybody", is, as I said, characteristic. It proves at bottom its affiliation to the anti-democratic tradition. From the relief of being emerges a direct way to the 'relief function' of the institutions in Arnold Gehlen and also to the 'reduction of complexity' through system formation in Niklas Luhmann. Here the talk ultimately is about 'relief' by heteronomy; the 'advantage' not to be free arises for us from habitualization and institutionalization: It is just as characteristic that the power of *outis*, of nobody, also mentioned by Castoriadis, can only be negatively connoted. The anonymous collective, seemingly, can always only be thought of as a negative, coercive, overwhelming instance, but not as a self-determining, democratic collectivity. Han summarizes his discussion of the 'semantics of the power' roughly like this: Power, in contrast to naked violence/force, bounds up / connects with meaning. By means of its semantic potentials it inscribes itself in a horizon of meaning or even produces a new one and can thus effectively regulate the process of understanding and action in its sphere of influence. "The power achieves a high stability, if it appears as 'everybody', if it inscribes itself in 'everydayness'. Not the violence, but the automatism of the habits increases its effectiveness. An absolute power would be that, which never would make its appearance/would never be forthcoming, never refer to itself, but which rather would totally merge with self-evidence. Power is conspicuous by its absence [*Macht glänzt durch Abwesenheit*]" (Han 2005: 64).

Thus, a limit of the mentioned concepts of power seems to be indicated. Because – after the discussion with Castoriadis – it should have to be said precisely: *Heteronomous* power is conspicuous by its absence (its absence *qua power*; it is certainly present in a multitude of effects). Autonomy has as its aim the greatest possible *presence* of infra-power; it is the permanent attempt to make the power of the imaginary visible and shapeable. The imaginary background radiation, of which I spoke, is suspected by these authors and noticed vaguely in its power effects. But their views apparently do not go beyond its pseudo-natural, heteronomous forms. The semantics of power seem to be thinkable by those authors as productive and creative, but nevertheless only as heteronomous. That *outis* could turn out to be the collective of the free and equal, instituting itself as such, seems to lie beyond the horizon of such a way of thinking.

3. Imaginary perspectives of autonomy?

I will now refer to some results and draw conclusions. The project of autonomy aims at bringing forward the instituting power in order to make it explicit by reflection (as far as possible); and it aims at merging the political, the explicit power, into politics, the object of which is the explicit institution of the society. 'More explicit power – with equal participation of everyone in its exercise' may perhaps be a fitting formula. Politics thus reaches 'deep', but must reach deeply – into the infra-power. Politics is thus not only *not* limited and limitable to the 'political system': because all forms of social, not least economic distribution of power, are necessarily its 'objects'. Above all, it also aims at the imaginary background or underground of society. This has to be opened up as widely as possible, reflected, put into question and made accessible for common decision-making. This means also that power constantly becomes "contested power" with a permanent "public confrontation of alternative claims to and uses of explicit power" (Arnason 2007: 100).

If we turn from this abstract analysis – so to say from the form analysis of power – to its concrete analysis, it becomes especially important to elucidate more precisely the heterogeneity of the infra-power. Castoriadis stresses above all the forming forces of the capitalist project and the project of autonomy, the specificity and the interaction of which he examines in some detail. However, are these the only relevant ones and/or can all relevant tendencies of modernity be reduced to these two? Take the imaginary complex of the nation state or of gender: they can hardly be subsumed without force under the problematic of capitalism. Or take the indeed frightening return and binding and destructive power of religious delusions. We should take the understanding of the heterogeneity of the modern imaginary seriously, in order to determine more precisely the limits, overlaps, conflicts – and also the relative power and related forming (or instituting) 'strength' of its heterogenous complexes (cf. Castoriadis 1993: 216–21).

Furthermore, it seems important for such an analysis to highlight the concrete interplay between ground-power and explicit forms of instituted power, which is specific for every society. This seems, not least, crucial for the possibilities of an autonomization of power for the society in question, as Arnason points out: "The modalities of institutional ground power vary with the imaginary content of the institution in question; imaginary foundations also shape the structures of explicit power, and may make them more or less amenable to changes that would lead to the institutionalization of contested power" (Arnason 2007: 101).

Now, what is today the state of the power of the autonomous imaginary, its instituting power? Obviously, Castoriadis was more and more pessimistic about the chances for a direct practical realization of the project of autonomy. Of the two imaginary core meanings, the conflict of which seemed to him to be the characteristic of the modern world – the capitalist project of unlimited expansion of pseudo-rational control and the project of autonomy – the former triumphs all the way, while the latter experiences a long decline.

One finds this diagnosis of decline in, for instance, a text like "Democracy as Procedure and Democracy as Regime", where Casto-riadis poses the question of present prospectives of democracy (Casto-riadis 1997b). There he shows on the one hand that for the most part contemporary political philosophy, with its fixation on models of democracy reduced to formal procedures, entangles itself in unresolvable contradictions. And he also shows that a real democracy would constitute a whole social order, which makes the equal participation in shaping and regulating the common affairs possible for all. That includes democracy, i.e. self-determination, in the economic sphere. Likewise it includes an equal distribution of power, which means effective equality of politically relevant resources. And Castoriadis demonstrates in this text that the existing social order withdraws more and more from such elementary preconditions of democracy. We do not live in a democracy, but in a 'liberal oligarchy', as he calls it.

This drifting away not only reflects the decline of the project of autonomy. The imaginary perspectives of autonomy become, so to say, increasingly 'imaginary' in the ordinary, common sense of the word: it becomes illusionary. This decline especially paralyses also the social and political conflict - so far vitally necessary for the development of modern capitalist societies. This paralysis is part of, and contributes for its part to, a deep crisis of today's western societies in general. This crisis Castoriadis sees, of course, not as an economic one, but as one of increasing 'insignificancy'. 'The rise of the insignificancy' as a central diagnosis of crisis refers particularly to the erosion of values, norms, social roles, which seemed up until now necessary for the functioning of the system. In one of Castoriadis's s seminars he uses the term "destitution" (see Castoriadis 1986: 16). It is not the instituting/installation of meanings, but the depositing/deinstallation, the erosion, the loss of significations that, according to this mere speculative idea, in a sense become the main activity of the imaginary. Formerly central imaginary significations – like that of the classical entrepreneur, the responsible worker, the traditional gender roles etc. – seem to erode and to be 'destituted' (which *per se* may not be that bad) but leaving nothing real behind them as solid alternatives.

One may object that such alternatives emerge anew in the framework of the so-called anti-globalization movement; and there are already new up-to-date imaginations of emancipation on the way to power. With respect to the new movements, I am also, of course – as Castoriadis surely was – very curious,, but also, to be honest, very uncertain with regard to the perspectives and prospects of success and sustainability. But since the outset I promised you that as a conclusion: open questions.

References

Arnason, Johann P. (2007) „Imaginary Significations and Historical Civilizations", in: Magerski, Christine; Savage, Robert; Weller, Christiane (eds.) *Moderne begreifen. Zur Paradoxie eines sozio-ökonomischen Deutungsmusters.* Wiesbaden: Deutscher Universitäts-Verlag, 93–106.

Castoriadis, Cornelius (1987) *The Imaginary Institution of Society,* trans. Kathleen Blamey. Cambridge, Mass.: MIT press.

Castoriadis, Cornelius (2002 [1986]) "Séminaire du 26 novembre 1986", in *Sujet et vérité dans le monde social-historique. Séminaires 1986-1987. (La Création humaine, 1),* ed. par Enrique Escobar et Pascal Vernay. Paris: Seuil, 15–37.

Castoriadis, Cornelius (1991) "Power, Politics, Autonomy", in *Philosophy, Politics, Autonomy.* ed. and trans. David Ames Curtis. New York/Oxford: Oxford University Press, 143–74.

Castoriadis, Cornelius (1997a [1993]) "Complexité, magmas, histoire. L'exemple de la ville médiévale", in *Fait et à faire. Les carrefours du labyrinthe V.* Paris: Seuil, 209–25.

Castoriadis, Cornelius (1997b) „Democracy as Procedure and Democracy as Regime", trans. David Ames Curtis. *Constellations,* 4:1, 1–18.

Foucault, Michel (1980) "Truth and Power", in *Power/Knowledge. Selected Interviews and Other Writings 1972-1977.* New York: Pantheon Books, 109–33.

Han, Byung-Chul (2005) *Was ist Macht?.* Stuttgart: Reclam.

Weber, Max (1972) *Wirtschaft und Gesellschaft. Grundriss der verstehenden Soziologie.* Tübingen: J.C.B. Mohr (Paul Siebeck).

Castoriadis, Education and Democracy

Ingerid S. Straume

In the 1989 essay "Done and To Be Done" (*CR:* 361–417), Cornelius Castoriadis mentions three questions that he has not been able to address to the degree he had wished. One of these concerns an "education oriented toward autonomy" (*CR*: 380–81). This interest in education is not extrinsic to the rest of his thought, but tightly interwoven with his approach to political democracy as an embodiment of the project of autonomy. Castoriadis is among the few contemporary philosophers who acknowledge the political and philosophical importance of pedagogical concepts such as education and *paideia*. In a characteristic passage, he places these notions right at the centre of political philosophy, claiming that:

> ... it is no accident ... that, contrary to the poverty in this respect of contemporary 'political philosophy,' grand political philosophy from Plato to Rousseau has placed the question of *paideia* at the center of its interests. Even if, practically considered, the question of education has always remained a concern of modern times, this great tradition dies in fact with the French Revolution (*PPA*: 162).

But even though 'education' and '*paideia*' play central roles in several of Castoriadis's most programmatic essays,[1] the concepts are somewhat underdeveloped, and tensions exist between these and other concepts. In this essay, I will take a closer look at these questions in order to set out some premises for further discussions of Castoriadis's thoughts on education. This investigation is placed within the framework of the philosophy of education – more precisely, in discussions about *education in a democracy*, where Castoriadis's ideas about a democratic *paideia* are able to open up the field in unprecedented ways.

In the philosophy of education, the concepts of 'democracy' and 'education' are closely related. Traditionally, democracy – the self-rule of the people – has been legitimated by education of some sort, from the *paideia* of the Greeks to contemporary citizenship training programmes. Education makes the difference between mob rule and legitimate majority rule. It adds to the argument of fairness – 'it is fair that people rule themselves' – a dimension of utility: 'people are in fact capable of ruling wisely'. Thus, education becomes, in the words of Castoriadis, "the permanent labor of the institution of society ... to render individuals such that one might *reasonably* postulate that their opinions all have the same weight in the political domain" (Castoriadis 1997a: 11; emphasis added). Many would also say that education should be democratic and empowering in itself. In this connection, John Dewey's classical work, *Democracy and Education* from 1916 is frequently invoked (Dewey 1997).

The expanding, international regime of educational policy frequently invoke ideals of democracy, inclusion and active citizenship figure as guidelines for national policies and curricula. The focus here is mainly on the exercise of citizenship, usually conceptualized in terms of three factors: *democratic knowledge*, *democratic skills* and *democratic values* or *culture*

---

1 "Democracy as Procedure and Democracy as Regime" (Castoriadis 1997a), "Power, Politics, Autonomy" (*PPA*), "Psychoanalysis and Politics" (*WIF*), "The Greek *Polis* and the Creation of Democracy" (*CR, PPA*) and "Psychoanalysis and Philosophy" (*CR*). See also the interview "Psyche and Education" (*FT*).

(see, e.g. Gutmann 1999, the Civic Education Studies[2] and the EU-programme for Lifelong Learning). The term 'democratic competence' is also used in this connection. On the practical side there is a vast and growing literature on the teaching and practicing of corresponding skills such as critical rationality, communication, conflict solving and inclusion in a changing and complex, multicultural world. Important as these factors undoubtedly are, however, this article argues that we need to widen the discussion of education and democracy in order to realise the *political* dimension of democracy. The teaching and practicing of skills, values, competences, etc. does not take us very far in seeing democracy *as a political system* of people consciously ruling themselves. For this we need a concept of democratic agency that indicates *power*. Not only does the 'skills-and-values-approach' fail to address democracy's political and creative dimensions, it could also be said that the idea of 'democracy' is reduced to more formal ideals like social integration and peaceful coexistence, thus stripping the concept of its potential for actual self-rule.

In the thought of Castoriadis we find a more radical conception: "We ... define politics as the explicit and lucid activity that concerns the instauration of desirable institutions and democracy as the regime of explicit and lucid self-institution, as far as is possible, of the social institutions that depend on explicit collective activity" (Castoriadis 1997a: 4). Democracy is seen as a regime, based on the collective capacity for questioning the social order and its foundations, which could be summed up as institutionalised self-questioning and self-limitation. The members of such a collective are actively involved in setting the political agenda and in positing laws. Democratic agency thus involves much more than voting and what is usually called participation. It involves criticising and questioning the social institutions, but more importantly, the ability to create new institutions. The modus operandi of democratic

2 The Civic Education Study was conducted by the International Association for the Evaluation of Educational Achievement in 30 nations to assess "students' civic knowledge and their civic attitudes and engagement". See http://www.iea.nl/cived.html

politics, then, is *change as creation*. This definition is certainly normative – even revolutionary – but even has a pragmatic side to it: without the creative dimension, it is hard to see how citizenship education can ever succeed in motivating the young. This is especially true under the current political atmosphere in most Western societies, where politics has lost much of its capacity for psychological investment (Castoriadis 2005, Fisher 2009, Žižek 2010) – an insight that forms the basis for many citizenship programmes.

The text proceeds in three parts. The first part traces two common conceptions of democracy and education, inspired by John Dewey and John Rawls respectively (although not limited to these thinkers). Both conceptions are found in dominant perspectives on democracy education (see e.g. the works of the liberal philosopher of education, Amy Gutmann [1987, 1991], who draws on both thinkers). These conceptions serve as the backdrop for developing a more radical notion of democracy education, building on the thought of Castoriadis (part two). In the third section, I discuss the concepts of *'paideia'* – and, in less detail 'education' – as used by Castoriadis, and point out some of the strengths and weaknesses in his understanding. Finally, I suggest further developments of Castoriadis's contribution to theories of democracy education.

I   Conceptions of Democracy Education

Let me set out by discussing two central conceptions of democracy education (or better, education in a democracy). First, I consider a conception of education that is influenced by one of the foremost philosophers of education, John Dewey (1859–1952). For Dewey, democracy is characterised by *openness*, the ideal of *self-improvement*, and *communication* both within groups and between groups. This communication serves to secure a variety of shared viewpoints and common interests (Dewey 1997: 83ff). In *Democracy and Education*, he famously asserts that "democracy is more than a form of government; it is primarily a mode of associated living, of conjoint associated experience" (Dewey 1997: 87). Through this much cited definition Dewey strengthens the justification for a democratic education. Democracy is not just something that takes place in parliament and other institutions assigned for political purposes: democracy concerns everyone, and rests on the education of everyone. But 'democracy', for Dewey, first of all denotes a society that aims at *growth* for all its members. If there are oppositions between groups, or if some are excluded from collective actions and processes, this growth cannot be realised.

> Democracy is a way of life controlled by a working faith in the possibilities of human nature. Belief in the Common Man is a familiar article in the democratic creed. That belief is without basis and significance save as it means faith in the potentialities of human nature as that nature is exhibited in every human being irrespective of race, color, sex, birth and family, of material or cultural wealth. This faith may be enacted in statutes, but it is only on paper unless it is put in force in the attitudes which human beings display to one another in all the incidents and relations of daily life (Dewey, *The Later Works*, electronic source).

According to Wilfred Carr and Anthony Hartnett (1996), Dewey was arguing against those who thought that democratic politics had become so complicated that one could not expect everyone to participate. They further point out that, in the processes of implementation and evaluation, Dewey's radical motives were toned down and more or less forgotten (Carr and Hartnett 1996: 65). It is easy to agree that Dewey held a more radical political programme than its received version has maintained. But even in Dewey himself we can witness a displacement of the political aspects of democracy: from democracy as a form of rule to democracy as a form of life. In Dewey's view, greater openness and interaction between groups could release the human potential to create and improve the social and physical environment.[3] His concern is a flexible society that is able to handle tensions and to change itself. His aim, however, is stability and integration, not radical change. In 1916, Dewey was very worried about the threats of destabilization and social fragmentation, especially class war (Dewey 1997). This was a time of social unrest, marked by rapid political and social changes and uncertainty. A main concern for Dewey was to secure social cohesion and integration, albeit not at the cost of the less privileged; on the contrary, he seems truly concerned with issues of fairness and social problems.

It is important to remember that at his time of writing, one had no way of knowing whether class struggles would lead to total disintegration or socio-economic compromises. It is therefore understandable that Dewey operated with such a selective definition of democracy. But even if *his* reasons were good, we should examine our own reasons to adopt this definition. Dewey's conception of democracy as "internal and external communication", "shared interests" and a "mode of associated living" provides a rather meagre conception of democracy, especially in political terms. Why, then, are Dewey's words about democracy being "more than a form of rule" (Dewey 1997) so frequently cited today, in literature on democracy education?[4]

Today, it seems more important to raise the opposite argument: Democracy is more than a conjoint experience, more than a mode of associated living; it is *also a form of rule*. Uncritical use of Dewey's conception today can give rise so several problems connected to de-

---

3 Like Gutmann (1999), Castoriadis (*CR*) and others, Dewey points out that the institutions of democracy – and abstract knowledge about these institutions – are worthless without practicing, active citizens. Dewey (1997), moreover, underlines the importance of a democratic *paideia* in terms of certain *attitudes*: questioning, researching, creative, and not least, active attitudes.

4 The use of Dewey as a major source of inspiration for democracy education is pronounced in the Nordic social democracies.

politicisation. One of the more obvious problems is that when democracy is defined primarily as communication – like Dewey does – it becomes difficult to distinguish between democracy and plain social adaptation. 'Everything nice' may be fitted into this kind of definition, and democracy becomes a concept emptied of political contents.

My objection is that democracy, in the field of education, is frequently conceptualised *without democratic politics*. In fact, many of the definitions in use do not reach beyond the capabilities of individual selves (values, skills, knowledge); they do not grasp the dimension of collective organisation, a necessary dimension if we want to create new institutions. My impression is that there might now be too much focus on democracy as an 'associated form of living'; at the expense of *demos kratein*. Educational thought thus deflects from the difficult arena of politics and discord toward more manageable social and socio-emotional issues like how to function together in the (multicultural, diverse) classroom. In the same move, 'democracy' is reduced to a Panglossian theory for the best of all possible worlds, namely our own, that is, to *status quo*.

The second position I want to discuss has cultural or religious beliefs/values/doctrines/identities as its main focus. The question here is not so much how to conceptualise democracy in relation to classroom activities, but rather the question of *who decides* over education, curricula, etc., and more philosophically, on what grounds should they do so, i.e. *which principles apply* when these questions are decided. These are central concerns for the philosopher of education Amy Gutmann, for John Rawls (whose main interest was not education), and much of the Anglo-American literature on democracy education. The discussion arises from the key assumption that education contains or transmits certain cultural values. Accordingly, the most important political discussions about education concern which, or rather, whose values should prevail in the educational system. In Gutmann's words:

> A democratic theory of education focuses on what might be called 'conscious social reproduction' – the ways in which citizens are or should be empowered to influence the education that in turn shapes the political values, attitudes, and modes of behavior of future citizens (Gutmann 1987: 14).

Influence over education is seen as the power to shape the future (citizens). To Gutmann, "[t]he central question posed by democratic education is: Who should have the authority to shape the education of future citizens?" (1987: 16). With this as the central question, the political discussion is orientated around issues such as multiculturalism, rights, religious questions, group interests and identity politics.

One of Rawls' premises is that societies are easily *divided* by the cultural – and, in particular, religious – outlooks of individuals and groups (Rawls' 'substantial doctrines'). Political and philosophical discussions turn around *who should decide, on what grounds,* to ensure a stable and legitimate or just order. What is *not* up for discussion, however, is the framework itself, i.e., the central institutions in existence. The approach leaves little room for political agenda-setting or creation of new institutions. Like the perspective described above, it mirrors existing institutions and practices throughout the Western world, which of course provides it with a certain robustness.

The objectives of political liberalism have varied over time. While the concern of early political liberalists was to discuss – limit and justify – the exercise of state power (Hobbes, Kant) and protect individual ownership rights in early capitalism (Locke), theories of liberal democracy since Rawls are mainly a *system* for handling cultural differences; for peaceful coexistence between groups that might in principle be in disagreement over ethical and moral issues, such as religion (Wolin 2004). Contemporary political liberalism is not so much a theory of democracy as a set of principles for *governance* in a modern world marked by mobility, complexity and global capitalism. For John Rawls in particular, the 'handling of differences' is of great philosophical importance. Since substantial-normative issues are seen as (potentially) contentious, they are delegated to the sphere of particularity, i.e., the private. The theory itself carefully avoids substantial notions of 'the good' while ensuring justice for the holders of different beliefs – thereby securing peaceful coexistence and loyalty to society's central institutions. Political liberalism then becomes a political super-theory, whose neutral framework is made up of *just institutions*.

Rawls's model of the political is unusually resilient to criticism. Any objections to political liberalism, e.g., communitarian ones, are easily fitted under the political liberalist's cloak as perfectly legitimate – yet, unpolitical – substantial doctrines. Moreover, it is utterly irrational to argue against the idea of just institutions – such arguments will only undermine the standpoint of the speaker, who, by depriving others of their freedom takes away her own. Peaceful coexistence is thus assured by filing all standpoints, even the illiberal ones, into a system that divides the political from the private, the relevant from the irrelevant, keeping as 'politically relevant' only the principles that secure the common interest, those that maintain peaceful coexistence, such as welfare arrangements, the rule of law, etc. It may seem that such a system cannot be superseded by rational or legitimate arguments, only ignored or sabotaged, by *illiberal* practices (Wolin 2004).

Notwithstanding its merits, there are certain things that a liberal political theory cannot achieve in the domains of political philosophy and education. For instance, in Rawls' thought, the notion of the *demos* is undeveloped, and may in fact be disposed of as soon as just and fair institutions are in place. Due to fears of destabilization, e.g. the tyranny of the many over the few, political liberalists have traditionally been wary of popular sovereignty (Müller 2006, 2011 Pulkkinen 1996, Wolin 2004). This fear has led to the defensive mechanisms found within liberalism, and a conflation of democracy and the rule of law (*Rechtsstaat*). Against this defensive orientation, radical leftist thinkers such as Chantal Mouffe and Jacques Rancière have developed an acute awareness of the importance of the *demos* that often combines with a sceptical attitude towards the state.

To sum up, these brief considerations show that the dominant positions in the field of democracy education are more orientated toward stability and *status quo* than political change. Notions of politicisation, power, the demos and political creation are poorly developed. In order to theorise these dimensions, alternative perspectives are needed.

II   Creating Institutions: *Paideia* and Autonomy

We now turn to Castoriadis's conception of democracy, which is more radical than the ones we have considered so far. 'Radical' here indicates an orientation towards social and institutional *change*. For Castoriadis, democracy is a form of rule that acknowledges, yes, cherishes the fact that societies are self-created. Democracy, thus understood, is committed to politicisation and self-limitation, where no guarantees are possible. It is a project with tragic undertones, since there is no way of securing that the people will always decide to create the best alternatives (Castoriadis *CR:* 267ff). Although this seems like stating the obvious, the implications of this perspective are rarely reflected in mainstream political theory or in democracy education. Or perhaps more correctly, the fear of majority rule has led to a series of restrictions on democracy that has reduced its political potential (Rancière 2006, Mouffe 2005, Wolin 2004).

Castoriadis's political philosophy turns around the concept of 'creation' – as does his philosophy of time, language, society, meaning, being (ontology) and almost all the other themes he worked on. His political and social thought has a phenomenological dimension, underlining that societies are first and foremost characterised by, held together by, and understood through the *meaning* that they provide for their members. This meaning is upheld by the 'social imaginary significations' of the society in question, and embodied in its institutions. Castoriadis's philosophy is rich, complex and highly original; hence, it is a challenge to present only a few aspects or concepts in a general argument. Many of his concepts can only be explained by invoking other concepts; other aspects of his thought. With these reservations, I shall briefly examine Castoriadis's approach to *creation within a democracy*. What does it mean to say, as Castoriadis does, that a society creates itself? To answer this, we will review an unusual view of the individual, the collective and societal creation.

Let me set out by noting that the traditional conception is that *only individuals can be creative*. The individual can – and for some thinkers, should – be able to act independently *vis-à-vis* the collective. The collective, on the other hand, traditionally represents stability, institutions and traditions. Based on these assumptions, many political discussions turn around *how much* creativity and subversive activity a society can and should bear from individuals and groups. In political liberalism, 'the individual' is a figure that is free in principle, bearer of certain interests and preferences that belong to the individual and not to the social sphere. These interests then need to be mediated and negotiated in a socio-political context, to secure sufficient (individual) freedom within the framework of fair, just and stable institutions.

With Castoriadis, these premises become highly questionable. Unlike political liberalists, Castoriadis sees the individual and the collective neither as polarities, nor in tension with each other. The individual is not, and cannot be, in ontological opposition to the collective or the society, since to become an individual for him means to become socialised. The individual is not something outside the social institution, but rather, its foremost product:

> We are all, in the first place, walking and complementary fragments of the institution of our society – its 'total parts,' as a mathematician would

say. The institution produces, in conformity with its norms, individuals that by construction are not only able but bound to reproduce the institution (*WIF*: 7).

Accordingly, the resources for becoming an individual are always social. Individuals do not 'decide' or 'agree' to use language, language is a mode by which these individuals are what they are:

> There is no such thing as an extrasocial human being, nor is there, either as a reality or as coherent fiction, any human 'individual' as an a-, extra-, or presocial 'substance'. We cannot conceive of an individual that does not have language, for example, and there is language only as creation and social institution (Castoriadis 1997a: 1).

From these statements it would seem that Castoriadis's individual is determined by the social, and, hence, that freedom is impossible. But several modifications apply that contradict this interpretation. Firstly, there is Castoriadis's notion of the polarity between the psyche and the social-historical; secondly, the notion of an undetermined significational surplus; thirdly, the radical imaginary; and fourthly, the variable character of 'the social'. All of these points need some explanation, and they will be addressed below – albeit briefly, in order to move on to my main point, which is to discuss Castoriadis's thoughts on education and *paideia*.

A) The Psyche and the Social

'The individual' is not the only concept that denotes the human being in Castoriadis's thought, equally or more important is the concept of the human 'psyche'.[5] While the individual, to Castoriadis, is always socialised – a full-fledged product of society the psyche is not, and never can be, fully socialised. The key to understanding the status of

---

5 Note that in order to discuss the question of democratic *paideia* and education we will also need a third concept: the *subject*.

the individual is found in the relationship between 'the psyche' and 'the social-historical'. For Castoriadis, the polarity is "not that between individual and society, since the individual *is* society, a fragment at the same time as a miniature – or, better, a sort of hologram – of the social world" (Castoriadis 1997a: 2).[6] Rather, the raw material for socialisation is the individual psyche, which is socialised in each instance. The polarity thus consists of the psyche on the one hand and the social-historical on the other. This move is more than a change of terminology: the nature of the psyche is different from that of the (always socialised) individual, as the psyche represents the radical imagination, the representational flux and psychical investment of meaning (*cathexis*). "[T]he psyche of each singular human being is not and can never be *completely* socialised and rendered exhaustively conformal to what institutions demand of it," Castoriadis holds (1997a: 3), partly because there is always a remaining part of the radical imagination, a wild part of the psyche, and partly because the instituted society is itself under pressure to change. Through the socialisation process, the psyche is 'persuaded' in each instance to accept the significations of the instituted society, and in return, it finds *meaning* – something that the psyche cannot produce by itself – in the social imaginary significations.

B) Undetermined Surplus of Meaning

Societies, to Castoriadis, exist as both instituted and instituting – socially created and socially creating. This means that the social field is not simply closure or structure; it is also *that which creates* all social phenomena; things that cannot be produced by the psyche, such as meaning, language, etc. This creative dimension of the social is given many names by Castoriadis,[7] where one is as good as the other, for

---

6 Note that in order to discuss the question of democratic *paideia* and education we will also need a third concept: the *subject*.

7 Various terms used by Castoriadis are: 'the social-historical', 'the instituting society', 'the instituting social imaginary', 'the radical anonymous collective', 'the social imaginary' and 'the

example 'the social instituting imaginary' (*CR*: 374). The psyche, on its part, is not capable of producing anything of a social nature. Rather, the psyche needs to be socialised to become the social individual. Specific to the social sphere are the *social imaginary significations*. Social imaginary significations make things and phenomena appear as they do, i.e. as themselves, through the associated principles of *existence, value, thought* and *action* (*WIF*: 313). The psyche becomes socialised by accepting these significations as its own, and in return it finds meaning. Thus meaning is a social phenomenon, provided by the social imaginary significations.[8] But instituted society is not a closed system of significations; it exists in more or less unstable forms and is always threatened by the chaotic nature of Being. Moreover, there is always a surplus of meaning in the social domain, an undetermined surplus that exists as instituting:

> [There cannot be] any question of a society that would completely coincide with its institutions, that would be exactly covered, without excess or deficit, by the institutional fabric and which, behind this fabric, would have no flesh on it, a society that would be a network of infinitely flat institutions. There will always be a distance between society as instituting and what is, at every moment, instituted – and this distance is not something negative or deficient; it is one of the expressions of the creative nature of history, what prevents it from fixing itself once and for all into the 'finally found form' of social relations and of human activities, what makes a society always contain *more* than what it presents (*IIS*: 113–14).

Henceforth, since the social is itself partly undetermined, the individual cannot be totally determined by the social situation.

---

imaginary of the social-historical'.

8 Examples of social imaginary significations are gods, God, nation, freedom, liberty, capital, fascism, tradition, power and so on.

C) The Radical Imagination

The created and creative nature of the human world is highlighted by Castoriadis's notion of 'the radical imagination' (*l'imagination radicale*). The 'radical imagination' denotes the ability to create something that does not stem from – in the sense of being assembled from, combined by, or grown out of – something else. The 'radicality' points to the fact that something is created 'out of nothing' (*ex nihilo*). If this were not so, Castoriadis contends, we would not witness all the varieties of social forms, i.e. societies, whose universes of significations are unique, and not reconstructible 'from scratch'. Just think of the Roman Empire, the city states of Florence, the vast array of tribal cultures etc. (see "The Greek Polis and the Creation of Democracy", *CR:* 267–89). The radical imagination in its societal form is *the social instituting imaginary* mentioned above. In the singular psyche, the radical imagination constantly produces representations that have no reference in the Real, such as dreams, phantasms and works of art (*WIF; CR:* 349–60). As long as the radical imagination is able to operate, in society and in the psyche, the individual can never be fully determined.

D) The Character of the Social

Society, in each case, institutes itself as something, namely *itself*, with its specific significations. Through the social imaginary significations, a certain society is what it is, and everything that can be experienced in this society is contained within its instituted 'horizon' of meaning. Now, some societies are acknowledged as the products of society itself. Through this insight, both the freedom to create and the responsibility for one's actions are also instituted. In such societies, individuals are *even less* determined by their social situation, since the social situation itself is seen to be the creation of individuals' actions, for which they are responsible *de facto* and *de jure*. But still, these individuals are the *products* of this society, where freedom and responsibility are instituted as meaningful. The specific point here, which does not make sense within an individualist ontology, is that even though individuals are products of society, fully socialised by it, their socialisation implies the significations of freedom and autonomy, along with responsibility and political agency.

III   *Paideia* and Freedom

The logical implication of all the above – most clearly exemplified in the last case – is that for individuals to be politically creative, something in their socialisation and the social institution must allow for this creation to make sense, to be meaningful. If this were not so, every society throughout history would have fostered more or less the same amount of creative inventions, radical ideas, etc., something which is clearly not the case. There have been social-historical periods with a great amount of new inventions, like the European renaissance, but more common in history are long periods of repetitive life-forms, both in art and politics.

The 'co-resonance' of individuals and societies is mirrored in Castoriadis's concept of 'individual and collective autonomy,' which he would always use as *one* concept. A main point for Castoriadis is that freedom (or autonomy) for the individual is not possible without an already existing freedom of the collective – and correspondingly, collective autonomy means freedom of the individuals concerned. Most importantly, without the socially instituted capacity (or ability) to act upon the social structures and change them, individuals can never be free in more than a narrow, private sense. In liberal democracy theory, by contrast, the idea of socially instituted freedom is seen as a contradiction in terms. Autonomy is here placed wholly at the 'pole' of the individual. To be autonomous in the liberal meaning means to be able to act independently of societal structures.

Castoriadis does not contest the idea that autonomy for the individual is possible, such as the ability to think for oneself, to challenge *doxa* and existing institutions, to problematise and criticise. His point is that the conditions for valuing – and hence, exercising – this kind of activity must be *socially instituted*. Society is primary:

> [O]ne cannot see [the social institution] as resulting from some deliberate cooperation between 'individuals' – or from an addition of 'intersubjective networks': for there to be intersubjectivity, there must be human subjects as well as the possibility for these subjects to communicate – in other words, there must be already socialised human beings and a language that they could not produce themselves qua individuals ... since they must receive language through their socialisation. The same considerations hold for a thousand other facets of what we call the individual (Castoriadis 1997a: 2).

On this background, we can now approach the concept of *paideia* as it is used by Castoriadis: "[T]here is a 'part' of almost all institutions that aims at the nurturing, the rearing, the education of the newcomers – what the Greeks called *paideia:* family, age groups, rites, schools, customs, laws, etc." (*PPA*: 149). '*Paideia*' is thus closely tied to the socialisation process whereby the psyche internalises the social institution. This internalisation consists in the psyche's investment (*cathexis*) of instituted significations and their meaning. The socialisation of the psyche that forms the individual is vital to societies' existence as such. It entails the psyche's acceptance of the institution of the society as a whole, ensuring its 'effective validity'.

In a certain sense, the power of *paideia* is the greatest political power of all. Every society is held together by it: "Thus, before any explicit power and, even more, before any 'domination,' the institution of society wields over the individuals it produces a *radical 'ground power"* (*PPA*: 150). This "ground power" is defined by the central imaginary significations of a society: what makes sense and what does not make sense, what has meaning and what does not.[9] Individuals' desires and needs are shaped by it. Accordingly, in contemporary societies, we do not aspire toward social types that make little or no sense in current social structures: "These [psychogenetic] processes are irreducible to purely social processes; but at the same time they logically and effectively presuppose them, since what is in question here is forming the individual as capitalist or proletarian, and not as lord, patrician or Amon-Râ priest" (*IIS*: 318). Nor could parents in ancient Athens or Rome even wish to raise their kids to become president of General Motors. Nothing in the psyche as such can produce the *world* of significations, the *mode of being* of these significations as instituted.

According to Castoriadis, the same logical relation applies to the significations of 'freedom' and 'autonomy'. These significations are only possible – meaning that they only make sense – in certain societies and not in others. For an individual to be able to invest psychic energy in, e.g., a 'quest for freedom', this person must live in a social-historical setting where this idea is thinkable and makes sense. As Castoriadis points out, however, this is *not* the case in many instances. He argues that the significations of freedom, autonomy, etc. were created in the "twin birth" of political democracy and philosophy in ancient Greece (*CR:* 267ff). To him, a close connection exists between philosophy and democratic politics, as both disciplines are concerned with investigating the limits and 'grounds' of norms, principles and ideas. To question a law means – in the full consequence – to question its grounds, foundations and validity, in other words, to practice philosophy. Similarly, a culture where political creativity based on questioning, reflexivity, responsibility, etc. *makes sense,* must be in place before we can talk of individuals becoming politically creative. Castoriadis denotes this state as 'individual and collective autonomy.' At this point, where

---

9 The radical ground power is the power of no-one – its source is the radical imaginary: "the institution of society wields a radical power over the individuals making it up, and ... this power itself is grounded upon the instituting power of the radical imaginary ..." (*PPA*: 150).

heteronomy is transformed to autonomy, the capacity (or capabilities) of the individual changes:

> The autonomy of the individual consists in the instauration of an *other* relationship between the reflective instance and the other psychical instances as well as between the present and the history which made the individual such as it is. [...] This means that the individual is no longer a pure and passive product of its psyche and history and of the institution (*PPA*: 165).

At this point, Castoriadis no longer talks about the 'individual' and the 'psyche', but introduces the notion of the 'subject'. I will not elaborate on the notions of autonomy or heteronomy here, but in stead focus on the more restricted concept of '*paideia*'. As we have seen, Castoriadis's *paideia* is closely related to socialisation, and the two are in fact often conflated. However, he sometimes also talks of a 'true *paideia*,' or a 'real education'.[10] This is the *paideia* and education that take place in an *autonomous* setting (political democracy), and aims at autonomy. Here is an example:

> We want autonomous individuals, that is, individuals capable of self-reflective activity. But, unless we are to enter into an endless repetition, the contents and the objects of this activity, even the developments of its means and methods, must be supplied by the [psyche's] radical imagination. This is the source of the individual's contribution to social-historical creation. And this is why a non-mutilating education, a true *paideia*, is of paramount importance (*WIF*: 133).

In "Democracy as Procedure and Democracy as Regime," Castoriadis writes about *paideia* "in the strongest and most profound meaning of the term" as "aiding individuals to become autonomous" (Castoriadis 1997a:

---

10 Castoriadis (*CR*) talks about "schooling" as the bad (heteronomous) kind of education and a "non-mutilating education" as the desirable one (*WIF*: 133).

15). The notion of a 'true', 'strong' or 'profound' *paideia* is not very well developed. The meaning seems to be that a 'true' *paideia* leads individuals toward autonomy, while 'non-true' *paideia* is heteronomous. But this is insufficient, since *paideia* for Castoriadis is also a necessary element in all societies; as we saw in the definition further above. It denotes the way societies are reproduced from one generation to the next; hence all *paideia* is *paideia* (non-*paideia* being impossible in a society lest it breaks down *qua* society). It would probably be very difficult to develop the notion of a *non-true paideia*. On this background, a 'true *paideia*' does not bring us very far. I think the reason for this arguably weak conceptualisation is simply lack of a better alternative. In my view, the term that Castoriadis lacks in order to flesh out his points exists in the Scandinavian and German languages, in the more or less synonymous terms *danning* and *Bildung*.[11] These terms – which in this connection can be treated as one concept – denote a subject's conscious work upon the self. *Danning/Bildung* indicates improvement, conscious cultivation of the self in a reflective relationship to one's own cultural and political situation. The concept is clearly normative: It does not make sense to say that one regrets having been subject to *danning/Bildung*, whereas this could – in theory – be possible for Castoriadis's '*paideia*'. I am not, however, claiming that Castoriadis is unaware of this idea. In "Psychoanalysis and Philosophy", for example, he talks about a similar state – "a reflective and deliberate subjectivity" (CR: 360) – as the end of the psychoanalytic process.

Further problems with the distinction between '*paideia*' and 'true *paideia*' (and similarly for education) emerge, however, in situations where subjects are *uneasy* with their own existing socialisation, e.g. in times of cultural ambivalence, anomie, insignificance, social conflicts, etc.[12]

---

11 *Danning* is the Norwegian term, *dannelse* is Danish/Norwegian, *Bildung* is German and *bildning*, Swedish.
12 Castoriadis does not deal with this situation directly, and might even object to this type of diagnosis. However, he comes close in his diagnosis of 'insignificance' (Castoriadis 2005).

In such situations, when the social imaginary significations of a society do not provide sufficient meaning for its members (Castoriadis 2011), the distinction *paideia* vs. real *paideia* appears to be both too coarse and too idealistic. Moreover, in matters of education it must be possible to distinguish the (intentional) educational setting from ordinary (mainly unintentional) socialisation. On the other hand, the *Bildung* tradition is problematic for Castoriadis due to its reliance on German idealism and the philosophy of the subject.

In the larger picture, Castoriadis's notion of *paideia* is able to highlight the societal side of *Bildung* in a manner that traditional *Bildung* theory cannot do. His insistence on the importance of *paideia* makes it clear that education and *Bildung* cannot be separated from society's *shaping*, nor can the individual be separated from the institution of society (culture and civilization). Thus, without using the term, Castoriadis clarifies why goals such as 'political *Bildung*' will make sense in certain societies, but not others. In order for a notion to make sense – and to be a legitimate, educational goal – certain cultural or civilizational resources must be in place. This is why it does not make sense to reproach someone for overlooking matters that simply do not make sense in their *own* cultural context. In Castoriadis's words: "Freedom and truth cannot be objects of investment if they have not already emerged as social imaginary significations" (*PPA*: 166).[13]

Closing Remarks

Castoriadis's thought on education is rich, even though the conceptual apparatus is somewhat underdeveloped, as we have seen. In addition to the themes discussed in the above, I see various areas where his thought can be developed as a philosophy of education, for example, the nature

---

13 Following this line, we could ask whether 'political creativity' provides sufficient meaning for us (Westerners) today, and accordingly, whether we are able to follow this as an educational goal. There are many indications that this is not the case, see, e.g., Mark Fisher (2009) and Slavoj Žižek (2010).

of human (significative) learning,[14] the educational import of social imaginary significations, the nature of the pedagogical relationship (*FT*: 165–87) and the development of subjectivity (the subject and its world), to mention a few themes.

In the above sections, I have tried to demonstrate why Castoriadis's political and social-philosophical thought provides a fuller understanding of what it implies to educate for political democracy than the traditional (liberal and communitarian) approaches. Let us recall the concept of 'individual and collective autonomy', which is well suited to conceptualise the notion of a politically active *demos*. Building on Castoriadis, the focal point for such an education would be the social imaginary significations, within which another world is seen as possible, desirable, and feasible. Through this perspective, the 'knowledge, skills, and values-approach' is given an additional, social dimension whose meaning consists not only of representations, but also intentions, drives and affects (*PPA*: 337). This can only enrich democracy education, since without belief and investment in politics, the traditional democratic 'skills' and 'values' cannot really motivate to action. Moreover, democracy must be conceptualised as a political project involving decision-making, power and often struggles, and not just a 'mode of associated living' (Dewey). But if education in a democracy is set out to educate a politically active *demos* – a question that needs more elaboration than the place here allows – one of the problems we must face is that, in the socialisation and education of the next generation, the institutions in existence will necessarily have to be used, even though the aim of education is to be able to create new and different institutions. In other words, we want the existing – and at least partly undesirable institutions – to produce individuals who are different than ourselves, and the society in which they are produced. According to Castoriadis:

---

14 Cf. Castoriadis's critique of 'learning' as a biological category (*CR*: 381ff).

Only an autonomous collectivity can shape autonomous individuals – and vice versa, whence the paradox, for ordinary logic. Here we have one aspect of this paradox: autonomy is the ability to call the given institution of society into question – and that institution itself must make you capable of calling it into question, primarily through education (*FT*: 176).

This is a paradox, which cannot be foreseen or explained, but it still happens. A similar leap takes place when the social-historical and the individuals change simultaneously:

> Individuals aiming at autonomy cannot appear unless the social-historical field has altered itself in such a way that it opens a space of interrogation without bounds [...] But the concrete embodiment of the institution are those very same individuals who walk, talk, and act. It is therefore essentially with the same stroke that a new type of society and a new type of individual, each presupposing the other, must emerge, and do emerge, in Greece from the eighth century B.C. onward and in Western Europe from the twelfth and thirteenth centuries onward (*PPA:* 166–67).

That a new type of individual and society should emerge, in one and the same stroke, is "unthinkable" from the traditional viewpoints of philosophy, "the inherited logic of determinacy", according to Castoriadis. However, this has happened in actual history, and still can, through "the creative work of the instituting imaginary, as radical of the anonymous collectivity" (*PPA*: 167). The paradox cannot be solved by logic, only acted out as a creation, a political act. This way history is created. A final example of the paradoxical character of autonomy is found in "Psychoanalysis and Philosophy" (*CR*), this time on a one-to-one level. In his discussion of the 'end' of psychoanalysis, Castoriadis talks of helping another person towards autonomy by "'using' for this purpose the potential elements of this same autonomy", before it is actually in place. The autonomy of another person cannot be *installed* by, e.g., the educator. All we can do, according to Castoriadis, is to act *as if,* and make use of the autonomy that is not yet fully developed. Again, there is a leap, where something new – a reflective subjectivity – is created 'out of nothing'.

On the societal level a parallel leap can be traced in the relationship between education and democracy. Consider that, for Castoriadis, autonomy is a *project* whose 'effective embodiment' is democracy. Its mode of being is open-ended, with no 'guarantee' beyond the citizens' capacity for self-limitation. Democracy can only be lived, enacted, practiced and filled with purpose – not once and for all, but through the continuous engagement of citizens who actively cultivate themselves and each other as political subjects. The essential relationship between education and democracy thus concerns the development of a will, through collective, political and creative action – a collective will that is capable of creating new institutions and significations. Whether these significations will also house the quest for truth and freedom is, of course, an open question.

References

Carr, Wilfred and Hartnett, Anthony (1996) *Education and the Struggle for Democracy: The Politics of Educational Ideas.* Buckingham/Philadelphia: Open University Press.

Castoriadis, Cornelius (2011) *Postscript on Insignificance. Dialogues with Cornelius Castoriadis.* Edited with an introduction by Gabriel Rockhill, trans. Gabriel Rockhill and John V. Garner. London: Continuum.

Castoriadis, Cornelius (2007) *Figures of the Thinkable*, trans. Helen Arnold. Stanford: Stanford University Press *(FT)*.

Castoriadis, Cornelius (2005) *Une société à la derive, Entretiens et débats.* Paris: Seuil.

Castoriadis, Cornelius (1997a) "Democracy as Procedure and Democracy as Regime", *Constellations* Vol. 4 No. 1, 1–18.

Castoriadis, Cornelius (1997b) *The Castoriadis Reader*, ed. and trans. David Ames Curtis. Oxford: Blackwell, 349–60 *(CR)*.

Castoriadis, Cornelius (1997c) "Psychoanalysis and Politics", in *World in Fragments*, ed. and trans. David Ames Curtis. Stanford University Press, 125–36 *(WIF)*.

Castoriadis, Cornelius (1991) *Philosophy, Politics, Autonomy*, trans. David Ames Curtis. New York: Oxford UP.

Castoriadis, Cornelius (1987) *The Imaginary Institution of Society*, trans. Kathleen Blamey. Cambridge Mass: MIT Press.

Civic Education Study, available at: http://www.iea.nl/cived.html

Dewey, John (1997 [1916]) *Democracy and Education. An introduction to the philosophy of education.* New York: Simon and Schuster.

John Dewey: The Later Works 1925-1954, Vol. 14, available at http://dewey.pragmatism.org/

Fisher, Mark (2009) *Capitalist Realism.* Winchester/Washington: Zero books.

Gutmann, Amy (1999) *Democratic Education*, 2nd edition. New Jersey: Princeton University Press.

Gutmann, Amy (1987) *Democratic Education.* New Jersey: Princeton University Press. Howard, Dick (2010) *The Primacy of the Political.* New York: Columbia University Press.

Mouffe, Chantal (2005) *The Return of the Political.* London: Verso

Müller, Jan-Werner (2006) "Fear and Freedom: On Cold War Liberalism", working paper. Available at: http://www.princeton.edu/~jmueller/ColdWarLiberalism-JWMueller-2006.pdf

Müller, Jan-Werner (2011) *Contesting Democracy. Political ideas in twentieth-century Europe*. New Haven/London: Yale University Press.

Pulkkinen, Tuija (1996) *The Postmodern and Political Agency*, Doctoral dissertation in philosophy. University of Helsinki.

Rancière, Jacques (2006) *Hatred of Democracy*. London: Verso.

Wolin, Sheldon S. (2004) *Politics and Vision; Continuity and Innovation in Western Political Thought* (expanded version). New Jersey: Princeton University Press.

Žižek, Slavoj (2010) *Living in the End Times*. London: Verso.

The Wreath of Subjectivity and Time

Kristina Egumenovska

For reasons we can partly deduce but cannot fully know, the question of the subject and the question of time have often been thought together. Just as often, the endeavor itself has been fraught with pitfalls, twists and turns. Woven, as if in a wreath, subjectivity and time usually ended up being sacrificed to the 'pure', the 'given'. In this paper I will specify the most prominent snares in order to link subjectivity and time. In doing that, Castoriadis's idea of time as an emergence of otherness will be treated as substantially linked to Aristotle's idea of time as a number of change (*arithmos kineseos*).

Time as emergence of otherness

There is a passage in *IIS* which can open our discussion *in medias res*. Castoriadis writes:

> ... space exists prior to the figure as its *a priori* condition. There is nothing like this in the case of time, which would be *nothing* if it were the mere possibility of iteration of the identical. An 'empty' space is a logical and physical *problem*; an 'empty' time is an absurdity – or else, it is simply a certain name given for no particular reason to a spatial dimension (*IIS*: 193).

The position that space, unlike time, exists *prior* to the figure is not something we would agree with unconditionally in terms of the relation between matter and space (see Einstein, [1952] 1954), but time truly would be nothing, as Castoriadis emphasizes in this quote, had it merely been a possibility of iteration of the identical. The question of time is here posited basically as a question of otherness, because it argues against the premise of time as pure possibility. In fact, in "Time and Creation" (*WIF*: 374–401) Castoriadis defines time as unfolding of otherness, but thinking in terms of otherness and difference is not exclusive to the concept of time in Castoriadis's edifice. Let us reiterate his understanding of these two categories. On one hand, something is *different* with regard to something else as far as it can be deduced or produced from the given elements and following certain laws (cf. *IIS, WIF*). On the other hand,

> [...] to say that figures are *other* (and not simply different) has a sense only if figure B can in no way derive from a different arrangement of figure A – as a circle, ellipse, hyperbole or parabola derive from one another and so are the *same* points *arranged* differently – in other words, only if no identitary law, or group of laws, is sufficient to produce B starting from A (*IIS*: 124).

What is important to emphasize is the thesis of intractability of these two irreducible-to-each-other dimensions, which in my view is implicit in the claim made by Castoriadis that multiplicity formally entails unity (cf. WIF: 399), or by the claim that otherness entails difference (ibid: 400). To give a tangible example, *Feminine Grace* or any other artwork in its unrepeatable (poietic, creative) 'otherness' has to rely also on perspective, or on the positing of objects that can be simply numbered and which rely themselves on geometric forms, etc. Language in its poietic dimension, where one uses an idiomatic phrase or writes "infinite is not that (τι) where nothing is outside, but that, where something is always outside (ἀεί τι ἔξω)" (see Aristotle, Physics: 6.206b33-207a1-2), has to rely on language as a code as well. In other words, deployment of otherness as otherness is not separate from difference (the identical, repeatable, etc.), but the reverse is not necessary (i.e. repeating the same tone does not make for a song, and yet the later cannot be made by excluding identical notes or phrases). In any case, both categories were used by Castoriadis to help elucidate ontological questions and are relevant not only for thinking time, but also space, language, the social-historical, politics, subjectivity, art.

As we see from the opening citation, difference and otherness are used also to spell out more clearly the distinction between time and space, i.e. on one hand the possibility of space to exist simply as repetition of the identical (i.e. abstract space), on the other hand, the need to recognize that time is nothing if defined only in those same terms (i.e. as difference: extension, repetition). However, what we have encountered historically is thinking difference and otherness in exclusive terms, and therefore both time and space (but also subjectivity) have been thought as being deployed only through the one or the other category. Two most prominent snares of this kind are the spatialization of time and the mathematization of space (i.e. the reduction of space to abstract space).

Specifically, the spatialization of time made anew by physicists is certainly valid as long as one remains in an abstract mathematical space, but when this reduction is implicitly related to the question of the subject, time becomes an extension of the soul (e.g. Augustine and his famous passage on time as extendedness of the soul itself, cf. Augustine, XI, 26) or pure *a priori* form of knowledge (e.g. Kant). The reduction of time to spatiality, succession and extension was recognized and criticized by Henry Bergson at the end of the 19th century in his *Essai sur les données immédiates de la conscience* ([1889]1921). But despite his intricate analysis of time, Bergson's slippage was that he *identified* space with abstract space. One might wonder in what way does this reduction affect one's definition of the human subject, but consider for instance Bergson's radical dissociation between reciprocal exteriority specific for the world outside us, the homogenous space, and the opposite 'tension', *'la durée pure'*, the absolute heterogeneity inside us or the successiveness *without* reciprocal exteriority. Fortunately, not much is needed to argue that space cannot be exhausted by the quantifiable, but to 'vulgarize' this point: the (embodied) coexistence of you, me and our friend is a far cry from the coexistence of three triangles in an abstract space. This point is made by Castoriadis and the French mathematician Alain Connes in *Entretien Cornelius Castoriadis–Alain Connes*[1] and is concerned with the irreducibility of physics to mathematics and vice versa.

The problem of the enigmatic link between the question of time and the question of the subject is only enlarged when the fact of private and common time are brought into the debate. For instance, in Heidegger we read many pages on how the world-time becomes leveled off and covered up. And yet, how is it that this world-time, precisely as 'the time for something" (cf.*H*: 414),[2] becomes *effective*? In other words, if public time "has its source in factical temporality" (*H*: 412), is this a necessary *and* sufficient condition for the public time to be *public*? Heidegger is clear on this point: time is made public because *Dasein* "is already disclosed" (*H*: 411, emphasis in the original). Therefore, it is not surprising that Heidegger has to write that with the disclosedness of the Dasein and the world, the world-time is 'more subjective' than any possible subject and 'more Objective' than any possible Object (*H*: 419). For how to choose a better way to pass in silence that one is unable to allow fully a common time whose condition is found in itself (i.e.

1 With other interviews (from the same series broadcasted in November-December 1995 and July 1996 on France Culture) published as *Post-scriptum sur l'insignifiance* (1998) La Tour d'Aigues: Editions de l'Aube, 121–48. English translation: *Postscript on Insignificance, Dialogues with Cornelius Castoriadis* (2011), ed. Gabriel Rockhill, London: Continuum, 74–92.
2 To help readers find the cited passages from Martin Heidegger's *Being and Time* (hereafter *H*), regardless of the edition or translation used, here and later I do not give the pages, but the section where the citation is to be found.

common time as consubstantial with society) rather than in *Dasein's* 'care-structure' grounded in temporality (in the known order: reaching out towards the future while taking up the past and therefore yielding the present)? Perhaps in a philosophy which must start with, or come back to, the so called subject, it is admissible to spell out temporality (i.e. the being of *Dasein* who understands being) as a condition for the possibility of world time. Heidegger does not *deduce* objective time from the subjective reckoning of Dasein, but his approach is nonetheless exemplary of the difficulties to account for the fact of common time and private time whenever they are seen as a context for anything but their own inherently conditioned formation.

Clearly, questions and attempts at an answer cannot be simple when we are specifying complex phenomena in all their plurality, common and private time notwithstanding. Even the systematic Aristotelian analysis of time, which has become the point of departure for the whole European tradition later on, seems to cause more questions than answers. It is not questionable that in Aristotle's account time *is not* change, but is one of the essential determinations of change. The dilemma seems to be how to understand the 'before and after' in Aristotle's definition of time.[3] Castoriadis is right to note (*WIF*: 379) that 'before' and 'after' are taken to happen originarily in space, but misses to add that according to Aristotle we also say 'before' and 'after' with reference to now (*Physics*: 223a5). In fact, according to Castoriadis, a subjective element "inevitably creeps into Aristotle's cosmological view of time" (*WIF*: 379) and to support this claim he cites a passage[4] from *Physics* 4.2 (*WIF*: 379–80).

---

3 Aristotle understood time as "the number of movement according to the before and after" (*Physics*, 219b1–2, 220a24–25), where movement is of course not only local movement but change in general (cf. 4th book of *Physics*).

4 For readers' convenience, the passage from Aristotle is: "we take cognizance of time, when we have defined the movement by defining the before and after; and only then we say that time has been [has elapsed] when we perceive the before and after in the movement ... for, when we think [*noesomen*] that the extremes are other than the middle, and the soul pronounces the present/instants [*nun*] to be two, the one before, the other after, it is only then that we say that this is time (219a22–25, 219a26–29)" (*WIF*: 379–80).

Castoriadis then concludes that "the after and before becomes thus a primitive notion, the understanding of which must appeal to some subjective ordering by the soul" (*WIF*: 380). But given that Aristotle's definition of time as a number of change [*arithmos kineseos*] implies that time is essential for change to be countable, Castoriadis could have been less quick in focusing on the 'before and after', without linking them back to *arithmos kineseos* (moreover, the cited passage seems to be outright concerned with stating the essential condition 'now has to be two if we were to say this is time'). Let us not dismiss the known deliberateness for which Aristotle's writings are known and let us linger a bit more on his choice of 'number' [*arithmos*] rather than 'measure' [*metron*] in the definition of time. It is essential to contextualize that our own concept of number is simply radically different from the concept of number in Ancient Greece (which did not include negative numbers, fractions, or irrational numbers, only positive integers greater than unity were *arithmoi*). At that time, *arithmos* was a count *of* things, linked to that of which it is a number (Klein, 1968).

Furthermore, the count of which Aristotle writes is the count *of change*, movement [*kineseos*] which is change in general. In fact, change is not prior to time, for the essence of time is the now [*to nun*] as *arithmos kineseos,* as a number of movement/change. Finally, time is a kind of number, a number in the sense of *what* is counted or what is countable/ what can be counted, but not in the sense of what we count with (cf. *Physics*: 219b5–9).[5] Only as a reminder, just as a limited length is a line, a limited width a surface, a limited depth a body, so a limited [*peperasmenon:* definite, determinate, defined] plurality is an *arithmos* (*Metaphysics, Delta* 13, 1020a12–14). And plurality is, so to speak, a genus of *arithmos* (see the section in *Metaphysics Iota* (I)6,1057a2–3). The emergence of something with regard to something is a criterion which Castoriadis

---

5 Also compare *Metaphysics*, Nu(N)1, where the same distinction for number is made: *arithmos* signifies a plurality which has been measured and a plurality of measures (N(1)1088a6).

himself uses to distinguish time from space, i.e., I cannot distinguish the *mode* of 'moments' (time) from the mode of 'points' (space) unless what is essential to time is that *something* in respect to another something appears, time in terms of *that*, which emerges (see *IIS*). Castoriadis too, links time with the deployment of otherness, time as essential to *this* (here-and-now, always anew) alteration.

In this sense, Aristotle's notion of time as a number of the now being two cannot be read separate from the imploding context of plurality from where *arithmos* as multitude of indivisibles was taken (nor from the fact that number in Aristotle's time was essentially linked to content, a count of things). It seems that Aristotle's appeal to number can be seen as essentially informative to Castoriadis's notion of time as unfolding of otherness.[6]

In any case, our concept of time will be impoverished if we disregard or take as 'self-evident' the manifoldness of our experience in terms of the plurality of time's phenomenology in a human lifetime, despite the fact that human subjectivity (in all its repetitiveness and richness) is not all there is to being. Perhaps for all of us, summers lasted longer when we were children and the nights before a vacation never seem to have reached the morning. In other words, the way things become *this 'counted' plurality in the now* is inherent to how they can *be*. Due to this, we might be tempted, for a moment, to think that time can be best conceptualized in a formal sense, i.e. as a generic mode of being (generic as a passage from being to non-being and vice versa). This formal reformulation of time in terms of being, would allow us, again only for a moment, to think

---

6 Perhaps in this informed context we can read Aristotle's question 'would there be time if there were no soul?' which brings to the open the relation between time and the activity of the soul. There would be no time in the full meaning of the term Aristotle has given to it (see *Physics*: 223a21–29), unless there is no 'counting'. Time would not exist as a number *of* (change), but *as* before and after. There will be *change*, or in our broader context said, there will be plurality (as "that which is divisible potentially into parts which are not continuous, *Metaphysics*:1020a12–13), but not a *defined* [*peperasmenon*, which derives from *peras*, limit] plurality [*plethos*] of change. Obviously, time *is not* qua *limited plurality* whenever the *numbering subject is not*.

the plurality of times without privileging one over others, by recognizing the fact that time *is* differently configured for the human subject and, for instance, the whales; and by avoiding the danger of succumbing to the wavering between the objective and the subjective approach, or subsuming the one to the other. However, formalized as a mode of being, 'time' is not sufficiently differentiated from a four dimensional manifold (as a topological space), which is why the mode of being would have to be further specified as engendering new conditions.

The essential link between time and subjectivity is the plurality of change, of alterations. Subjectivity is time as *otherness*, because time (and subjectivity) *is* emergence of other determinations, *creation* proper. And this was captured by the idea of *self-dilation* (see Castoriadis *IIS*; *WIF*), i.e. that the 'world' accessible to us is never given once and for all. It seems one should never tire from emphasizing that this 'self-dilation' is not self-dilation of a self-transparent mathematical ellipse, but of a time-bound heterogeneity.

Subjectivity beyond algorithms

It is common today to model personality in terms of cognitive multi-level patterning, which relates human behaviour to biases in processing certain types of information or attaining personal goals. Cognitive models relate personality to a variety of neuronal, computational and self-regulative processes; they acknowledge that 'subjective belief and objective reality' may diverge, sharply in the case of mental disorders, but they give an account of personal dynamic patterns by referring to adaptive and maladaptive elements. To give one example, we read that "[a]daptive significance of these biases is typically indirect (except, perhaps, at the *extreme* of abnormal personality) in facilitating or hindering skill acquisition" (Matthews 2008: 69, my emphasis). These models are *adaptational*, rather than psychological, and as such, they have trouble accounting for the 'extremes' in a substantial way.

The question is what are the logical (transcendental) conditions for the empirical-psychological 'extreme' to be *effective* at all? But first of all, what about this extreme? Is it *only* an extreme (which would amount to saying it is not relevant for understanding human personality)? The latter claim is evocative of the historically predominant large sample approach in psychological research, where the 'unit' of analysis is not individuals, but populations, and where the single individual variation is generally not being considered 'important' unless that variation appears in many individuals[7]. Surely, it is another topic whether or why a researcher is puzzled more by the fact that we rest when tired, eat when hungry, perform badly under condition x, or more by the fact that we resist *and* obey authority, undergo plastic surgery when the nose is functioning just fine, paint and write, or *talk* regardless of the hour. This is not to say that we do not have biological limits, but that we *can* thwart, detach from or refuse to accept these limits, oftentimes to our own peril, for we are not bound exclusively by the 'functional' logic. The logic we are bound by is *consubstantially* social and psychical. In other words, a proper *psychological* account recognizes that human psychism is viable only in and through the social, and that the psychical and the social are mutually amenable, even if irreducible to each other (subjectivity as having its positive condition in both language and imagination).

Castoriadis emphasized that the human psyche sustains effective livability of the domination of representational pleasure over organ pleasure (cf. "Logic, Imagination, Reflection; The State of the Subject Today", *WIF*: 246–72) and articulated this detachment in canonical

---

7 Historically, the research interest which depends upon substantial change in considerable numbers – inherent to the evolutionary framework – was a legacy of Francis Galton, the founder of differential psychology, who interpreted individual departures from the average as hereditary deviations essential to natural selection in light of his cousin's theory of evolution, Charles R. Darwin. For a more contemporary account of historical implications and related issues see Desrosières (1998), Rabinowitz (1984) and Borsboom (2005). See also Molenaar (2004) for an insightful account on the ongoing paradigmatic shift in psychology, of a Kuhnian type, related to the large sample approach in psychology.

coding of biological satisfaction as one of the necessary conditions for various human phenomena to be possible (e.g. the above mentioned 'extreme', psychosis, language, art, reflective thought, deliberate activity or the disconnection of sexuality from reproduction). But this 'break' in instinctual regulation, as I want to read Castoriadis, *is* consubstantially psychical and social-historical.

When articulating the logical (transcendental) structure of subjectivity – and related to our discussion of time and the essential link between content and a count of things in *arithmos* – Castoriadis writes in the *IIS* that there is no thinking subject except as the disposition of contents (cf. "every particular content can be bracketed but not any content as such" *IIS*: 247). They are, as if, the '*hyle*' (Gr. ὕλη)[8] of our thinking. This is only another way of saying that there are no 'pure forms of intuition' cleaned up from *any* content, containing nothing at all. But what exactly does it mean to say that content is an effective condition for 'subject' (cf. *IIS*)? Put simply, it means that subjectivity is not a neutral medium (just as time is not a neutral, purified medium of successive coexistence). Subjectivity attests that time, space and *that* which unfolds are separable only, to use Aristotle's language, in account, but not in extension.

Subjectivity cannot be explained in terms of an 'algorithm', however elegant the algorithm might be. In this sense, and in light of today's advance of technology and the possibility to map extremely subtle processes on anatomical, molecular or functional level of the human brain, it is important to emphasize that the human psyche implies the intractable representation-affect-intention mode. I presume this is why Lev Vygotsky (1896–1933) wrote in 1933 that thought is not begotten by thought, but engendered by the affective-volitional tendency, which holds the last 'why' in the analysis of thinking (cf. Vygotsky 1986: 34–35). The intractability of the representation-affect-intention is perhaps

---

8 I am using the term *hyle* (Gr. ὕλη) as in Aristotle, which in the English translation of the term as *matter* partly loses the active aspect implied in *hyle*.

more overt when we consider the presentment proper to dreams: their intertwined and here-and-now way of 'saying' that the person whom I look at and who looks-at-me-and-salutes-me-while-holding-a-glass-of-red-wine, is a half-man half-owl; or that out of the snowy forest landscape a covered-with-snow but beautiful-and-big deer awakens just in front of me.

Conclusion

The 'trace' of traditional ontology where the 'pure' (Being/being, multiple, Truth, etc.) is conceptualized Elsewhere (perhaps 'before counting has taken place', cf. Badiou 2001) fortunately cannot dismiss the fact that mathematics cannot explain the world. The thematized snares in this paper were only 'structurally representative' of why that is so, whereas Castoriadis's understanding of time as unfolding of otherness was seen as substantially linked to Aristotle's usage of number in his definition of time. Evidently, the way we are as subjectivity is woven in this time-bound alterity, for the way things become *this heterogeneous multitude in the now* is inherent to how they *are*. Awakened or asleep, the passage from being to non-being and from non-being to being, at least for us, is not 'numerical' in important respects of our lives, and certainly not given once and for all.

References

Aristotle (1995) *On the Soul* (Ancient Greek text with an English translation by W. S. Hett). London: Harvard University Press.

Aristotle (1936) *Aristotle's Physics. A Revised Text with Introduction and Commentary by W.D. Ross* New York: Clarendon Press.

Aristotle *Metaphysics* (Ancient Greek text with English translation by Hugh Tredennick) 2 vols. Ed.G.P. Goold. Loeb Classical Library. London: Heinemann (1956–58).

Augustine (1963) *The Confessions of St. Augustine,* trans. Warner Rex. New York: Penguin.

Badiou, Alain (2001) *Ethics: an Essay on the Understanding of Evil,* trans. Peter Hallward. London: Verso.

Bergson, Henri (1889[1921]) *Essai sur les données immédiates de la conscience.* Paris: F. Alcan.

Borsboom, David (2005) *Measuring the Mind: Conceptual Issues in contemporary psychometrics.* Cambridge: Cambridge University Press.

Castoriadis, Cornelius (2007) *Figures of the Thinkable,* trans. Helen Arnold. Stanford CA: Stanford University Press.

Castoriadis, Cornelius (1997) *World in Fragments: Writings on Politics, Society, Psychoanalysis, and the Imagination,* ed. and trans. David Ames Curtis, Stanford CA: Stanford University Press.

Castoriadis, Cornelius (1993) "The Institution of Society and Religion", *Thesis Eleven* 35:1, 1–17.

Castoriadis, Cornelius (1987) *The Imaginary Institution of Society,* trans. Kathleen Blamey. Cambridge, Mass.: MIT Press.

Desrosières, Alain (1998) *The politics of large numbers.* Cambridge: Harvard University Press.

Einstein, Albert (1952) "Relativity and the Problem of Space" appendix five in 15th edition of *Relativity: The Special and the General Theory,* trans. Robert William Lawson. London: Methuen & Co.Ltd. [1954], 135–57.

Galton, Francis (1901) "Biometry", in *Biometrika,* Vol. I, No.1, 7–10.

Galton, Francis, Pearson, Karl, Weldon R.F.Walter, and Davenport, B. Charles (1901) "Editorial", *Biometrika,* Vol. I, No. 1, (Oct.1901) 1–6. Biometrika Trust.

Heidegger, Martin (1962) *Being and Time,* trans. John Macquarrie and Edward Robinson. Oxford: Blackwell.

Klein, Jacob (1968) *Greek Mathematical Thought and the Origin of Algebra*. Cambridge, Mass.: MIT Press.

Matthews, Gerald (2008) 'Personality and Information Processing: A Cognitive-Adaptive Theory', in G. J. Boyle, G. Mathews & D.H. Saklofske (eds.) *The Sage Handbook of Personality Theory and Assessment Vol.1 Personality Theories and Models*. London: Sage, 56–79.

Molenaar, C.M. Peter (2004). "A manifesto on Psychology as idiographic science: Bringing the person back into scientific psychology, this time forever". *Measurement* 2(4), 201–18.

Rabinowitz, F. Michael (1984) "The heredity-environment controversy: A Victorian legacy". *Canadian Psychology*, 25(3), 159–66.

Autonomy and Self-Alteration

Stathis Gourgouris

To think is not to get out of the cave; it is not to replace the uncertainty of shadows by the clear-cut outlines of things themselves, the flame's flickering glow by the light of the true sun. To think is to enter the Labyrinth; more exactly, it is to make be and appear a Labyrinth when we might have stayed 'lying among the flowers, facing the sky.' It is to lose oneself amidst galleries which exist only because we never tire of digging them; to turn round and round at the end of a *cul-de-sac* whose entrance has been shut off behind us – until, inexplicably, this spinning round opens up in the surrounding walls cracks which offer passage.[1]

Cornelius Castoriadis, *Carrefours du labyrinthe* (1978)

Castoriadis's rumination disengages thinking from all Platonic derivatives that map the journey to Enlightenment, which would pertain to a whole range of transcendentalist aspirations, revelations, epiphanies, but also intensions of perfectibility, including any pretensions to arrive at a clearing (*Lichtung*). He sees thinking as a peculiar mode of architecture in which the instrumental is always secondary to the creative. That this architecture is labyrinthine means that it is ultimately without end,

---

1 Translated by the author.

despite its many, its ubiquitous, dead-ends. It is without end because, on its own terms, it is interminable and boundless, because the limits that emerge on every turn are of the thinker's own making. Castoriadis's mode is to leave behind the elegy-inducing Rilke for the enigma-provoking Kafka, recognizing in the latter's vein that the labyrinthine galleries of one's burrow are one's thoughts in-the-making, with yet an important deviation: not as ideal projections of self-making (as for Kafka's paranoid architectural creature) but as wondrous openings of self-othering. In this respect, thought becomes quintessentially *poietic*, that is to say, creative/destructive: a (self-)altering force that sometimes produces *cul-de-sacs* and other times opens windows onto chaos. Indeed, Castoriadis's description of how a dead-end becomes a window onto chaos is one of the most dramatic encapsulations of his entire way of thinking. To think is thus to enact an alterity both toward yourself and toward the world. It is not to derive or emerge from an alterity, and surely not to desire alterity as *telos* – the labyrinth, a space resplendent with otherness, is always one's own.

The coveted object in this statement is some measure of the impossible, of what indeed appears impossible because the horizon of possibility in the perception is rendered inadequate by the reigning preconception. The impetus here is to imagine that human beings are characterized precisely by their daring to make the impossible happen, which has nothing to do with making miracles but it does have to do with encountering and acting in the world with a sense of wonder. Enquiring what animates and encapsulates this daring for the impossible will lead us to the fact that *human-being*, as a living condition, is immanently differential, which is to say that alterity is intrinsic to it.

The way of this inquiry is to contemplate an admittedly impossible concept: *self-alteration*. Strictly speaking, self-alteration signifies a process by which alterity is internally produced, dissolving the very thing that enables it, the very thing whose existence derives meaning from being altered, *from othering itself*. In terms of inherited thought, this is indeed an impossible concept – at least, within the conceptual framework that identifies alterity to be external, a framework, I might add, that is essential to any semantics (and, of course, politics) of identity. Such framework cannot but vehemently defend, by contradistinction, the bona fide existence of what can thus be called without hesitation 'internality,' even if, in a gesture of cognitive magnanimity, it may accept a fragmented, fissured, indeterminate, or even boundless internality. But internality thus conceived, however 'open-ended' it claims to be, cannot enact self-alteration because alterity will always remain external to it, precisely so as to secure its meaning. Having said that, let us also concede that this framework of an internally/externally conceived distinction of identity and difference gives meaning to the language I am using at this very moment. It is, inevitably, the framework that enables us to build communicative avenues by positing totalities and identities that we consider recognizable even if we might significantly disagree over their content. I understand that, in this framework, self-alteration is an impossible concept, but I have a hunch that it is nonetheless possible, that it *takes place* in the only way anything can take place in the world – *in* history, *as* history. At the limit, the conceptual inquiry I am suggesting, labyrinthine though it is in its own turn, configures its groundwork in the world of human action, not in the universe of concepts and propositions.

I

Self-alteration is a central concept in Castoriadis's thought, and we could say that he understands it as essential to all living being – perhaps even go so far as to say that it is tantamount to *physis* itself. In this first order, the concept owes a lot to Aristotle's notion of movement as change – in Greek *alloiosis*. But though Aristotle may be Castoriadis's favorite philosopher, Castoriadis is by no means an Aristotelian; for him there is no *physis* without *nomos*. This comes into play particularly when we discuss the world of the human being – the most peculiar of all living beings. In this register, one other word for alteration in the Greek, which we find in Castoriadis's Greek texts, is more provoking: *heterōsis*. It is this meaning that I use as an anchor, in order to examine self-alteration, in the world of the human being, both as a psycho-ontological and as a social-historical dimension.

A basic kind of starting point would be to consider self-alteration in the context of Castoriadis's persistent view of the living being as self-creative and of the human being, specifically, as a social-historical being that exists via its interminable and indeed unlimited capacity for the creation/destruction of form in the world. Hence, self-alteration is articulated in direct connection with self-creation as an ontological standpoint that Castoriadis understands as *vis formandi*, a kind of morphopoietic force or life-power that reconfigures the world by creating radically new forms or indeed, more precisely, radically other forms. It is important to understand the *co-incidence* of this notion of self-creative being with a destructive, catastrophic, element. Castoriadis is not consistent on this matter, but one often sees in his writings the formulation *creation/destruction*. Certainly, in his analysis of tragedy (*Antigone* especially) and in much of his discussion of pre-Socratic cosmology, where the emphasis is on an ever-present dyadic cosmological imaginary (*apeiron/peras, chaos/kosmos*), no notion of creation can be configured without a simultaneously enacted destruction.[2] The crucial element here is the simultaneity of two distinct forces. We are certainly not speaking of some monstrous concept, like the neo-liberal notion of 'creative destruction' or some such thing. Nor are we speaking of any sort of simple dialectical relation, despite the inherent antagonism of such originary dyadic frameworks; in Castoriadis at least, the matter of dialectics as preferable epistemological mode is ambiguous.

---

2 See "Aeschylian Anthropogony and Sophoclean Self-Creation of *Anthropos*" (*FT*: 1–20) and *Ce qui fait la Grèce I* (Paris: Seuil, 2004).

This simultaneous or *co-incident* double figure elucidates one of the most controversial of Castoriadis's philosophical figures, the notion of creation *ex nihilo*. Given the texts, we do not really need to wonder why Castoriadis insists on this figure. His entire anthropo-ontological framework is based on the idea that what distinguishes the human animal specifically is the capacity to create form (*eidos*) that is entirely unprecedented, previously inconceivable, and indeed nonexistent in any sense prior to the moment and fact of its creation. He insists time and again that creation does not entail the production of difference but the emergence of otherness. This capacity for the wholly new, wholly other, is what distinguishes the radical imagination. The *ex nihilo* is there to accentuate the fact that we are not talking about reformulation, or infinite variation, or creative assembly or rearrangement of already existing forms. His example that the invention of the wheel is a more radical and splendorous creation in the universe than a new galaxy is well known, for every new galaxy emerging in space is ultimately but another instance of the galaxy form, whereas the wheel is entirely unprecedented.[3] The often used idiomatic injunction in English encapsulates what Castoriadis has in mind: 'you're reinventing the wheel!' means you're not being creative, you're not using your imagination, you are wasting your effort in reproducing what exists (however we are to consider the merits or inevitabilities of this kind of effort).

But Castoriadis – especially in late years and in order to defend himself from likely misunderstandings – insisted on the clarification that *ex nihilo* did not mean *in nihilo* or *cum nihilo*. Unprecedented radical creation *out of nothing* does not mean with(in) nothing, *in a vacuum*. On the contrary, what makes it radical is precisely that it takes place in

---

3 "The wheel revolving around an axis is an absolute ontological creation. It is a greater creation, it weighs, ontologically, more than a new galaxy that would arise tomorrow evening out of nothing between the Milky Way and the Andromeda. For *there are already* millions of galaxies – but the person who invented the wheel, or a written sign, was imitating and repeating *nothing* at all" (*IIS*: 197).

history, *as* history – that indeed it makes history anew. There is no way such creation can register as history anew without destroying, in some form or other, what exists in place, whether we conceive this as simply what resists the new or merely what resides there unwitting of whatever will newly emerge to displace it or efface it. New social-imaginary creations do contribute to the vanishing of social-imaginary institutions already there. That is why we do not have Pharaonic priests, Spartan warriors, or Knights of the Round Table running around in the streets of New York or the suburbs of Paris. That's why the North American Indians, who now exist in the impoverished universe of the reservation, cannot possibly imagine themselves as free roaming and proud warriors, and even if they could – beyond the patented clichés of Hollywood Westerns – they certainly cannot be it.

In retrospect, it is possible to construct a description – to write a history – of how and what elements and processes characterize the creation of new social-historical being. A common example in Castoriadis, discussed at various junctures in his work and arguably culminating in the years that made up the seminars of *Ce qui fait la Grèce I* (1982–83) is how the specifics of the Cleisthenes reforms that encapsulate the creation of Athenian democracy as new social-historical being are 'traceable' – if that is the proper word – in the complexities of the social-imaginary institution of the Greek *polis*, which Castoriadis duly points all the way back to the earliest Greek textual documentation – Homer, Hesiod, Anaximander, Sappho. In other words, Castoriadis's theory of creation *ex nihilo* is not entirely unrelated to various theories of discontinuity in history. I cannot pursue here this line of comparison, but it is a worthwhile path of reflection to consider the line, otherwise alien to Castoriadis, that extends (in the French tradition at least) from Bachelard to Foucault. If we do not adhere dogmatically to the notion of the 'epistemological rupture' characteristic of this line – in the same way that we would not heed the accusations against Castoriadis that creation *ex nihilo* ushers some sort of theology in the back door – then we might arrive at a more nuanced understanding of the notion.[4]

But there is also another dimension to this issue that I do not think has been adequately attended to. In his classic essay "Done and To Be Done" from 1989, Castoriadis speaks of what grants validity to creation – its encounter with the world. I quote extensively:

> Newton certainly did not 'discover', he invented and created the theory of gravitation; but it happens (and this is the why we are still talking about it) that this creation *encounters* [*rencontre*] in a fruitful way *what is*, in one of its strata. […] We create knowledge. In certain cases (mathematics) we also create, thereby, the *outside time*. In other cases (mathematical physics) we create under the constraint of encounter; it is this encounter that validates or invalidates our creations (*CR:* 396).

And later on:

> To the extent that we can effectively comprehend something about a foreign society, or say something valid about it, we proceed to a re-creation of significations, which encounter the originary creation. […] A being without the re-creative capacity of the imagination will understand nothing about it (*CR:* 396–97).

Let us focus for a moment on two elements: "the constraint of encounter" and "the re-creative capacity of the imagination". The first is precisely to emphasize that *ex nihilo* does not mean *in nihilo* or *cum nihilo*. Not only is radical creation out of nothing always enacted in the world, but it is enacted as and constrained by an encounter. The 'nothing' out of which radical creation emerges exists, in the most precise sense, *in* the world; it is not, in other words, some sort of transcendental nowhere. And though we should not at all compromise the notion – we indeed mean out of

4 For a recent such example, see Van Eynde (2008).

nothing; we mean, in the ancient Greek sense, to note the passage 'out of non-being into being' – we have to allow ourselves the paradoxical capacity to imagine both that this nothing, this non-being, is worldly and that, instantly upon coming to be something, this newly created being registers its worldliness by an unavoidable encounter with what exists, whether in the dimension of logic and calculation (what Castoriadis calls, by means of a neologism, *ensidic* – ensemblist-identitary) or beyond it, in the *poietic* dimension as such.

Second, it is not enough to stick to a kind of straight surging forth of the new, of the other. We need also to put our imagination to work on re-creating the entire domain of the surging forth, the full dimensions of emergence of the new. This too can be understood in different ways. One recognizable instance of imaginative re-creation is the hermeneutical act itself, as Suzi Adams has pointed out acutely (see Adams 2011). This is at play not only in philosophical work but surely in historical work. The best historians are the ones who can re-creatively imagine the horizon of emergence of the historical shift they are investigating. But in both cases (philosophical and historical), as I have argued in *Does Literature Think?* (Gourgouris 2003), one engages in the work of *poiein* – of imagining form in the case of radical creation; of shaping matter into form (which is to say: of signifying form) in the case of imaginative re-creation. The *poietic* dimension in society's imaginary institution pertains indeed to society's creative/destructive capacity, and is essential both to the radical interrogation of (self-)instituted laws/forms that enables in turn the radical creation of new forms – in other words, both to the question of autonomy and the question of self-alteration.

II

This epistemological level of situating self-alteration – but also onto-logical, to the degree that it conceptualizes a *physis* – should serve as a certain groundwork, shifting though it is, which needs to be elucidated, however, by a psychic dimension, in order to lead us to the social-historical concerns that pertain to the *physis* of human-being as such. For Castoriadis, this is the crossroads between his psychoanalytic writing and his philosophical writing, where self-alteration becomes a key notion entwining the elaboration of a politics of sublimation, on the one hand, and the project of social autonomy, on the other.[5]

As an impossibly quick clarification, let me recount that, for Castoriadis, sublimation is not the transmutation of libidinal drive to the non-sexualized activity of the imagination, as is traditionally conceived in the wider sense of the so-called repression-hypothesis – in two ways: First, if nothing else, on account of an unquestionable human capacity for and proclivity toward non-functional sexuality that foregrounds sexuality first and foremost as a matter of the pleasure of fantasy (that is, the privilege of phantasmatic representation over simple organ pleasure). Because the pleasure of fantasy informs every aspect of human existence, it becomes difficult to contend in what sense sublimatory investment involves indeed desexualized pleasure. In other words, the primacy of phantasmatic (or representational) pleasure still occurs on the somatic or sensuous register. It is not meant to be understood as some sort of abstract spiritualization. Even ascetics experience pleasure in their asceticism, and the *jouissance* of mysticism over the ages is all too evident in a variety of expressions. What matters is the autonomization of desire, which goes hand in hand with the defunctionalization of desire – the *co-incidence* is precisely what makes the human imagination independent of instinct or drive and, in this respect, 'functional' in an altogether different sense of the term.

Second: because sublimation is the necessary mode of socialization –

---

5 Castoriadis elaborates on his own theory of sublimation at great length in his signature work *IIS*, but for a concise depiction of his psychoanalytic theory in general (in which sublimation and, of course, self-alteration play a central role), see also the psychoanalytic section in the collection of essays *WIF*: 125–212 and *FT*: 153–222. For an elaboration on this intricate crossroads in Castoriadis's work (and a predicate to this section here) see my essay "Philosophy and Sublimation" (Gourgouris 1997).

or precisely, as Castoriadis says, of humanization – that is, the mode by which the indomitable psyche cathects its primal desire for omnipotence onto the pleasure of social community, at the expense, of course, of this omnipotence but at the gain of the 'security' of ego-constitution through the provision of meaning (with all the traumatic elements this entails). Because, however, socialization/humanization is a social-historical process and sublimatory objects are always part of the imaginary institution of society (even when they are objects of radical interrogation of society, or indeed even when they are objects of society's destruction, suicidal or genocidal), sublimation is not some sort of natural process, with consistent and immanent elements, but always involves a politics. It is precisely the politics of sublimation that makes an inquiry of this properly psychoanalytic domain be at the same time an interrogation of the political ontology of subjugation and heteronomy against which the concept of self-alteration emerges as an emancipatory force.

The problem of heteronomy in sublimation is insurmountable within a certain Freudian register, insofar as it partakes of a basic contradiction in the psychoanalytic epistemological universe, which Freud never quite theorized, perhaps because he never resolved for himself the conceptual struggle inherent in the psychoanalytic project between the phylogenetic and the social-historical nature of the human. I'm obviously referring to Freud's inability to reconcile the fact that, on the one hand, civilization must be condemned for repressing human drives in the service of domination and exploitation, while on the other hand, this same repression of drives (according to the notion of the 'renunciation of instinct') must be accepted as a prerequisite for humanity's actualization of its higher potential, a prerequisite of civilization's very existence. This, in Freud, necessarily links sublimation with repression and, given his admitted lack of theoretical elaboration on the work of sublimation, becomes responsible for the dismissive (or at best, narrowly conceived) treatment of sublimation at the hands of many psychoanalytic and cultural theorists. Sublimation has thus been tainted with the mark of a perverse condition, as a sort of necessary evil inevitable for mental health. The implication can only be that the human animal is irrevocably perverse or pathological by nature. We can say a lot of things about the human animal's biological incapacity, but it is terribly problematic to consider it pathological; the very assumption of 'incapacity' renders impossible the very concept of the normal and thereby its critical dismantling.

There is indeed another implication, which I cannot address here, but deserves to be mentioned: the fact that a radical indecision arises at the core of psychoanalytic theory and practice, a split between the emancipatory project of liberating repressed libidinal potential and a kind of ingrained conservatism in recognizing repression as the necessary cost for the progress of civilization. Ego-psychology, as we know, bypasses the dilemma by making a conscious decision in favor of the second 'solution' and subscribing directly to what we could call the domestication of the unconscious, whereby 'liberation' of repressed desire is to be managed by an all-powerful 'healthy' ego that will, for all practical purposes, replace the injunctions of the superego with its own. To what extend this entails a double repression in turn, a repression not only of unconscious potential but also of superego activity – thereby occluding the workings of authority for the subject – should be evident. I hardly mean to disavow the standard thesis that recognizes the superego as the psychic locus of heteronomy. But at this point I am not concerned with sublimation as a proto-formative process but as a practico-poietic process, and here the ego (secondarily but for me essentially) becomes key. The ego is the locus of society's *conscious* agency, and a heteronomous ego becomes the agent of heteronomous sublimation on grand social-cultural scale. This is precisely a matter of the *politics* of sublimation and cannot be exorcised by some sort of 'pure' psychoanalysis.

An evocative way to consider this problem is the radical significance of Castoriadis's reversal of Freud's classic motto to *Wo Ich bin, soll Es auftauchen* (Where I am, It shall spring forth) (*WIF*: 128). That is to say, the creative/destructive capacity of the unconscious will emerge in the ego's location in such a way as to disrupt the ego's reliance on gaining signification solely from the social-imaginary institution present in the superego. This disruption hardly means the end of sublimation. Such an end is essentially impossible; were it to occur, it would signify the evolutionary regression of the human animal. But it does mean, potentially, the alteration of the standard ways of sublimation, as we know them in history. In a concrete sense, it also means an altered relation to history as such, meaning, as ceaseless flow of human thought and praxis.

Let us return to Castoriadis's insistence that sublimation is tantamount to humanization. The point is that sublimation is not merely the hand of civilization upon the human (the classic repression hypothesis), but the process by which one becomes human, insofar as the monadic core of the psyche cannot possibly survive on its own as an organism, driven by its insatiable desire for singular omnipotence at all costs. Sublimation, in other words, does not enact the agency of civilization and it surely involves something more than the creation of civilization: it is an element intrinsic to the process of human existence that makes human existence possible, an *autopoietic* element. Of course, from the standpoint of the monadic core of the psyche, sublimation will always appear as – and *is* in fact – heteronomous rule. From this standpoint, sublimation does entail violent disruption of the plenitude – the closure – of proto-psychic existence and its relentless refusal of reality. At this level, heteronomous sublimation is not a problem; it is a fact. But the level of the monadic core of the psyche is hardly a sustainable standpoint from which to understand (even to view) the complications of human existence. The problem arises precisely at the moment this elemental but *partial* fact is taken for the whole.

What do I mean? Castoriadis's insistence on the defunctionalized nature of the human psyche, even at the level of the monadic core – a point, by the way, entirely commensurate with Freud – enables us to understand that, though it is indeed the work of the social imaginary institution, sublimation is not enacted as external imposition (nor should we be tricked to think that it is a brute internalization of superego-type injunctions). What enables it to happen is the psyche's own ability to operate and respond at the level of representation, of imagistic flux (*Vorstellung*). The psyche's imaginary capacity exists already at the level of drives; it is not a meta-attribute, some sort of *cultured* capacity. It is already present at the moment sublimation is enacted. We might say, it enables sublimation precisely because it provides a language that can translate society's forms into psychic terms. In this respect, though the monadic core of the psyche experiences a violation and cannot but resist, it also experiences – against itself but from within itself – an elemental pleasure, which is what ultimately allows sublimation to work. Otherwise, given the insatiable autoscopic nature of the psyche, no sublimation would have been socially effective and one can only wonder what this would mean for human history.[6]

This tempers the sublimation-as-repression theory, if it does not render it inadequate, because simultaneously with the experience of radical violation of plenitude there is an equally powerful experience of elemental pleasure, an immanent pleasure one would say, in the object-investment that sublimation affords. One could choose to pathologize this double condition – which is actually to say, *naturalize* it – or one could choose to view it in social-historical terms, which would entail making a political decision as to the significance and distinction, indeed the value, among the multitude of sublimatory objects in the course of human history. In this respect, the heteronomy of sublimation, simply understood, does become a problem precisely because it is not a *naturally*

---

6 A learned and thought-provoking discussion of how the psychic monad may enact/be enacted by the autonomous subject is conducted by Klimis (2007: 25–54).

inevitable outcome, but is rather conditioned by the historical dimensions of social imaginary institution.

III

Already, given the terms of this rumination, a trajectory is set up to pass through the conceptual straits of alterity with the enormous body of heterological discourses that shadow it. Be that as it may, the impetus is to attain, in a certain dialectical sense, an *altered relation to alterity*, with an aspiration ultimately to counteract the allure of transcendence that has become elemental in the contemporary lexicon of the Other, to such an extent as to reproduce consistently a cognitive figure of transcendence that is itself untranscendable. At the same time, I am aware that this trajectory thereby plunges us into the chimerical waters of the Self, whose own conceptual lexicon has long been the target of the most radical tendencies in psychoanalytic and feminist theory, as well as today's insurrectionary politics.[7] This is all the more complicated by the often irresistible association of discourses concerning the subject with discourses concerning the self, which makes conspicuously evident indeed how problematic – that is to say, how political – becomes any theory of subjectification insofar as it must involve a theory (or, in essence, a politics) of sublimation, whether acknowledged or not. In the last instance, we must restate the utterly obvious because it is so crucial: subject-formation is a political matter, as it signifies the inaugural negotiation with power – indeed, with the power of the other, or with power *as* other, but also, inevitably, with power as altering (*othering*) force. It is this latter aspect that problematizes the entire equation, raising, by its very constitution, the question of the political pure and simple:

---

7 Foremost in the feminist deconstruction of the problematic of the Self, of course, has been the work of Judith Butler in the last two decades. As for the most ingeniously damning invocation of the chimerical abyss of the Self – 'whatever prosthesis it takes to hold on to an "I"' – in recent political texts I would select The Coming Insurrection pamphlet (The Invisible Committee n.y.), the First Circle of which should be ingested by us all as ineluctable pharmakon.

Where does the power of othering, of alteration, of transformation, reside? Wherefrom does it emerge? What is its referential frame? Its location? Its standpoint of interlocution? And finally, what is its mode and terms of articulation?

In *The Psychic Life of Power*, Judith Butler has made a bold intervention in response to these questions, working from the Hegelian basis of the negotiation of power in the dialectics of self-recognition but clearly exceeding it – or more precisely, altering its terms – so that the always theoretically precarious terrain of the construction of the subject can re-emerge in its full complicity with the construction of subjection. Butler's overall understanding of the forces involved in this complicitous relation is profoundly dialectical. Indeed, in a basic sense, it forges an altered relation to dialectical thinking, which demonstrates the capacity of dialectical thinking to frame questions and responses that outmaneuver the deadlock of identitarian logic. Let us traverse the terms of her argument for a moment, with an eye to their implications as groundwork for an inquiry into self-alteration.

Butler predicates her argument on the rather controversial assertion that subject-formation is always intertwined with subjection: that is, with subordination to the power of an other, or more precisely, to power as an other entity that retains the force of its otherness even when it is (as it must be) 'internalized' in the process of the subject's emergence into being. Internalization here does not mean the ideological assumption of the terms of external power, in the classic sense of all political and psychological figures of subjugation, precisely because, Butler argues, the moment of internalization is itself a formative moment – indeed, a *transformative* moment – whereby the subject's inaugural act of existence signifies both the 'absorption' of power as otherness and the enactment of the forming capacity of this power.

In other words, there is a foundational simultaneity at work in the inaugural moment of subjectification that points both inwardly toward the psychic nucleus and yet outwardly in excess of the determinant domain of the other.[8] This paradoxical simultaneity, whereby the other both forms the subject and yet is formed by the subject, plunges the entire ontological equation into uncertainty and makes signification enigmatic. Butler calls it explicitly a 'tropological quandary,' mining from language itself the full range of the Greek meaning of *tropē* (both turn and manner, shift and figure):

> The form this power takes is relentlessly marked by a figure of turning, a turning back upon itself or even a turning *on* oneself. This figure operates as part of the explanation of how a subject is produced, and so there is no subject, strictly speaking, who makes this turn. On the contrary, the turn appears to function as a tropological inauguration of the subject, a founding moment whose ontological status remains permanently uncertain (Butler 1997: 3–4).[9]

In this respect, the very language of subject-formation turns on a figure of uncertainty, whereby all structural and temporal order (of principles, elements, forces, loci, etc.) makes for an undeconstructible enigma.

Right away then, the discourse of subjection as discourse of subject-formation can hardly be mapped as a specifically directional vector force, the force of subjugation pure and simple. As order (*taxis*) is foundationally enigmatic, no paratactic or syntactic (or even tactical, in the context of strategic) arrangement of power can be assumed. Taking this rhetorical rubric to its full extent, I would argue here the same for subordination (the *hypotactic* element) in a grammatical but also philosophical sense, something that Butler does not address as such but, nonetheless, leads us to by implication. In any case, though power does exist 'external' to the

---

8 Reiterating what I mentioned at the outset, the inner/outer distinction is just a figure of rhetorical usefulness. This is not to say that the distinction is meaningless; rather, its meaning is a constructed condition of difference, as will become evident in the discussion that follows.

9 Henceforth cited in the text, as *P*, followed by page number.

subject – by definition, insofar as it is recognized as a formative force – its externality is impossible to determine, precisely because, in a dialectical sense, power is itself subjected to the transformative force of the subject's inaugural act of making this power 'internal.' Conversely, the subject's inaugural position, as itself 'external' to power (to whose formative force it is subjected), is also impossible to determine. There is no *a priori* subject. Rather, the subject enters the domain of determination at the very moment it 'internalizes' power as its own, thereby transforming – *altering* – power both in terms of its location and the elements of its force. It is crucial to keep in mind here that this alteration is a moment of rupture, an interruption. Otherwise, internalization would merely signify the worst aspect of heteronomous enslavement, and the significational alterity in the force of alteration would be entirely lost. This is why Butler repeatedly insists on the discontinuity between "the power that initiates the subject" and "the power that is the subject's agency" (*P*:12).

The logic in the figural encounter that Butler describes resonates uncannily with Castoriadis's own psychoanalytic account of both subject-formation and social-imaginary institution. The similarity of both registers is quite remarkable, with some important differences in language – Castoriadis does not grant such authorizing force to 'power' but prefers to keep in this position the term 'society' – and in this respect it deserves a study on its own. For our purposes, however, let me note the following: Whenever Castoriadis speaks of imaginary institution he always assumes a groundless, abyssal simultaneity at the origin, a simultaneity that thus forms a consubstantial, co-determinant, co-incident origin – what he explicitly calls "the primitive circle of creation" (*WIF*: 315). In his basic terms, every society is the 'subject' of its imaginary institution in the sense that every society emerges from the magma of its own significations: significations which society institutes as its own at the very time it is instituted by them, since, like the subject, no society can exist a priori to a social imaginary – there is no vacuum space in history. To say that society is the subject (and conversely, that the subject is an institution of society) is neither to imply a notion of collective consciousness (or for that matter, collective unconscious) nor to assume that subjects are, simply speaking, social-historical products. Society/subject is a dialectical form that has no a priori origin and no teleological meaning. Precisely because there is no historical vacuum, the subject is always instituted as a social form insofar as it assumes the imaginary significations particular to the social-historical moment that pertains to it. At the same time, however, social-imaginary significations at any historical moment are themselves meaningless (i.e., unsignifiable) without the subject that institutes them: confers upon them relevant meaning.[10]

Castoriadis conceptualizes this structure in the psychoanalytic terms that pertain to subjectification, as well as in the domain he calls 'the radical imagination,' which enables him to speak in terms of an ontology of society, of *physis* with *nomos*. At the level of the radical imaginary, the untamable core of the psyche encounters what appears to it to be the pure alterity of societal institution in a moment that signals simultaneously the psyche's defeat and emancipation: the inaugural moment of subject-formation. I'm reiterating that, for Castoriadis, the monadic core of the psyche remains insubordinate to the power of societal institution, while thus providing the nuclear energy, so to speak, that powers the institution: it is, at a foundational level, the *instituting* imagination – limitless, indeterminable, unsignifiable, untamable, abyssal flux of image/affect/representation: pure *Vorstellung*. This psychical insubordination, even if consequent source of radical imagination, preserves the constitutive internal schism on which it leans – the fact that the first real stranger that rends asunder the primal corporeal undifferentiation of the psyche is the ego itself, that is, the psyche's very own renegade ambassador to the

---

10 Of the numerous texts Castoriadis has written on these matters, the most essential is "The State of the Subject Today" in *WIF*: 137-71.

outside world. The later psychoanalytic work of Castoriadis elucidates especially this primary production of otherness within, which animates the psyche with an elemental self-hatred that always lies in ambush even in the most extreme manifestations of primary narcissism (self-love). For Castoriadis, the radical hatred of the other, observed indicatively in racist affect, leans precisely on this outmaneuverable psychical self-hatred. What averts racist desire is, in this respect, a specific politics of sublimation that enables an encounter with otherness as difference instead of as existential threat to the self – in psychical terms, radical treason of self. Conversely, a politics of sublimation that empowers racist hatred always bears an intrinsic genocidal potential, even if it does not always reach this extent.[11]

Obviously, the psychic monad as such (as pure *Vorstellung*) is a nonsensical entity in any sort of simple terms of human-being. It is entirely meaningless and its survival hinges on its being endowed with meaning, with signification. Going back directly to Freud, in this respect, Castoriadis speaks of the psyche's translation of the images/affects/representations of societal institution at the very moment of this encounter, which may be conceived as a moment inaugurally, but is obviously conducted again and again in an individual's lifetime, insofar as subject-formation is never exhausted in a single instance but is inevitably an open-ended (re)iteration, a historical enactment. In this translation, the psyche receives the instituted significations that signify it as a subject in a given social-historical domain, in which (significations) it then invests – as it must, in order to emerge out of its autistic monadic condition – but in such a way as never to be reducible

---

11 Castoriadis's distinctive mark for the racist relation to the other is the commitment to the other's inconvertibility, that is, absolutely barring the other from possibly entering the domain of the self, an important notion to consider in the historical inquiry into the politics of religious conversion. This particular discussion is useful in corroborating the dimension of internal otherness, but it speaks to a much broader domain that cannot be, in this context, adequately dealt with. See Castoriadis's "Reflections on Racism" in *WIF*: 19–31 and "The Psychical and Social Roots of Hate" in *FT*: 153–59.

to the overall instituted signification. Were it to be so, the psyche would be terminally defeated and an unconscious would be unimaginable. This translation is therefore a *poietic* performance, a transformative act that subjects instituted signification to alteration. By the same token, subject-formation is the limitless process (indeed limited only by the certainty of mortality) by which the radical imagination of the psyche retains its capacity to make and unmake (alter) the horizon of possibility of social-imaginary institution by accepting (and acceding to) social-imaginary signification, by accepting (and acceding to) the specific social-historical content it then comes to recognize as its worldly existence.

This relation renders any idea of absolute alterity unfeasible, un-signifiable, except as a condition of perspective. While from the radical standpoint of the psyche the institution of society does indeed appear as pure alterity – as does, conversely, the psychic core appear as absolute alterity to the logic of society (despite ceaseless efforts to explain it or conjure it away, whether by religion, philosophy, or psychoanalysis) – there is no way to signify a location external to these standpoints that would determine the other's existence. To put it in a rather clumsy way: there is no self to the other, or in another sort of language, the other is not a subject. The other is a force of alteration that enacts and is enacted by the subject – this is the position that power holds in Butler's conception: a force that brings the subject into existence, yet is nonexistent without the subject. Thus, the crucial element to determine is not the figure of the other but the force of alteration. Butler raises a succinct question in this regard: "how is subjection to become a site of alteration?" (*P*:11). The political ramifications of this way of phrasing the question should be obvious: subjection must be (re)considered not as site of enforcement of instituted power but as site of transformative power – in Castoriadis's terms, of *instituting* power. In Butler's words, "the act of [the subject's] appropriation may involve an alteration of power such that the power assumed or appropriated works against the power that made that assumption possible" (*P*:13).

In this respect, Butler's inquiry into the complicity between subject-formation and subjection demands that we reconsider the terrain of the other in a way that opens up the possibility of subjectification as self-alteration. This requires us to re-orient ourselves theoretically from attending to the internalization of the other toward recognizing the internal force of othering which, in the broadest sense, constitutes humanity's creative/destructive (*poietic*) capacity to alter the forms of its historical existence, for better or worse. The obstacle in enabling this reorientation resides in the indicative gesture of concealment that seems to occur at the subject's inaugural moment: in order for the subject to emerge as power – or, in order for the subject's power to emerge – the subject seems to conceal the formative force of power, so that, as Butler says, "agency [appears to] exceed the power by which it is enabled" (*P*: 15). In other words, the subject appears to enact a gesture of self-referentiality at the origin that actually occludes the autonomy of self-reflexivity to be achieved: this is the ideological content of all autopoetic figures in our post-Enlightenment and post-Romantic imaginary, whether variants of the self-made entrepreneur or variants of the autonomous genius of the Artist.

This dissimulation – or to quote Butler, "the metaleptic reversal in which the subject produced by power becomes heralded as the subject who *founds* power" (*P*: 16) – occurs also at the level of societal institution, except in the other direction, a point that Butler does not address. Namely, as history has shown it to be prevalent, societies tend to conceal their own instituting force, potential and actual, conferring thereby authorization of their origin and survival upon social-imaginary significations that are constructed as instances of transcendent rule: God, the father, the king, the nation, the constitution, the market, etc. Indeed, even in cases of nominally secular societies, these instances of transcendent rule are explicitly rendered sacred, and this sacralization becomes in effect the most profound expression of subjection as subjugation. In this respect, the force of subjection does not merely concern the psychic domain of subject formation, but pertains to the social-imaginary as such. Most social-imaginaries in human history enact a heteronomous institution; that is, most societies submit the self-altering force emerging in the internalization of power to self-occultation, as Castoriadis says all too often. They prefer to (re)institute the perspective of an 'external' authority of subjection into pure alterity, into occult heteronomous order.

IV

This raises the most salient political question of all: Can a process of subject-formation that takes place distinctly through a process of subjection conjured as pure subjugation produce an autonomous subject? To put it directly, can – or how can – an autonomous subject emerge out of a heteronomous order? Obviously, in risking the use of the term "autonomous subject," I do not mean to suggest a self-enclosed, self-supposing, narcissistic subject, suspended in the ahistorical void of its own essence. Pure autonomy is itself a theological concept, even in Kant's glorious rationalist mind. It pertains to a self-referential, tautological meaning that the monotheistic mind – in fact, any monomythical mind, as the German philosopher Odo Marquard (1989) has so incisively put it – attributes to the one and only power of signification. In a philosophical language, the name "I am that I am" is the name for the total attributes of Being, including, of course, all the possible languages of Being, the plurality of which is abolished by the monistic source that enables them. Thus, such pure ('autonomous') ontology cannot be named, cannot be represented. By extension, it cannot enter history because it cannot 'know' history – it cannot know anything other to what it knows absolutely, which is (and can only be) itself. Hence, it cannot change – not merely history, but anything at all, including itself. Not only does this Being not 'know' alterity; it has no altering – and most significantly, no *self-altering*

– powers. At its most extreme, it may be said to exist as absolute alterity for someone else, someone who believes his/her being to be determined by it, derived from it. In other words, this absolute and tautological equation of Being-in-itself has meaning only in a heteronomous universe of meanings, in a universe whose signification is guaranteed by the presence of an unreachable, unutterable, and unapproachable Other who precludes any alternative authorization.

In the way Castoriadis understands it, very much against the grain of traditional philosophy, autonomy can exist only as project: an ever-presently restaged project whose primary condition or rule (*archē*) is explicitly drawn from the capacity for self-alteration. This means an *archē* that always begins anew, *othered* – therefore, an *archē* that re-authorizes itself as an other. That is why autonomy as explicit self-alteration is not some fancy way of considering self-constitution, or *autopoiēsis*. In fact, as an ever-restaged and ever-interrupted *archē*, self-alteration renders all received paradigms of self-constitution unfeasible, unconstitutible claims. From the standpoint of self-alteration, the autonomous subject engages in a kind of interminable self-determination, whereby both the 'self' and the determinant elements are under perpetual interrogation. In literal terms, by autonomous subject I am considering here a subject who makes the law – a poet of the law – whose most prized achievement is the limitless interrogation of the law in its full range: first of all, law's emergence, and then its referential framework and justification, its authorization and canonical execution, and most of all, its metatextual presumption of authority. To be the poet of the law is first and foremost to recognize the existence of the law not as transcendental dimension but as historical privilege. This is tantamount to thinking of the subject (whether of oneself or one's society) as a historical entity, whose ground is otherwise abyssal, whose *archē* is indeterminate, and whose *telos* is nothing other than the very project of self-interrogated, worldly, mortal existence.

It is unclear what social-historical conditions are needed for subjectification to take this form. It is safe to say, however, that social autonomy is hardly a natural condition of human-being. It can only emerge as the *praxis/poiēsis* within a certain social-imaginary, which surely does not mean that it is the mere expression or application of a certain social-imaginary. On the contrary, in such an instance, the radical interrogation of the terms of one's existence would be itself the ground of *praxis/poiēsis*, in full cognizance of its otherwise ontological groundlessness. Autonomy is impossible without limitless self-interrogation, in the sense that autonomy cannot be attained once and for all but must be, by definition, open to reinstitution (i.e., alteration), whose limits cannot be set outside the process of alteration. Contrary, then, to traditional notions of autonomous subjectivity which, one way or another, cannot avoid equating self-determination with the self-presupposition of both origin and end, Castoriadis's notion insists on an open figure in which the limits of both 'subject' and 'autonomy' remain indeterminate as a matter of *physis*. The determination of limit that presumably distinguishes the domain of relation between subject and object, internal and external, individual and society, etc., is always a political determination, a matter of *nomos*.

To conclude, it would be essential to add, following this Castoriadian terminology, that autonomy signifies a particular sublimation: a politics of sublimation that confronts the definitional heteronomy 'experienced' by the psyche when it encounters the social-imaginary as the pleasure of/in the force of alteration itself. This sort of sublimation would enact a subject whose psychic reception of society's *Vorstellung* – enacted, in turn, by the psyche's translation of society's imagistic/affective/representational flux into its own terms – would consist in a *poietic* experience: a performative experience of self-othering, which moreover signifies the non self-referential poetic pleasure of altering one's world. In this respect, it seems apt to recall John Cage's often quoted phrase "Art is self alteration" – provided, however, that we do not take it to mean a sort of artistic redemption or self-actualization (in some New Age sense), but that self-alteration names the core process by which our worldly existence can be radically transformed, which is also, after all, the deepest significance of art: the radical transfiguration of form. To this end, self-alteration cannot be conceptualized or articulated if the self remains a notion within the signifying limits of identity. The process of self-alteration is deadly to the sovereignty of identity. It presupposes – it enables and performs – an *identicide*: the self-dissolution of the self, or in another idiom, the production of non-identity as self-transformative force.[12]

---

12 A key to understanding what is at stake here would be Anne Carson's sumptuous *Decreation* (2006). I mention it not only because it deserves to be mentioned, but also as a *bona fide* teaser – for it opens the way indeed to something else, of which at present I remain silent.

References

Adams, Suzi (2011) *Castoriadis's Ontology: Being and Creation*. New York: Fordham University Press.

Butler, Judith (1997) *The Psychic Life of Power*. Stanford CA: Stanford University Press.

Carson, Anne (2006) *Decreation*. New York: Vintage.

Castoriadis, Cornelius (1987) *The Imaginary Institution of Society*, trans. Kathleen Blamey. Cambridge: MIT Press.

Castoriadis, Cornelius (1997) *The Castoriadis Reader*, ed. and trans. David Ames Curtis. Oxford: Blackwell *(CR)*.

Castoriadis, Cornelius (1997) *World in Fragments. Writings on Politics, Society, Psychoanalysis, and the Imagination* (1997), ed. and trans. David Ames Curtis. Stanford, CA: Stanford University Press (*WIF*).

Castoriadis, Cornelius (2004) *Ce qui fait la Grèce I, D-Homère à Heraclite*. Paris: Seuil.

Castoriadis, Cornelius (2007) *Figures of the Thinkable*, trans. Helen Arnold. Stanford CA: Stanford University Press *(FT)*.

Gourgouris, Stathis (1997) "Philosophy and Sublimation", *Thesis Eleven* 49:1, 31–43.

Gourgouris, Stathis (2003) *Does Literature Think?* Stanford: Stanford University Press.

Klimis, Sophie (2007) "Décrire l'irreprésentable, ou comment dire l'indicible originaire", in *Cahiers Castoriadis 3*. Bruxelles: Facultés universitaire Saint-Louis.

Marquard, Odo (1989) *Farewell to Matters of Principle*, trans. Robert M. Wallace. New York: Oxford University press.

The Invisible Committee (2009) *The Coming Insurrection*. Indiana: Semiotexte.

Van Eynde, Laurent (2008) "Castoriadis et Bachelard: un imaginaire en partage", *Cahiers critiques de philosophie* 6. Paris: Éditions Hermann, 159–75.

About the Authors

Suzi Adams teaches social theory in the School of Political and Social Sciences, Flinders University (Adelaide). In 2010 she was the recipient of a Junior Scholar Fellowship at the Centre for Theoretical Studies (Prague) to pursue research on Jan Patočka. Her monograph *Castoriadis's Ontology: Being and Creation* was published by Fordham University Press in 2011, and she has recently guest edited a special issue entitled *Cornelius Castoriadis: Critical Encounters* for the *European Journal of Social Theory* (2012) (with Ingerid Straume), and another, entitled *Political Imaginaries* for *Critical Horizons* (2012) (with Jeremy Smith and Ingerid Straume).

Giorgio Baruchello: Born in Genoa, Italy, Giorgio Baruchello is an Icelandic citizen and serves as Professor of Philosophy at the Faculty of Humanities and Social Sciences of the University of Akureyri, Iceland. He read philosophy in Genoa and Reykjavík, Iceland, and holds a Ph.D. in philosophy from the University of Guelph, Canada. His publications encompass several different areas, especially social philosophy, theory of value, and intellectual history.

Kristina Egumenovska is a researcher at the Department of Psychology, University of Ljubljana. Her interests cover the question of beauty and good life, human imagination and politics and the philosophy of language. Her most recent publications are in *Social identities: Journal for the study of race, nation and culture* (2012) and the chapter *On the Spirit that buts into everything: George Herriman's Krazy Kat* (2011, Peace Institute: Ljubljana). She earned her PhD degree in psychology from the University of Ljubljana in 2012 with a thesis exploring the empirical relation between good life, life-narratives and personality. Egumenovska also specializes in Gestalt psychotherapy.

Andrea Gabler teaches sociology at the Institut für Sozialwissenschaften, Technische Universität Braunschweig, Germany. In her PhD thesis, published in 2009, she reconstructs the history of the group "Socialisme ou Barbarie" and analyses its work research. Her main research interests are sociology of work, ethnography, political theory, feminist theory and sociology of social movements.

Catharina Gabrielsson is Assistant Professor in urban theory at the School of Architecture KTH, Stockholm. Her doctoral thesis *Att göra skillnad* (Axl books, 2006) explores the material, spatial and imaginary dimension of public space through a series of cross-readings between political philosophy, art and architecture. Her more recent research, mainly conducted in London and Istanbul, revolves around the concept of 'beginnings' in architecture, encompassing notions of initiation, originality, process and emergence set against architectural claims of authorship and permanence. She currently collaborates (with Helena Mattsson) on "The Architecture of Deregulations: Politics and Postmodernism in Swedish Building 1975–1995", tracing the relationship between architecture, ideology and the neoliberal shift. Recent contributions to research publications include H. Frichot & S. Loo (eds.) *Deleuze and Architecture* (University of Edinburgh Press, forthcoming 2013) and S. Ewing et al (eds.) *Architecture and Field/Work* (Routledge, 2010). She is a member of the editorial board of *Arkitektur* and *Architecture and Culture* (AHRA & Berg Publishers) and was co-editor for *Nordic Journal or Architecture* (no. 3. vol. 3: 2012) on 'alteration'.

Stathis Gourgouris is Director of the Institute for Comparative Literature and Society at Columbia University. He is the author of *Dream Nation* (Stanford UP, 1996) and *Does Literature Think?* (Stanford UP, 2003), and editor of *Freud and Fundamentalism* (Fordham UP, 2010). In

May 2012, he gave the State Library Lectures in Philosophy and Society in Sydney, Australia, which were broadcast on Australian National Radio and published as *Lessons in Secular Criticism* in the "Thinking Out Loud" series of Fordham University Press in 2013. He is currently completing work on two other book projects of secular criticism and radical democracy – *The Perils of the One* and *Nothing Sacred* – while continuing to work on a long term project on music and the problem of listening.

Sophie Klimis teaches philosophy at the Université Saint-Louis-Bruxelles, where she is a permanent Professor and the head of the department of Philosophy. Her main interests are on Ancient Greek Philosophy, the relations between philosophy and poetry (especially Epics and Tragedy), reelaborations of ancient Greek thought by modern and contemporary philosophers, and the interactions between philosophy and performative arts. She earned her PhD in Ancient Greek Philosophy in 2000 at the Université Libre de Bruxelles (ULB). Klimis is one of the three founding members of the *Groupe de Recherche Castoriadis* at the Université Saint-Louis (2004-2012), as well as a co-editor of the *Cahiers Castoriadis* (8 volumes published). She is a member of the board of the Association Castoriadis in Paris since 2009. She is the author of two books: *Le statut du mythe dans la* Poétique *d'Aristote. Les fondements philosophiques de la tragédie* (Ousia, 1997; Prix Reinach 1998) and *Archéologie du sujet tragique* (Kimé, 2003).

Angelos Mouzakitis (MA, PhD University of Warwick, UK) was a Jean Monnet Fellow at the European University Institute, Florence, Italy (2003–2004). His research and teaching expertise lie in the fields of social theory and philosophical phenomenology. He currently teaches social theory at the University of Crete, Greece and for the Hellenic Open University. He is the author of *Meaning, Historicity and the Social.*

A critical approach to the works of Heidegger, Gadamer and Castoriadis (Dr. Mueller Verlag, 2008).

Ingerid S. Straume is a philosopher of education and a subject specialist at the University Library of the University of Oslo, Norway. In her PhD thesis Straume elucidates and discusses Castoriadis's thought in the frame of the philosophy of education, especially his notion of political *paideia*. Straume has published within political and educational theory, with critical essays on environmental politics, depoliticization, neoliberal capitalism and right-wing populism. Her latest work is an anthology on the history of the philosophy of *Bildung* (*Danningens filosofihistorie*, Gyldendal, 2013). Along with Anders Ramsay, she was coordinator of the NSU network Creation, Rationality and Autonomy (2007–2009).

Harald Wolf is senior researcher at the Sociological Research Institute (SOFI) at the University of Göttingen and teaches sociology at the University of Kassel, Germany. In his study *Arbeit und Autonomie* (Work and Autonomy) (Verlag Westfälisches Dampfboot, 1999) he examines the implications of Castoriadis's thinking for industrial sociology. Since 2006, he is co-editor of the German edition of *Ausgewählte Schriften* by Castoriadis (to date, 5 volumes) and editor of *Das Imaginäre im Sozialen. Zur Sozialtheorie von Cornelius Castoriadis*, published in 2012 by Wallstein Verlag.